While the City Sleeps

VIOLENCE IN LATIN AMERICAN HISTORY

Edited by Pablo Piccato, Federico Finchelstein, and Paul Gillingham

While the City Sleeps

A History of Pistoleros, Policemen,
and the Crime Beat in Buenos Aires
before Perón

Lila Caimari

Translated by Lisa Ubelaker Andrade
and Richard Shindell

UNIVERSITY OF CALIFORNIA PRESS

University of California Press, one of the most
distinguished university presses in the United States,
enriches lives around the world by advancing scholarship
in the humanities, social sciences, and natural sciences.
Its activities are supported by the UC Press Foundation
and by philanthropic contributions from individuals and
institutions. For more information, visit www.ucpress.edu.

University of California Press
Oakland, California

Library of Congress Cataloging-in-Publication Data

Names: Caimari, Lila M., author.
Title: While the city sleeps : a history of pistoleros,
    policemen, and the crime beat in Buenos Aires before
    Peron / Lila Caimari.
Other titles: Mientras la ciudad duerme. English
Description: Oakland, California : University of
    California Press, [2016] | Series: Violence in Latin
    American history ; 2 | Includes bibliographical
    references and index.
Identifiers: LCCN 2016026153| ISBN 9780520289437
    (cloth : alk. paper) | ISBN 9780520289444 (pbk. : alk.
    paper) | ISBN 9780520964105 (ebook)
Subjects: LCSH: Crime—Argentina—Buenos Aires—
    History— century. | Crime—Argentina—Buenos
    Aires—Sociological aspects—History—20th century. |
    Police—Argentina—Buenos Aires—History—20th
    century. | Crime and the press—Argentina—Buenos
    Aires—History—20th century. | Mass media and
    crime—Argentina—Buenos Aires—History—20th
    century.
Classification: LCC HV6885.B8 C3513 | DDC
    364.10982/11—dc23
LC record available at https://lccn.loc.gov/2016026153

Manufactured in the United States of America

24 23 22 21 20 19 18 17 16 17
10 9 8 7 6 5 4 3 2 1

Al grupo Crimen y Sociedad

Contents

Acknowledgments

This book has benefited greatly from the help of both individuals and institutions.

My first debt is to Argentina's National Council of Scientific and Technical Research (CONICET), which financed this long and complex project. That much-repeated expression is once again very much in order: this book *would have not been possible* without the stability provided by my position as a permanent researcher in this public institution. Also, in 2008 a Tinker Fellowship allowed me to spend several months at Columbia University's Institute of Latin American Studies. There, I began to follow the material trail of *pistoleros* and to reflect on the police in historical perspective.

The subject matter of these essays depended upon sources that were often difficult to obtain. I'm grateful to those who went out of their way to allow me access to information. Although some are named in respective passages of the book's text, I'd like to mention here Sonia Cortés Conde, whose good humor and generosity were a welcome antidote to some of the harshness of the police archives. The research team at the Criminal Policy Division of the Ministry of Justice and Human Rights gave me open access to their historical database. As usual, the wonderful librarians at San Andrés University were helpful throughout the entire project. Also, thanks to Liliana Ávila for her archival assistance, to Cecilia Allemandi for her support in the preparation of maps, and to Juan Pablo Canala for his invaluable assistance at the Biblioteca Nacional.

Friends and colleagues read passages of the drafts, making a writer's work less solitary. Thanks to Roy Hora, Isabella Cosse, Juan Carlos Torre, Diego Galeano, Mercedes García Ferrari, and Pablo Piccato. In the context of the PIP project "Interwar Buenos Aires: Revising an Interpretive Paradigm," Diana Wechsler, Sylvia Saítta, and Alejandro Cattaruzza read my long drafts on the *porteño* police and helped me to see many things in a larger perspective. I also benefited from my dialogues with Sofía Tiscornia, Ricardo Salvatore, Pablo Ansolabehere, Ruth Stanley, Sandra Gayol, Sergio Serulnikov, Marcela Gené, Gabriel Kessler, Alejandro Isla, Cristiana Schettini, Máximo Sozzo, Ernesto Bohoslavsky, Juan Manuel Palacio, and Diego Armus.

As the years go by, the wonderful spirit of intellectual challenge and interdisciplinary exploration at the "Oscar Terán" seminar on the history of ideas and culture at the Ravignani Institute (University of Buenos Aires) remains for me an important point of reference and source of inspiration. The company of friends and colleagues there—Hugo Vezzetti, Adrián Gorelik, Martín Bergel, Alejandra Laera, Fernando Rodríguez, and Jorge Myers—has been deeply gratifying.

Describing Sylvia Saítta's help would require all of the preceding categories, and a few more. No doubt, this project would have been very different without her personal and intellectual company. My long and uncertain path of city streets, policemen, and *pistoleros* was made easier thanks to her clever listening and her curiosity, even (or especially) for my strangest discoveries.

Pablo Piccato, Federico Finchelstein, and Paul Gillingham kindly invited me to publish a translation of this book in their series "Violence in Latin American History." At University of California Press, Kate Marshall, Bradley Depew, and Sue Carter were unfailingly helpful in their assistance during the editing of the book.

Due to thematic affinity and shared research experience, this book owes a vital debt to the students and colleagues of the "Crime and Society" group, which I've coordinated with Eduardo Zimmermann at San Andrés University for over a decade. We're a much larger group than when we began in 2005. We've also come a long way from our original research expectations. And I have no doubt that soon we will have progressed even further from the present context, which gave rise to this book. In the meantime, I dedicate it to those companions in the search for the hidden paths of crime, police, and penal law.

Buenos Aires, February, 2016

Abbreviations

AGN	Archivo General de la Nación
BA	*Bandera Argentina*
CC	*Caras y Caretas*
EM	*El Mundo*
GP	*Gaceta Policial*
HP	*Hogar Policial*
LL	*La Libertad*
LN	*La Nación*
LO	*La Opinión*
LP	*La Prensa*
LR	*La Razón*
LV	*La Vanguardia*
MP	*Magazine Policial*
OD	Policía de la Capital. Orden del Día
ODR	Policía de la Capital. Orden del Día Reservada
PA	*Policía Argentina*
RCSP	*Revista de la Caja de Socorros de la Policía y Bomberos de la Capital*
RP	*Revista de Policía*
RPo	*Revista Policial*
SH	*Sherlock Holmes*

Introduction

This book, dealing with the question of public order in 1920s and 1930s Buenos Aires, began as a detour. Over time, what started as an indulgence developed into an increasingly demanding distraction from another, more circumscribed, research project, itself a sequel to a still earlier investigation on the history of punitive ideas—wanderings on the way to the present work.

Its origin can be traced back to an interest in a late nineteenth-century set of concepts, images, and metaphors that grew up around the figure of the modern criminal. More precisely, I was trying to understand the link between criminological and "profane" discourses: between the voyeurism of psychiatric magazines and that of commercial newspapers. In order to capture the evolution of this slippery relationship, I consulted an extensive sample of press sources and came across an intriguing finding: in the mid-1920s, the local causes célèbres were overshadowed by a number of high-profile robberies offering a very different kind of spectacle. The great cases of the late 1800s were private crimes and were described in naturalist-scientificist language with overtones of detective fiction. Three decades later, however, in the thrall of cinema and comic strips, illustrators and journalists seemed to lose interest in recounting a suspect's biological past, for instance, choosing instead to focus on the details of the criminal performance: cars, weapons, clothes, and operational skills. For the enjoyment of readers, chronicles (usually consisting of photographs combined with short texts) sought to reconstruct, in the most exciting way possible, the shootings and manhunts taking place in the streets. There was much talk of Al Capone's *porteño* imitators. As I advanced into the 1930s, I noticed that the police also acquired a certain celebrity in the crime sections of newspapers and that the criminologists I had intended to follow were fading out of sight. Patrol cars, radios, and automatic weapons promised "around the clock" control of the city. I took note of all this, intending to return to the spectacle of *pistoleros* and policemen of the 1920s and 1930s.

When that moment finally arrived, I discovered that the research project I had envisioned—a cultural history of crime journalism, or perhaps a study on the figure of the modern criminal as portrayed in the languages of mass communication—called out for yet *another* project, one that restricted the original chronological boundaries in order to widen its thematic spectrum. Indeed, a little investigation showed that the transformations in the realm of journalism were insufficient to explain a body of evidence that was quickly becoming overwhelming. What lay behind the changes occurring in the crime section of newspapers represented much more than a shift within the journalistic field: it was a reflection of new criminal practices, new forms of violence, and new state technologies to detect disorder. Besides, the appeal of these episodes was much broader than the history of crime, or fear of crime, or police repression of crime. Many of the elements involved were central to the understanding of Buenos Aires in that period, although they had remained absent from historiographical narratives. In any case, they allowed for a history of crime, but also for a history *from* crime.

So I crossed (this time, in the opposite direction) the blurry line between practices and representations in search of a more satisfying interpretation of those headlines about assaults, shootings, and escapes. What I found constitutes the core of the essays included in this book. In a process of gradual adjustment, they were added to an initial project on the spectacle of crime in the era of mass communication, modifying and redefining its axis. The chapters are connected by a loose, nonchronological argument, as well as by some common themes: urban growth, some harsh and unsettling aspects of modernity, the multiple uses of technology at a time of increasing access to certain artifacts, the languages of mass culture. The archival foundation of these essays consists not only of commercial newspapers and scientific journals (as expected), but also the materials found in police archives, where I landed in search of information about *pistoleros*. Very soon, I discovered that those documents spoke more eloquently about the question of order in the city (and its environs) than about that particular form of disorder called crime (even if the police claimed this to be their specific turf). Following this thread, I touched upon research areas that had already been well traveled by historians.[1]

In the two decades between the world wars, the population of Buenos Aires jumped from about 1.5 to 2.5 million. As had been the case since the late nineteenth century, this extraordinary demographic expansion was the result of European immigration—Argentina was the nation of the Americas (north or south) with the greatest proportion of overseas immigrants in relation to its original population.[2] Demographic explosion brought great urban expansion as well. From the beginning of the century, Buenos Aires quickly extended outward following the design of public transportation (tramways and railways first, buses later). "My neighborhood is fifteen years old, and it's already old," observed a 1928 article in *El Hogar*.[3] This expansion was based mainly on the construction of single-family houses. As a result of the access to real estate and the rapid construction of basic urban infrastructure (electricity, sanitation, etc.), the surface area of the urban grid expanded, while average population by district decreased.[4]

The history of this extraordinary growth is captured in the saga of those many thousands who, after crossing the Atlantic, were able to leave the overcrowded tenement houses (*conventillos*) of downtown and move out to the new neighborhoods pushing the frontiers of the city limits. This scenario of rapid upward mobility has provided the framework for analyzing many dimensions of *porteño* life in the early decades of the twentieth century: its vital network of neighborhood associations, its literacy campaigns, its grassroots politics, its many reformist projects, and so forth.[5] This book returns to that same universe, with the help of sources that have thus far been marginal to the discussion: the popular press (particularly its "small" sections, the local police and municipal pages) and a large body of documents produced by the Capital Police (Policía de la Capital), the state agency most present in public spaces, everyday occurrences, and "low" politics.[6]

Following the *porteño* street cops is an exercise fraught with methodological challenges, as we will see. Still, this book assumes that the problems are worth the risk, as these records provide access to a street-level point of view, in which so much of the detail—some of it momentous, some of it trivial—of everyday life is documented, where circulation is monitored, and where many expressions of popular culture are kept under close observation. More importantly: as the archive yielded its treasures, information on certain forms of disorder, such as crime or political protest, showed themselves to be intertwined with larger questions about the construction of street order and social order.

How does this evidence change the interpretation of life in Buenos Aires during those years? Certainly, it is not the "hidden story" behind an essentially optimistic narrative. Neither does it replace this narrative with the darkest data from the police archive. It doesn't reverse the plot, then, but it does inject tension into it, calling attention to the intrinsic violence that characterized a society where quick social promotion could be followed just as quickly by demotion, and where success coexisted with the frustration of many dreams. It explores the question of order at a time of material achievements and radical transformation, a time also when the limits of that transformation became apparent. It observes the cultural expressions of the vast majorities which have remained marginal to historical narrative insofar as they don't correspond to what has been described as a main feature of this society (that is, the belief in the transformative powers of public instruction) and are not relevant to the historical debate about the origins of political citizenship. The resulting image of *porteño* society may be less photogenic than the one we have cultivated so far. It is certainly less virtuous and optimistic. There are gambling joints around the corner from some of those community libraries. I hope that at the end of this road, these essays will have contributed to a more recognizable picture, one painted with many hands.

In the 1920s and 1930s, Buenos Aires was considered a modern city by both those who observed it and those who lived in it. This characterization persisted, regardless of the variable (building infrastructure, urban equipment, patterns of material and cultural consumption, etc). One way or another, the episodes analyzed in this book are a product (albeit unforeseen, or undesired) of this modernity. That Buenos Aires was seen as uneven, unequal, or incompletely modern, a society of contrasts to be critiqued on moral grounds, only confirms the inescapable effects of its modernization.

As we know, that process was loaded with subjective effects—in other words, with *modernity*. Precocious and at the same time "peripheric," *porteño* modernity has been well described in some influential cultural studies on the 1920s and 1930s.[7] The essays in this book are indebted to those works, though they stem from a different intersection between journalism, literature, and urban transformation. Their hypotheses are in tune with a brand of cultural history that remains closely interwoven with social history, one strongly committed to archival evidence. Their interest in representations does not preclude questions about practices. In turn, some of these practices are observed with a phenomenological eye that betrays an interest in the difference between past and present modernity. Reflecting on practices, says Pierre Bourdieu, allows us to see "all that is inscribed in the relationship of *familiarity* with the familiar environment, the unquestioning apprehension of the social world which, by definition, does not reflect on itself and excludes the question of the conditions of its own possibility."[8] In history, such an operation of "defamiliarization" focuses on what must have seemed most familiar and unremarkable to those who inhabited the reconstructed world, and would seem strange if narrated in our present. Likewise, it observes the perplexity of those who lived in the past in the face of situations that we now take for granted. With this in mind, the following essays examine the appropriations of technologies such as the automobile or automatic weapons (both closely associated with the diagnosis about "new crime"), and to some extent, the legal and illegal "social life" of these artifacts.[9] Those Ford Model Ts and Colt pistols that garnered so much fascination (and complaints) are followed as a *material trail* that conditioned the experience of urban modernity, underlying several of the subjects analyzed here: the circulation between the city and the suburb, forms of violence, and techniques for detecting and perceiving disorder.

Buenos Aires, the modern city, was the scene of many opportunities for broad sectors of society, even if "broad sectors" should not be take to mean "all sectors," or everyone within a given sector. Processes of social mobility need to be considered in relative terms, as they always contain selective logics. In this case, studies agree that this upward selection favored European immigrants at the expense of the native population, a distinction that had geographical connotations given the uneven distribution of these two groups. Immigrants accounted for a substantial portion of those who lived in Buenos Aires and in the *pampa* region, where the category of "native" came to include large numbers of first- and second-generation descendants of these newcomers. According to Susana Torrado, by 1914, more than 50 percent of the Argentine "middle sectors" were foreigners. The rates of upward mobility were substantially higher in the city of Buenos Aires—where the middle class became dominant. Provinces at a distance from the export economy were not usually a destination for immigration.[10] The rise of a large, heterogeneous social group benefiting from the economic bonanza of the 1920s, as well as from access to education and housing, is also in the background of this book. From that process, much attention will be paid to the mixed consequences of modernization and social change: the attractions of modern life along with its discordant edges, the fruits of integration along with clear evidence of the limits of social inclusion.

Because it was more modern, Buenos Aires was also more complex and more explosive. Newspaper stories about "new crime" threw sparks into what was already an uncertain, heterogeneous, and unstable society, igniting much more than concern over rising crime. They also produced a fair amount of stupor at the "perverse" uses of technology, disgust at transgressions that reflected unbridled materialism, condemnation of those forms of violence that ignored time-honored codes, and ominous forecasts about the unreflective cult of Hollywood.

These changes, which were more intense and occurred more quickly in Buenos Aires than in any other Latin American city, soon led to much lamenting about the loss of a golden age of harmony. In contexts of modernization and rupture, the melancholic listing of lost values is a rather common way of organizing temporality. Those who live in times of rapid change, with all the disorientation and sense of dispossession it provokes, tend to compensate by constructing an imaginary past, and, with it, a "desire to return."[11]

We know the contours of the kind of anti-modern thought that arose as a reaction to the vertiginous *porteño* modernization. In the booming years around the Centennial of the Revolution of Independence (1910), writers from the provinces of the interior, like Leopoldo Lugones and Manuel Gálvez, introduced a set of topics that would often be invoked in the decades to come: the cosmopolitan dissolution of the national essence, the mercantilization of urban life, gross materialism, and moral debilitation.[12] This book calls attention to less articulated strands of critical thinking on *porteño* modernity. Moving the lens from elite authors to everyday street talk, it will try to evoke the major themes of anti-modern reaction as manifested in the interstices of everyday life. An analysis at this level seems particularly useful for explaining some important developments of 1920s and '30s anti-liberal reaction, such as the rise of Catholicism as an ideological reference and the reinstatement of the death penalty.[13] Though these trends were not articulated by a distinct, recognizable voice, it is possible to identify the moment of their crystalization in the anticlimactic sequence of the economic crisis in 1930.

Although the Great Crash did interrupt the curve of prosperity in the *pampas,* its consequences were not as deep or lasting as in other societies. The economic growth of the previous decade had produced tangible improvements in real salaries, benefiting a substantial portion of the regional population—and more particularly, those who lived in the city of Buenos Aires.[14] The sequence (an expansion and sudden retraction in the distribution of wealth) challenges our conception of the effect of the crisis beyond statistical data or exercises in comparative history. The horizon of personal risk does not always coincide with objective data or international comparisons, and we still need specific studies on the relative condition of *porteños* in order to understand the impact of the crisis with greater precision. Meanwhile, the following essays assume that a society where upward mobility was such a recent phenomenon, and therefore a state of affairs that *could not be taken for granted,* would perceive the threat of economic decline with a greater sense of fragility. They also assume that the consequences of the crisis in everyday life—certainly not as deep as in other countries, or even in other regions of Argentina—were in no way negligible. Because the crisis interrupted the promise of social mobility—a promise that remained strong in the collective imagination, even when it had failed—it encouraged previous frustrations and generated important defensive reflexes. This is why the "difference" of the 1930s that stems from these essays is closer to generic social conservatism than to the more drastic reactionary programs trumpeted by the extreme right. As a social mood, it imagines a protective barrier around the modest house (heavily mortgaged), it defends the kind of respectability that comes from hard work, and it projects an ideal of domestic order onto public space. If these essays draw a line at the final years of that decade, it's because by then the great "storms of the world" had taken over the headlines, and international politics had upstaged many of the less structured issues of order and disorder.[15]

The *porteño* society portrayed in these pages is less peaceful than in other reconstructions. Of course, it's not the turbulent Buenos Aires of the economic boom and the great wave of immigrants. It's not the turn-of-the-century city with thousands of new arrivals every week, half-built public works projects, overcrowded tenant houses, the ever-present threat of strikes, and panic around the "social question." Precisely because it was *no longer* that city-laboratory, there was an expectation that the fruits of that experiment would lead to change. Despite its association with nineteenth-century politics of "order and progress," the modernizing project had generated its own forms of disorder. And half a century later, social demands pointed to the end of that tumultuous era.

From the broad repertoire of violence associated with the "hard" 1930s, Argentine historiography has focused on what was politically legible: the repression of communism, the execution of anarchists, and

Radical Party uprisings. In other words, it has followed the path that goes from 1920s democracy (dominated by the Radicals) to the September 1930 military coup, and from there to the fraudulent politics during the "decade of infamy."[16] From the outset, these essays assume the solid grounding of this historiography, both factual and metaphorical. The profile of the post-coup state that arises from these pages is if anything more violent than it is in other works, seeing a sequence and a repertoire of violence that seems longer and more complex than has been previously assumed.

One thread added to the established narrative of 1930s violence concerns the cycle of *pistolerismo,* which peaked between the end of the 1920s and the late 1930s. This aspect of the study might well be labeled "cultural criminology" since it shares with this interpretive school the belief in careful historical, social, and cultural contextualization in the understanding of crime.[17] Conceived in the context of criminological studies, such an agenda is, in fact, bringing to the analysis of crime what has long been second nature for sociocultural historians. More historiographical than criminological in their interests, these essays employ this approach while reversing it: rather than arguing for the integration of historical context into the understanding of crime, they seek to understand crime as a window into the societies in which it occurred. Thus, in their relationship to technology, public performance, social fantasies about wealth, the languages of cinema, and the world of celebrities, *pistoleros* are followed here in order to illuminate another path to understanding modernity.

Of course, the violence that dominated the scene after 1930 was not that of *pistoleros* but that unleashed by the repressive apparatus of the state—by the police. At various points in this book, this agency becomes the object of analysis, constituting the main thematic shift away from its original subject. I'd prefer to avoid the introductory commonplace of dwelling on ways in which the book remedies certain deficiencies in our knowledge. Nevertheless, our ignorance regarding the Buenos Aires police, a subject of primary importance for these essays, must be addressed. Virtually unknown outside the narrow world of institutional laudatory historiography—unknown even in studies that do acknowledge the severity of the repressive forces of this period—the Capital Police played a key role in the political repression of the 1930s. The critical event here is the birth of the Special Section (Sección Especial) within the department, devoted to the persecution (including torture) of communist activists. The reader will find original information on this topic, although it's not this aspect of the police (which I've examined in previous studies) that defines the contours of the reconstruction.[18] The record of political persecution—which official archives provide in surprising detail—occurs in a broader context of brutality at the hands of a fraudulent political order. Despite the lack of information on the Buenos Aires case, I soon realized that it was comparable to that of other police systems for which there already existed an important tradition of study and conceptualization.

For reasons no less unfortunate for being obvious, the development of a history of the police has been long time coming to Latin American academia. Contemporary periods of intense police repression (that of the 1970s in particular) conditioned the ways in which that institution's past was conceived. If it appeared at all in historical narratives, it was as a plain, self-evident subject. When it received any attention at all, it was only to point out what was readily visible and intelligible: the police as a docile instrument (a *pure* instrument) of the chief forces of domination—a tool to neutralize social protest, to quash dissent.[19]

For many years, the combined effect of institutional secrecy and reticence on the part of academics kept this important subject relegated to the margins of historiographical reflection. Too despicable to deserve complex analysis, the study of the police degraded any social scientist who undertook it.[20] Now, we're beginning to assess its relevance and complexity by means of a growing multidisciplinary body of local studies on the subject. This book appears in the context of an investigative boom that will soon render these statements obsolete. Meanwhile, studies produced in other societies (most of them also quite recent) have yielded conceptual frameworks and hypotheses that may be put to good use here, assuming (as this work does) that the *porteño* police was no exception to the rule.

As the long shadow of military dictatorship recedes, the most brutal and explicit forms of coercion (those that belong in the genealogy of state terror) are being connected with other practices as the most conspicuous element of a larger repertoire. And with the advancement of research, the "empty" spaces between the most traumatic uses of force begin to acquire meaning. If conceived as a loose, amorphous entity, spread between the most visible public areas and the most obscure corners of the city, the history of the police is more than the chronicle of the regular ordeal of repression in the service of the powerful.

In numerous Latin American academic settings, the question of urban order has been "discovered" as a criterion of observation of the police thanks to the late work of Michel Foucault. Using an all-encompassing definition of the police as the multifaceted instrument of the "government of men and things," Foucault assumes the essentially hybrid nature of this agency, as well as its intimate relationship with the control of urban space. His attention to "governmentality" in the context of eighteenth-century capitalist development focuses on those techniques devoted to the management of populations, techniques used to monitor and channel circulation. Governments (that is, their urban police) attempted to maximize positive (mercantile) circulation and to minimize negative (criminal or epidemical) circulation. "The space of circulation," says Foucault, "is a privileged object of the police."[21] Policing is a practice with an interstitial nature; it spreads in series, over long periods of time.

The belated publication of Foucault's conferences on territory and population has inaugurated an immanent perspective for police studies, one grounded in the city. Despite limited access to documents, which curtails the research agenda of Argentine social scientists, this perspective is beginning to yield results.[22] After a little bibliographic research, it becomes clear that in those geographical or disciplinary contexts where Foucault's influence has been less dominant, techniques of police intervention in urban space already have a considerable tradition of analysis. "Because the history of the police is so much part of the history of the city," said social historian Eric Monkkonen three decades ago, "it is essential that the history of the city provide the first and most dominant framework within which to analyze the police."[23]

Within this framework, which takes a long-term perspective, this study is interested in a definition of the mission of the police as emanating from a utopian principle of the *abolition of disorder*.[24] Suggesting the persistence of a police agenda of "ordering" may seem anachronistic in the context of a centralized state where this institution defines its modernity around the struggle against crime. Nevertheless, the extent to which the old, diffuse social mandate to preserve order remained crucial to understanding urban police in the twentieth century soon became apparent. The Buenos Aires Capital Police proved to be, first of all, the principal manager of circulation, whose problematic areas were in the much-congested downtown and in the jurisdictional border separating the city from the province of Buenos Aires (a separation increasingly conceived in terms of order and disorder, as we will see). It was also the main agent of "domestic" order: cleaning the urban space, granting protection for certain subjects and artifacts (while rejecting others), street police emerged as a key to the shaping of the city. The police also monitored morals, suppressing unacceptable impulses and forms of behavior: excessive displays of pleasure and passion in public, excessive noise, and so on.[25] Finally, it was a "pastoral" police. I borrow this late Foucauldian concept in order to observe the beat cop in far-flung neighborhoods, where police presence had an individualizing quality, turning abstract state power into a force that promised to care for one and all: *omnes et singulatim*. There was room for everything in this all-encompassing yet essentially singular point of view: the whole of life and population in their ground-level interactions.[26] We'll see the extent to which this grassroots perspective also provided a repertoire of symbolic meaning for the institution, where the cop on the urban frontier was portrayed as a figure closer to personal bodyguard than to enforcer of the law.

As the following essays develop the notion of the police as a multitask agent dealing with circulation and order, they use a less abstract perspective than other "Foucauldian" studies dealing with the same categories. Indeed, when describing police agency, this study strives to be as specific as possible. It follows regulations and practices rather than treatises on police theory. It uses the concept of "technology" in a narrow sense to designate artifacts like patrol cars, blueprints, radios, and Colt .45 pistols in their applications in such straightforward tasks as the perception of disorder, the speeding of movement, information gathering, offensive power, and the conquest of public opinion. While taking advantage of the many conceptual and comparative possibilities offered in the field of "police studies," it attempts to consider the subject of "police" beyond this context, to discuss arguments about more general social, political, and cultural trends of the period.[27]

Not everything in *porteño* police practice responded to a negative impulse or was geared toward counteracting disorder. Beyond reaction, the capacity to *produce* meaning is also considered in these essays. It is embodied in two main issues: one touching on the problem of legitimacy of police work and the other dealing with the ability of the police to generate specific ways of looking at urban space. This last point reopens the question of the relationship between the police and the press, which I have written about elsewhere.[28] If those analyses stressed the autonomy of the sensationalist press in relation to its police sources, this more systematic comparison of newspapers' *policiales* with police archives has led me to consider more seriously the degree to which police-generated content and perspective managed to survive despite the mediation of reporters.

Although this book touches upon all of these dimensions of the Buenos Aires police, it is worth noting that at no point does it offer an institutional history, let alone a political history of its hierarchical figures (fortunately, these much-needed projects are currently being undertaken). Rather, the analysis focuses on the police's relationship with the city, which is why subjects like patrolling the street, maintaining public order, and producing collective imaginaries have been given priority.

The evidence for the multidimensional nature of this agency—the ways in which it modified a rapidly changing urban landscape; how it treated customs and habits with a mixture of repression, coexistence, and complicity; the tension between the fairness and unfairness of the social order that it was monitoring—seemed too important to ignore. All these subjects provided another way of understanding that society of extraordinary vitality that so fascinated me. Ultimately, my long detour prevailed over the original research project. Yet, it is still grounded in questions about Buenos Aires and its people, and about the everyday construction of order.

CHAPTER I

Pistoleros

October 2, 1930: the Palermo woods. It's a pleasant morning. Neighbors are riding down the street on horseback. Others enjoy the day at a nearby sporting club. In just a moment they will witness the following chain of events (to be reconstructed later by police investigators): first, a car speeds up Vivero Avenue, coming from the direction of downtown Buenos Aires. The driver, the witnesses later find out, is transporting money—salaries for the workers at the National Office of Public Works. The car carrying the payroll is then cornered by another automobile, carrying two members of a seven-person gang. The remaining five quickly descend upon the scene in a third vehicle, the getaway car. Both the assailants and their targets are armed, carrying Winchesters and high-caliber revolvers. A brief shootout leaves a few wounded, and one dead. The assailants rush to the getaway car with the money in tow and speed off in the direction of Belgrano. It all takes place in a matter of minutes.[1]

Naturally, those *porteños* who followed the news about the public works payroll holdup saw this episode as only the latest in a wave of similar crimes that had been the talk of the town: a subject of worried debate in police stations, a favorite topic in the press, and a fixture of conversations in cafés, on the trolley and in stores, social clubs, and neighborhood associations. By the end of the 1920s, the crime problem was common knowledge in Buenos Aires. Said one observer in 1927, "The outrages of the criminal underworld are generating alarm among all social classes; it has even become common to hear it said that people live better out on the *pampa,* where there is some guarantee of safety, than in any corner of our cultured and opulent metropolis."[2] No one would argue that the people of Buenos Aires were unaccustomed to living with crime. Gruesome chronicles had been circulating for years. Portraits of delinquents and dangerous perpetrators were regular elements of the city's newspapers. Yet midway through the 1920s, a change began to insinuate itself into the nature and intensity of society's anxiety over crime, swelling by the beginning of the next decade into a growing sense of imminent crisis. Editorials decried that the police and the penal system were ill-equipped to face the city's increasingly arrogant bandits. Neighborhood petitions called for more police in the streets. *La Prensa, La Nación, El Mundo,* and *La Razón all* pushed for firmer laws and stronger enforcement. Some called for Congress to reinstate the death penalty; others demanded that the police be armed for all-out war.

Talk of the "new" crime bound together a range of anxieties and concerns, most frequently connecting it to the perverse effects of modernity: a decaying moral order (in the realms of family and sexual mores), an identity crisis brought about by the city's rapid growth, the unbridled expansion of consumer culture, the rise of the entertainment industry and its cornucopia of dangerous fantasies and seductive stimuli, and so on. It activated a host of fears regarding the moral abyss besetting modern society. Crime was also perceived as an indicator of political decadence, suggesting a connection between power and rampant corruption. The illegal structural framework of *caudillo* control over vast territories of the province of Buenos Aires was, in the 1930s, part of the political landscape of any regular reader of newspapers, where anecdotes and scandals drew a picture of official complicity (both political and police) with crime or its related activities, particularly on the outskirts of the city of Buenos Aires. A complementary reading of the problem took the form of a more general critique of the state's weaknesses and inefficiencies. The climate of anxiety and distrust left in the wake of certain high-profile cases cannot be ignored when we consider the context in which broader challenges to the liberal state were flourishing.

This chapter looks at a specific aspect of this phenomenon: the material evolution of illegal practices in the city of Buenos Aires. This emphasis suggests a hypothesis: that the motor of change can be found in interactions between technological modernization, the expansion of consumer culture, and the rise of a performative dimension of crime. New criminal practices emerged within the context of different local practices and traditions, but their performative quality allowed them to

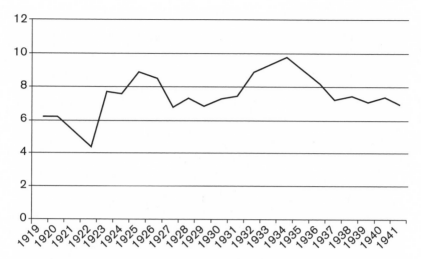

GRAPH 1. Number of crimes, per thousand residents, Buenos Aires, 1919–41. Source: Policía de la Capital, *Memorias correspondientes a los años 1919–1941;* Policía de la Capital, *Boletín de estadística: Delitos en general; Suicidios, accidentes y contravenciones diversas, anuarios 1920–41.*

be superficially grouped together and homogenized under a single conceptual mantle.

Was crime really on the rise in Buenos Aires? Police data provides no easy answer. The methodological problems in using these kinds of statistics are well known, but they warrant review. First, we should recall that police information only reflects reported crimes, which are themselves a highly uneven selection of real crime. Second, such data is labeled and filed according to institutional definitions of crime, which can skew perceptions. Third, crime reporting is gathered irregularly across time. Statistics thus reflect the typical problems of institutional data collection, including failures of efficiency, structural incentives to skew data, and the typical failings of information gathered by small offices. We should also note some specific problems associated with the Buenos Aires Capital Police's methods of data collection during this period. The data most cited in the press and by state agencies was not disaggregated in any way—the numbers were simplified as a global rate for reported crimes. Contemporary observers who sought data on crime noted that official information was insufficient to either confirm or deny perceptions of high crime. Yet, these figures remain the only numerical data available for analysis, and it is still the only quantitative information we have to map out these broader trends.

These are the kinds of rather placid statistics that police authorities cited when they cast doubt on the public perception of a crime wave. The data, they said, "shows that public opinion sounds a false alarm; it confuses a rise in news about crime with a rise in crime."[3] These same statistics were used by those who defended the 1922 penal code against those who argued for harsher punishments. The graph suggests, in effect, that crime rates per capita remained relatively stable throughout the period, with a brief upswing during the early 1930s. This rise, as we shall see, was consistent with disaggregated statistics on violent crime and should be considered within the context of global economic depression. Just as in other societies, including those in which the consequences of the Depression were more profound and sustained, the relationship between the economic downturn and criminal activity is far from clear.[4] Moreover, public perception of rising crime actually preceded the escalation marked out in the statistics in 1930. Even if we isolate the period in which reported crime did rise (between 1931 and 1937), it is apparent that Buenos Aires's crime rates were still far lower than those in other major cities. There was certainly less crime per capita than in Chicago, which represented the vanguard in the trend toward urban crime, with double the homicide rate of New York or Philadelphia. But Buenos Aires did not even approach the crime levels of European cities like Berlin or Paris—cities with which *porteño* authorities were most inclined to compare themselves. This was confirmed in statistics of "crimes against property," a category that actually declined over the long term. The numbers consolidated at the beginning of the 1920s at a relatively low rate, between 3 and 4 per thousand, and did not change considerably during the crisis.

Rising crime? On the contrary, the statistics suggest years of relative calm after the wild peaks accompanying the rapid urbanization of the first two decades of the twentieth century. What, then, made *porteños* of the 1920s so certain that they were in the midst of a crime wave? Sociological literature describes a "crime wave" as a series of complex changes in social perception that can be independent of rises and declines in crime rates. The first studies on crime waves began to appear in the United States in the late 1950s, and hypotheses about the nature of the disconnect between real crime and perceived crime have become increasingly complex since. This literature shows that no matter how large the gap between perceived and real crime, perceptions generate a very real impact: social pressure can change laws, increase the presence of police on the street, and cause a dramatic change in the number of convicted

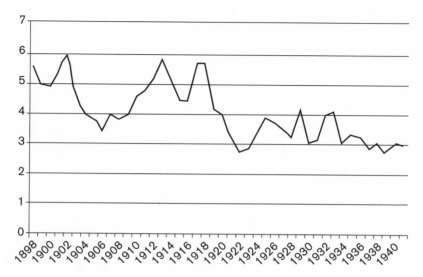

GRAPH 2. Number of crimes against property, per thousand residents, Buenos Aires, 1898–1941. Source: Policía de la Capital, *Memoria correspondiente al año 1941*, 227. Policía de la Capital, *Memoria correspondiente al año 1941*, 227.

criminals.[5] Thus, the ways in which crime was perceived and represented are crucial to our understanding. Yet before focusing on perceptions and representations, we must take a deeper look at criminal practices, because the symbolic renovation of the discourses and imaginaries of crime would not have occurred if *certain kinds of crime*—crime with high visibility and with great potential for sensationalism—had not actually been on the rise. Indeed, the relative stability suggested by the available statistics was hiding notable qualitative changes. The comparatively moderate (and relatively steady) crime rate in Buenos Aires was overshadowed by pronounced and evocative new kinds of crime that confirmed the feeling that the streets were becoming more unsafe.

Unsafe streets: this simple commonsense perception was, in fact, confirmed by statistics. But danger in the streets seemed to come more from negligence than criminal intent, from accidents rather than premeditated crime. Taking only homicide as a point of reference (since it is the crime that is least likely to escape police detection and that involves less symbolic construction), we can compare, for example, deaths caused by stabbing, by automobiles, and by firearms. The relatively stable rate of homicides by stabbing is the first point of reference. The two other sets of data, however, follow divergent paths: we see a rise in mortality from auto accidents that neatly correlated with the rise in number of automobiles present in the city

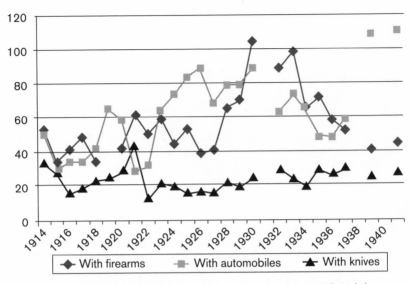

GRAPH 3. Homicides in the city of Buenos Aires, 1914–1941. Source: Policía de la Capital, *Boletín de estadística: Delitos en general; Suicidios, accidentes, contravenciones diversas, anuarios 1914–1941*. Policía de la Capital, *Memorias correspondientes a los años 1914–1941*. I removed data on homicides for the year 1919, as it includes the massacre of the Semana Trágica (Tragic Week) in its count. As the event was exceptional, the numbers would create an outlier that would detract from an analysis of more general trends.

during the 1920s. The rise in shooting deaths made them the number-one cause of violent death by the beginning of the 1930s.

As we can see, at the end of the 1920s traffic accidents were the principal cause of violent death in the city. They were also the number one cause of nonfatal injury, of which there was a dramatic rise during the decade.

In this case, there are few reasons to doubt the trends suggested by the numbers. The spike in "crimes against people" caused by car accidents was so swift that the category was soon subdivided further. Authorities found it necessary to disaggregate involuntary and voluntary manslaughter (car chauffeurs lead this group) and introduce distinctions between vehicles (trolleys, buses, taxis, private cars), the location of accidents, and so on.

Maps of violence produced by the automotive transport authority at the end of the 1930s, when accident rates had stabilized, showed that downtown streets were covered by a dense cluster of accidents. On some streets the concentration was so great that the trail of yearly accidents created an uninterrupted outline of the street plan. They became more widely spaced as they moved away from the downtown area, though no jurisdiction saw less than tens of wounded from accidents per year.

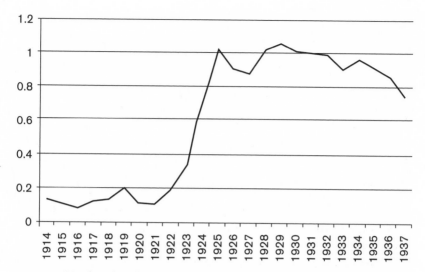

GRAPH 4. Number of nonfatal automobile accidents reported in the city of Buenos Aires, per thousand inhabitants, 1914–1937. Source: Policía de la Capital, *Boletín de estadística: Delitos en general; Suicidios, accidentes, contravenciones diversas, anuarios 1914–1941; Policía de la Capital, Memorias correspondientes a los años 1914–1941.*

As this data suggests, the feeling that violence in public places was on the rise was a perception rooted in reality, although the principal culprits were the new cars rather than the new crime. These two trends were not unrelated, however. As we will see in the next section, the rise of "new" crime was closely linked to the transformation of urban transport.

CRIME, CONSUMER CULTURE, AND TECHNOLOGY

"Not in Any Hurry" is pure Argentine.

—Jorge Luis Borges, "Inscriptions on
   Wagons" 1928

Changes in crime practices during the 1920s and 1930s illustrate the challenges that modern technologies posed (and continue to pose) to the established order.[6] They are testimony to the functional and semantic multiplicity of artifacts, to the repertoire of unforeseen appropriations, and to their potential use. They also reflect a context in which the structures of opportunities for crime were transforming—a historical moment in which engaging in illegal activity suddenly became easier. Telephones, radios, autos, firearms, and improved photography—to name only a few of the most relevant technologies of this period—were readily available tools. The history of the relationship between the state and crime in the early decades of the century was, by and large, a race to discover the most avant-garde application of each new artifact.

It was often said that the era's greatest threats resided in mass access to certain goods and the subsequent misuse of these technologies by sectors of the population. Audacity, boldness, and vertigo: crime's descriptives emanated from the changing material conditions of the times. The "new" criminal became most closely associated with the automobile. The account of motorized robbery that opened this chapter serves as one window into the changes brought on by new forms of transportation. In 1917 and 1925 (respectively), local subsidiaries of Ford and General Motors opened dealerships, introducing U.S. automobiles into the local mass market. Argentine car consumption expanded drastically. In 1920, there was one vehicle for every 186 residents of the country. A few years later, the number had climbed to one car for every 27 residents, more cars per capita than in Germany. By 1926, Argentina placed seventh in the world in automobile ownership, with numbers comparable to those in France and Great Britain.[7]

The car was the most important consumer object of the 1920s—far more relevant than any domestic artifact. Mass production, financing opportunities, and the diffusion of advertising in the media transformed the public's perception of car ownership. The automobile shifted from being a luxury object to being an accessible consumer item that, while not cheap, nevertheless marked an aspirational horizon for a growing segment of the urban populace.[8] Car ownership was also a dream for those who, barring a stroke of good luck, could never hope to acquire one. With a mixture of compassion and disgust, Roberto Arlt described the poor characters who gathered at dealership windows to gawk: "They stop at all hours, implausibly unkempt, stealing glances at a machine priced over 10,000, as if seriously considering whether this was the brand that they should buy—all the while stroking in their pockets the only sad coin they have, which will likely be spent on lunch and dinner at an Automat."[9]

Argentina began constructing a network of national highways and roads in the 1930s. Until that time, automobile traffic was largely confined to urban centers, and most specifically, to their central commercial and financial districts. Traffic was an important issue for city officials and, in the emerging field of urban planning, controlling street traffic became a primary objective. In 1927, the weekly magazine *Caras y Caretas* announced that the city was being "invaded" by automobiles.

With Model Ts occupying half of the road, avenues were no longer avenues: "With their overwhelming ambition, the metallic coaches run up and over the sidewalks and drive into empty lots," the article reports. Not even the sidewalks are free from the "plague" of "rubber-footed [beasts] with breath that smells of gasoline."[10]

Thanks to "the madness, the vertigo of velocity that like an infectious micro-organism, is carried in the blood of every man who takes the wheel of a car," a swift rise in speed transformed every intersection into a danger zone. The hurried anxiety unleashed by individual control of the accelerator prevailed over any punitive measure that the city might impose. For many witnesses, this new means of transportation reflected a culture of instant gratification and morally questionable modernity, where the tyranny of desire impaired new drivers' capacity for self-control, spinning into a perceptual frenzy, an intoxicating stream of light and shadow. In 1927, the writer Manuel Gálvez published a story that put his protagonist—a marginal writer who rarely experienced such luxury—in the backseat of a rental car moving through the downtown streets of Buenos Aires. "It is a thrill to see corners crashing with each other and streets cowardly escaping. . . . The collapse of colossal buildings in the distance, houses built one on top of the other, automobiles flying away, pedestrians swallowed up by the somber caves of dark doorways, the quick combat of shadow and light, reflection upon reflection—my eyes devour all of this as I ride in the automobile."[11]

For the police in charge of managing city traffic, the automobile was not a joy, but a burden. The authorities observed that even though drivers left behind a nearly constant trail of infractions, their violations were sanctioned less and less. Many of the drivers were men of such social and political importance that they simply refused to accept that their "triumphal, loud and unchained" new habit should be interrupted by a lowly police officer. The tension reminds us of another novelty of car culture: the sudden rise in interactions between police and members of the upper class—that is, men and women who were not accustomed to being stopped or questioned in public areas. And if police did not issue enough fines against the rapidly increasing number of traffic transgressions, this was also because the traffic cop was immersed in a broader acceleration of street activity. Indeed, authorities noticed that the police were losing the ability to even *perceive* violations amid the rising chaos of the street.[12] The noise of heavy tires on pavement, of brakes and motors, all raised street noise to new levels. Likewise, the blow of the officer's whistle seemed to dissolve into thin air, no longer commanding attention. It would have to be far louder if it was to be heard over the traffic, police authorities observed. The cars speeding through public streets transformed the experience of public space, as well as the acoustic ecology of the street, its traffic rules, its power hierarchies, and its risks.

None of this did anything to hinder the rise of this new consumer fetish. The car was associated with ideological prestige, the dynamism of U.S. postwar production in contrast to the decay of British railroad monopolies. It contained all of the glamour of the same lifestyle on display in entertainment and new advertising. Many were dazzled by the new consumer culture, but not everyone. On his return after a seven-year stay in Europe, a young Jorge Luis Borges deplored the ideological triumph of speed in the city of his childhood. Lamenting the new velocity of cosmopolitan urbanity, he treasured a certain unchangeable *criollo* essence where a slow possession of time and space was still a virtue. Ignoring the dizzying speed of traffic on Las Heras Avenue, Borges described a horse and cart moving at its own pace. At the reins was a "hefty criollo driver":

> There the plodding wagon is continually overtaken, but this very lagging becomes its triumph, as if the speed of other vehicles were the anxious scurrying of the slave, whereas the wagon's slowness is a complete possession of time, if not eternity. (Time is the native Argentine's infinite, and only, capital. We can raise slowness to the level of immobility, the possession of space.)[13]

The rush ("the anxious scurrying of the slave") had begun in Borges's city, with the trolley and the subway by then already incorporated into a new transport network. The *auto*mobile, as its name reflected, bestowed on the driver the power of acceleration. This sense of independence was the great novelty of the 1920s. While car advertisements typically connected automobile ownership to an ideal family life, rising tourism, and weekend trips, its freedom also opened new opportunities for clandestine affairs and sexual escapades. Like the bicycle during its heyday, the car gave women more independence. In Buenos Aires, as in other major cities, the "modern girl" who drove with a bobbed haircut and cigarette in hand emerged as an icon of modernity.[14]

The era's mass-produced cars also became protagonists of the "new" crime. Crime stories were flooded with references to automobiles: "Authorities are searching for a suspicious car"; "The automobile used in the assault has been found"; "They say a phantom car appeared"; "The *voiturette* went that way!" "The automobile taken by the assailants is a Studebaker." As a central component of criminal investigations, the car emerged as a new subject in police chronicles.

FIGURE 1. *La Razón*, October 12, 1927.

Not just any criminal group had easy access to an automobile, of course. But, by the end of the 1920s, this obstacle could be overcome with relative ease by stealing a car off the street, or hijacking a taxi. Both practices grew exponentially, introducing a new word into the modern lexicon: a "*spiantador,*" or car thief. *Spiantadores* became the police investigator's primary target for raids in Buenos Aires and in neighboring towns.[15]

Writer and journalist Roberto Arlt portrayed this drifting "union of thieves" in his vignette "The Art of Stealing Cars," printed in the daily *El Mundo*. In it he described the modus operandi of a band of thieves who were able to make 250 cars vanish "into thin air" over the course of two years. Unable to hide his fascination and envy, Arlt viewed these gangs as part of an equitable business arrangement, born of the "*reducidero*"—a most perfect consumer society, where everyone worked some and no one was exploited.

> It is the most perfect because, as in the hive, there is one bee that brings the pollen and another that builds the honeycomb. In this case, there is one who changes the motor's number, another who repaints the body or modifies a

FIGURE 2. "Cars Stolen by a Group of Bandits: Police Found
These Two Ford Automobiles Completely Disassembled and in
This Curious Position." *Caras y Caretas* archive, January 19,
1921; AGN, Department of Photographic Documents.

closed coach car into a "voiturette"; and then one, far away, who goes out
into the street to get the goods; and the leader who watches over his accomplices and thanks God for making such good men. And then the guy comes
in to say he's found a buyer, and everyone rejoices, and there is no yes or no,
or more or less; and one hand cleans the other and both wash the face, and
they all celebrate the good things in life with generous drinks; and everyone
works their own hours, without complaining, in perfect and total harmony;
and there is no accounting book listing income and expenses; there are no
dreaded tasks, no one buys on credit, not even Christ, but there are smiles
and praise to God, for filling this land with fools.[16]

The car became a symbol of group crime. Each thief had a particular role to play: one handled the gun, one took the loot, the driver waited with the motor running, and so on. This type of organized or semi-organized plan, the police observed, began to attract cultivators of more individual illegal activities. One symptom of the rise of group crime in the 1930s was the recurring use of the term *"hampa,"* a word for a gang with a collective modus operandi, internally established codes and language, and a certain level of hierarchy and specialization. Emerging within an illegal world of practices that the police and the press described as professional, or at least internally coherent, this type of organized crime could only be defeated in a "war," one for which the state would have to prepare and organize itself.

The car raised the tempo of crime, adding to the element of surprise as well as the incredulity left in the wake of any given episode. The quick sequence of events during these robberies, escapes, and disappearances, often followed by a car chase, fell into synch with the new rhythm of the street. The acceleration and independence of movement also increased the chances that a crime could occur at any moment. The protective cloak of night, so critical to the imagination of nineteenth-century crime, was no longer a necessary condition, regardless of whether a robbery was important or routine, meticulously planned or poorly conceived. Darkness had once accommodated an entire spectrum of stealth crime, creating dangers for the law-abiding city that were latent and invisible. The *punguista* (cat burglar) and the *escruchante* (a stealth lock picker) presided over an imaginary underworld of urban robbery, with a range of professional tools at their disposal: toolboxes were filled with picks, hooks, files, bulbs, molds, and pins, a "Martín Pescador" (used to fish through open windows), gloves, and other utensils. These small tools were those of a professional who cultivated his skills of invisibility and anonymity under the protection of night. With quick, soundless footfalls he moved across rooftops, jumping, climbing, until he disappeared into a busy intersection or vacant construction site. The obsession with false identities was pervasive in the late 1800s, when servants with exotic accents, prostitutes, and other "accomplices to crime and vice" troubled police and criminologists. The conman's hits were imagined as part of a network of underground social exchanges that, in turn, helped him cover his tracks.

Robberies conducted in broad daylight during the 1920s and 1930s contrasted sharply with this tradition. In this new economy of public performance, the fleeing criminal left behind plenty of witnesses who could then help the press reconstruct the sequence of events. In this way, criminals' performances became the object of public opinion, and, as we will see, the most renowned figures of the underworld began to take their public audiences into consideration. Of course, nocturnal crime persisted, as did scams and cons. But each holdup, each robbery or event taking place in the light of day, enacted a powerful new grammar of violence. In this context, mounting anecdotes and cases of visible crime contradicted the police's placid quantitative data.

"The robbery happened just next door to the commissioner's office, or in front the Police Headquarters on Moreno Street? My good man! Do you think the audacious thief cares about such details, knowing his accomplice in the driver's seat is a master of his trade and the motor is running?"[17] This show of resignation on the part of the police suggests that in the late 1920s there was a close association between "new" crime and the figure of the skilled driver. Indeed, the driver had become an archetype of modern virility, with tales of escaping gangsters echoing the sport of car racing and reinforcing the link between driving and masculine prowess. One creative policeman went as far as designing a tool to stop getaway vehicles: a scissor-like device, studded with nails, that an officer could take with him and fold out across the width of the car, closing off the criminal's escape path.[18] The device apparently did not work very well. Escape cars prevailed, generating a fundamental change in the modalities of crime as well as in the conceptualization of police intervention. The car, along with the development of a network of roads during the 1930s, propelled crime into a larger radius of action.

The automobile also gave mobsters an ability to pass easily through the capital city and enter the far less monitored corridors of Buenos Aires Province. This newfound mobility was crucial to the development, in the 1930s, of large-scale operations like those led by "Pibe Cabeza," "Mate Cosido," and the mafia king "Chicho Grande," whose crimes exposed gaps in the law and caused innumerable jurisdictional clashes between police.

The car extended the geography of crime far beyond the city limits, dispersing into spaces as wide as the nation itself (and beyond). Their creative use of the automobile also allowed these new criminal celebrities to engage in some daring escapades, moving from the city to the suburbs, and then from the suburbs into rural areas, crossing jurisdictions and escaping authorities in each one. Pibe Cabeza (Rogelio Gordillo's alias) and his band "made a hit one day in Córdoba, then the next day in Rosario, then the next in Buenos Aires, disorienting the police, who were left looking for him in the suburbs of the cities where he had last been seen," one experienced police officer recalled.[19] In his objectives, technologies, and public relationships, Gordillo was a typical *pistolero* of his time. He and his band were also in constant motion. At the peak of his fame, in 1936, he might steal two cars to use in a holdup, escape into a nearby province, sell his stolen *voiturette,* and rob a third vehicle to get to his next target. After his robbery of the Nobleza de Tabaco Company, in the center of the city of Rosario, he escaped in a "magnificent car" with a license plate from the town of Moreno, in the province of Buenos Aires. The police began an interminable search for the gang. They raided hideouts and confiscated a long list of stolen vehicles between Buenos Aires, Rosario, and Santa Rosa. The band, meanwhile, kept moving, occasionally stealing trucks and even hearses or, most often, hijacking a rented car and disposing of the driver.[20]

All of this was made possible by the network of paved national roads that was constructed during the 1930s. As in the United States, this infrastructure made possible a quick escape and expanded the geographical range of criminal operations in a manner never before seen.[21] An intimate knowledge of possible escape routes from the cities, and the connections between large and secondary roads, became indispensable. Pibe Cabeza's band was considered nearly untraceable because he counted on the services of drivers like Caprioli, or Ferrari "El Vivo," who the papers noted was a skilled navigator with a detailed knowledge of roads. Caprioli knew "the neighboring streets and interprovincial routes between Santa Fe, Córdoba, Buenos Aires, and La Pampa thanks to his extensive travel as a car salesman and from his previous escapes."[22]

The newspaper *El Mundo* reported that "city police, along with police from Buenos Aires, Santa Fe, Córdoba and even Montevideo are mobilized and searching for the gang led by Pibe Cabeza, the author of the cinematic raid that ran from Córdoba to the suburbs of this city."[23] The art of pursuing criminals had changed dramatically, leading to demands for a federal police force with jurisdiction across the entire country. The needed reform would be passed in 1943.

Taken together, mobile banditry and interprovincial car chases bolstered arguments for a national police force and an organ of federal power that could preside over provincial authorities. The subject first arose when the famed North American bandit Butch Cassidy appeared in Argentina. Escaping the United States, Cassidy fled to Patagonia, where he committed a series of surprise attacks on regional banks. These robberies spurred some of the first public calls for a national police force.

After one particularly stunning episode, a police magazine commented that the proliferation of such imported criminal behaviors posed a challenge in Argentina: "Is this not, then, the purpose of a *national* police force, which is to say a police force that can operate across the entire national territory, with a centralized authority, and not be bothered, nor slowed, nor inhibited by the inconveniences and obligations that arise in our current federal system of government?"[24]

In the 1930s, as organized crime went from being a rare occurrence to occupying the center of attention, policing also began to change. The First Police Congress (Primer Congreso de Policía) in 1933 prioritized methods of action against interjurisdictional criminal activity. In 1937, following several failed attempts to capture mobile gangs—in this case, the crew run by "Mate Cosido"—the chief of the Division of Investigation, Vacarezza, presented the National Executive Office with the first proposal for the creation of a federal police force. In July 1938, in response to a new wave of *"pistolerismo"* in the provinces, the government created the Gendarmería Nacional, a semi-military force with national jurisdiction.[25] We will return to these reforms at other points in this book.

Paradoxically, the expanding geography of crime, which moved from the metropolis out into smaller provincial towns, was also the result of the government's extension of a network of national roads and the production of detailed maps of the countryside. The men who advocated for the road network, who wrote guidebooks, made maps, and lobbied for infrastructure investment argued that a national road network would stimulate tourism and foster the economic integration of the country. They were unaware, of course, that they were also helping the nationalization of crime.[26] Nevertheless, like the radio broadcasts of automobile races, the press coverage of the era's high-profile chases through the *pampas*, Patagonia, the Chaco desert, and mountain towns, accompanied as it was by maps and detailed chronicles, added significantly to the public's growing consciousness and knowledge of national territory.

ARMED MEN

You can tell how modern a city is, the detective thought,
by the weapons you hear going off in its streets.
—Élmer Mendoza, *Silver Bullets*

The mobile bandit, escaping into neighboring towns after every hit, was of course armed.[27] It's almost not worth pointing out, since his stylized figure—pistol-pointing, fedora, double-breasted suit—had become an emblem of mob-era modernity. Among civilians, the circulation of firearms was no novelty in the 1920s and 1930s. On the contrary, the idea of the "armed citizen" was a critical component of the Argentine political imaginary in the nineteenth century and, despite initiatives to eradicate the practice, upper-class *porteños* long resisted giving up the time-honored practice of dueling.[28] Nonetheless, the mass production and sale of revolvers—which coincided with the decline of the gentlemanly duel—spoke to changes in the market and in modern, popular codes of male violence. Amid these changes, gun ownership lost its previous association with political citizenry.

Aspects of this phenomenon can be traced to changes in technology and the economy of the global arms trade. The privatization of the assembly and sales of arms dates to the end of the nineteenth century and is an example of triumphant capitalism, as evidenced in the trajectories of arms manufacturers such as Krupp, Vickers, and Remington. Representatives of these and other companies traveled the world, selling their products to state and private entities. Then, World War I saw advances in the design and manufacture of quicker, more precise guns. The war had not even ended when the technology developed to produce this arsenal migrated from the battlefield to broader society, expanding the market and making prices more accessible than ever. Until the mid-1930s, when the laissez-faire system that these companies had benefited from began drawing criticism, leading to calls in most western countries for greater oversight and the enactment of laws restricting gun ownership, commerce flourished for the gun manufacturers, whose only obstacle to growth was the law of supply and demand.[29] Even if we limit our analysis of gun sales to the realm of private consumption, leaving aside military sales in wartime (which also grew to unprecedented levels), we see that guns found a substantial market beyond the world of organized crime.

The effects of this phenomenon were already visible in Argentina at the beginning of the century. The magazine *Sherlock Holmes* noted in 1912: "Along with the agricultural machines, manpower, and tools that arrive in our country like an army and an arsenal of labor, an invasion of portable arms has been on the rise for some time, imported in great quantities, and made available to the public for easy acquisition."[30] Veteran police officer Laurentino Mejías remembered in 1927 that the revolver was not common during his early days on the force "because [the sound of its] thunder rattled the nerves of the *criollo*." It was a pricey instrument that was rarely seen on the streets—"not like later,

---

[when the revolver was] sold cheaply, on display in the windows of any used clothing store or junk shop, available for all tastes and budgets."[31]

A criminal seeking a gun did not need to turn to illegal trafficking to get it, since he was surrounded by thousands of completely legal offers. One need only peruse the illustrated magazines of the first four decades of the twentieth century to find advertisements for guns sold alongside other consumer objects. Payment plans made purchase all the more irresistible: "Free: without spending a cent you can obtain all classes of silver and 18 karat gold watches, rifles, revolvers of all kinds, fine footwear, electric lanterns, silverware, tea and coffee sets, and a great variety of other items," announced the American Import Company. Said one advertisement, "For only five cents in stamps, your only cost, we will give you a Colt revolver, camera, phonograph, etc. Just send your name and address."[32]

In 1920, Casa Rasetti tempted *Caras y Caretas* readers with automatic pocket revolvers for $50 and a .38 caliber for $90. If in 1920 a suit cost around $40, a pair of shoes around $15, a Kodak camera around $100, and a sewing machine around $150, it's safe to say that these seductive automatic pistols were within reach of many consumers (without even taking into account the market for used guns, even cheaper). During the Christmas season of 1920, Casa Masucci, a well-known department store, displayed gifts for men and women: a wide array of rings, bracelets, and necklaces for her, and for him, a shaving razor ("with three free replacement razors"), a flashlight ("with a free battery and replacement bulb"), and a .28 caliber Colt ("with a free box of bullets").

"Oxidized or Nickel-coated. Checkered walnut grip." Some advertisements for Colt pistols appealed to the aesthetics of design. Others evoked the dark magnetism of the undercover detective: "For the investigator's pocket: Colt *Detective*. Special Revolver (Double Action)."[33] Others appealed to militaristic martial law, calling their gun "the weapon of law and order." There were guns for discreet use, marketed to "respectable" men. The Orbea revolver was the "best gun for PERSONAL SECURITY and for THE DEFENSE OF ONE'S FAMILY." The "El Casco" brand offered its weapon to middle-class husbands who when they kissed their wives good-bye upon leaving home each morning, wanted to be comforted by the knowledge that they were starting the day with a gun in their pocket.

In Latin America, evidence of the circulation of guns is abundant, as is the familiarity of large sections of the male population with pistols and revolvers. Many of the guns that were bought and sold during this era were the product of the U.S. gun industry; the brands that had

FIGURE 3. *Caras y Caretas*, June 22, 1929.

developed pistol technology in the second half of the nineteenth century—Remington, Smith & Wesson, and, above all, Colt—had become synonymous with the advance of the U.S. western frontier. In Mexico City in 1917, for example, pat downs of men arrested for drunkenness yielded dozens of these brands of pistols. As in Buenos Aires, police statistics in São Paulo demonstrate a rapid shift away from stabbing to shooting homicides in the first decades of the twentieth century.[34] The Spanish essayist Rafael Barrett, who lived in Buenos Aires, Montevideo, and Asunción during the period, described the situation:

> In these streets each man carries five strangers' lives in the pocket of his trousers. The student [or] the mild-mannered employee cannot buy a watch, but can afford a revolver. The stylish youth leaves his Smith in the coatroom at the dance, next to his hat. Gentlemen go to the club to read the newspaper, armed with the artillery of a betrayed husband. Lawyers, doctors, even men of God leave their homes carefully armed. There is an air of tragedy; they think themselves heroes.[35]

Disturbing editorials and news articles noted that gun owners were unable to control their use of these new artifacts, as statistics clearly showed. In the 1920s, it became customary to celebrate the New Year with fireworks and a hail of gunfire. During the campaign preceding the election of Yrigoyen in 1928, shots were often fired during political rallies and street marches. Pistols and gunshots became part of clashes between unions. Conflicts that transpired "in the heat of the moment" also had a tendency to end in gunfire: citizens exchanged fire in bars, on street corners, and in the middle of domestic disputes. When cops and robbers

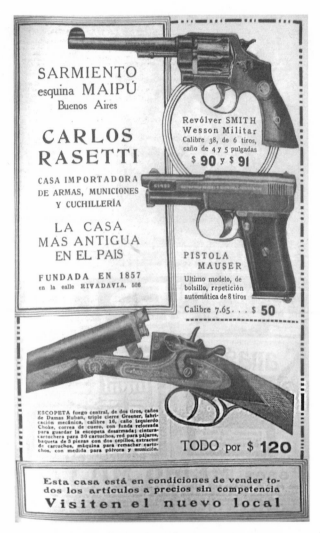

FIGURE 4. *Caras y Caretas,* December 11, 1920.

exchanged shots, onlookers often joined in, opening up a third line of fire. The more moderate anarchist leaders, for their part, felt obliged to remind gun owners to avoid engaging in "friendly" shootouts when out on a picnic, in order to reduce the number of weekend accidents. Routine violence interspersed the pages of Buenos Aires newspapers.[36]

Naturally, these gunfights called into question the state's monopoly on violence. This concept, however, should be understood as more figurative than literal: in no society does the state expect to maintain effective monopoly over violence, provided that it possesses sufficient means to regulate the arms used by other sectors of society.[37] The problem arises when the coercive equipment the state uses to guarantee a society's *perception* of a monopoly is more antiquated than that used by the subjects over which it exercises control.

A shift at this level, taking place gradually over the course of the 1930s, is shown in changes in the legal framework of the time (we will return to the changes in the police force in chapters 3 and 4). The availability of increasingly fast, precise, and powerful guns called into question the permissive context of their circulation, which was regulated by administrative edicts and resolutions. Buenos Aires's contravention code (which everyone ignored) was meant to regulate minor offenses, calling for fines between $15 and $30 and up to a month of jail time for publicly bearing arms in the street, in a store or in public space, or for shooting one's weapons within the confines of the city, including private property.[38] At the beginning of the 1930s, authorities modified this framework. The category of "arms of war" became part of the lexicon, designating any gun larger than 5 mm. Customs controls and regulatory taxes on armories became more severe. In 1932, a new, more zealous police edict limited the sale of individual arms over .38 caliber. Finally, in 1936 and 1939, two national decrees made it illegal to buy or sell automatic and non-automatic guns larger than a .22 caliber: "Practice has demonstrated that it is necessary to ensure, in the most efficient way possible, the lives of the population, continually exposed to the unpredictable danger of modern automatic repeating firearms and the effects derived from the caliber of its projectiles."[39]

In reality, the new mechanized speed of firearms was better represented by the machine gun than by the automatic handgun. Designed for trench warfare, the machine gun was the firearm with the most direct lineage to the battlefield. Its wartime connotations made it difficult to market in the postwar era—until organized criminals adopted the weapon during Prohibition.[40] The machine gun then became a weapon associated with the police and the most professional bandits, although it only occasionally made an appearance locally. In 1932, authorities categorized the machine gun as a weapon of "collective action," pushing its sale into the black market. There, it sold well. When authorities finally caught the anarchist gunman Severino Di Giovanni, for example, they found a small collection of an unknown model of Thompson machine guns. One observer remarked, "Only the devil knows how they got [them] into the country."[41] Anytime the rattle of gunfire broke out, the event was narrated in detail in the daily press. The machine gun had evocative power:

its presence in the urban and suburban scene paralleled the emergence of sound film and the arrival of gangster movies, which, in the early 1930s, enthralled the masses.

The availability of guns transformed the kind of duress associated with robbery and heightened the intimidating potential of each assault. Even if we accept the stable rates of crimes against property, as represented in police statistics, there is no doubt about the increase in the rate of homicides and nonfatal wounds—in other words, a rise in interpersonal violence. The rather placid curve in robberies and theft cannot be interpreted in isolation, nor should it be decontextualized from the rising number of persons killed by gunfire between the end of the 1920s and the beginning of the 1930s. The strong association between robbery and automatic weapons implied a transformation in the nature of "common" homicide, something previously presented as being confined to the private sphere.

On the one hand, the armed and car-driving bandits were connected to a professional model of organized crime, known locally as *"el hampa."* On the other hand, their rupture with certain codes of violence was perceived as a sign of the deprofessionalization of crime. Social sanctions often made reference to the form that violence took, not just its motivation. Thus, scenes of car chases and crossfire appeared as vain, amateur exhibitions. Control over firepower emerged as a central value in crime. With his public image in mind, the social bandit Mate Cosido pledged to do his best to avoid shooting civilians, including men who transported the money he was trying to steal. And if a robbery took a tragic turn, it was always someone else's responsibility. He told the magazine *Ahora* that he would "avoid violence whenever possible and, as is within my power, reduce the possibility of homicides and the sort of unfavorable commentary that dishonors me, and the comrades who accompany me."[42] A good (professional) *pistolero* was a man who knew when to use his coercive power, as distinct from the novice, who put at risk everyone but himself.

The increase in assaults called attention to the weakening of the rules of gun use among gentlemen. As was the case with so many changes brought on by modernity, the *pistolero* inspired nostalgia, a retrospective value placed on the more codified violence of the past. Amid yearning for the long-gone street corners of the old neighborhood, those sites of bravery and masculine ritual encoded in knife fights (the same fights that so fascinated Borges) acquired meaning in the context of the sudden irrelevance of those skills in an era of motorized armed robbery and the Colt .45. In a story published in the next decade, Borges would say:

"The singular style of his death seemed appropriate to them: Azevedo was the last representative of a generation of bandits who knew how to manipulate a dagger, but not a revolver."[43]

The demise of the knife at the hands of the revolver—that "mechanical, instantly fatal invention, child of modern industry, born of the spirit of speed"—led to a romantic appreciation for men of the dagger and the blade, for the gaucho and the suburban *compadrito*.[44] This new nostalgia was built on arguments dating back to the origins of the firearm. They were distant echoes, to be sure, but the essence of their moral critique was unmistakable. It celebrated the centuries-old skill of the knight of early modern Europe, who donned a sword and cape, and whose legendary abilities fell prey to the vulgar speed of gunpowder. The early disdain for firearms, at the very moment of their birth, when the age-old knowledge of the art of war and fifteenth-century codes of gentlemanly honor were being left behind, elevated the aesthetic and moral value of the violence of the past.

The *pistolero* of the 1920s and 30s did not need a dignified skill in order to impose his will, a fact that devalued his status in relation to the *compadrito* or the cunning gaucho, who used his entire body in a fight, and whose weapon (an extension of his arm) brought him into intimate contact with his foe. What was now being challenged was the balance of power between battling parties, and a certain moral economy of the interaction. Wounds from firearms, produced at a distance, giving no chance to the adversary, were mediated by a simple mechanism called a trigger. The bullet holes it produced were as small and monotonous as the era that mass-produced them. By contrast, the knife (the gaucho's constant companion, and thus Argentina's national weapon) opened a wound that produced enormous quantities of blood, leaving marks that were rife with meaning. Sarmiento, who in *Facundo* had described this cult of courage with such disdain, highlighted the significance of facial scars resulting from knife fights. The idea was not to kill, but to leave a record of defeat: "His object is only to mark him, give him a slash on the face, leave an indelible sign on him. This is why the scars one sees in gauchos are rarely deep. The fight, then, is engaged for show, for the glory of victory, for the love of fame."[45] Eighty years later, scarred faces were an anachronism and for that reason developed a positive connotation and a new association with national essence. The gunslinger knew nothing of the masculine codes honor of the knife fight. His reliance on firearms was proof that he had been weakened by the excesses of cosmopolitan civilization.

Overturning hierarchies, the automatic pistol was modern also because it lacked a genealogy. Whereas "the legends of the primitive age made gods the bestowers of the sword, the invention of the revolver looks like the work of a rushed North American."[46] Indeed, no criminal figure had ever been so clearly a product of foreign influences as the *pistolero*. His plebeian disdain for all pedigree—including his own poor and morally questionable heritage—was at the basis of the mounting audacity of these casual robberies and motorized bands, which made violence such a banal occurrence. If the *pistolero* enjoyed any social legitimacy at all, it derived from his vanguard status when it came to boldness. "Audacity": the term, which kept appearing in descriptions, alluded to the permission the *pistolero* gave himself to violate codes, as well as to the shock and ambivalent fascination of the public when he crossed that line.

In his influential (and controversial) book on the seductions of crime, Jack Katz argues that the study of crime must take into account its undeniably attractive elements, particularly its powerful emotional draw. Gang robberies and successful getaways in stolen cars, he says, have as much to do with the shared thrill of transgression as they do with the objective value of stolen property. To understand the experience of this kind of clandestine activity, one must appreciate how a society's sensual structure relates to the world of fantasy and how these pleasures play into the local culture of violence.[47]

Drawing on the criminological common sense of the lay observer, contemporary descriptions of *pistolerismo* drew links between the new forms of crime and the dizzying language of consumer society, with its celebration of ever greater and more immediate pleasure. The *pistolero*, it was said, was willing to burn himself out in his rush to experience all the pleasures of the world. For his hedonism and obsession with fame, he was the most extreme example of the subject contaminated by modernity. In its way, his individualism was in synch with the greedy consumerism of his age. He was its reflection—distorted, yet recognizable nonetheless.

THE CRIOLLO *PISTOLERO*: A TYPOLOGY

¡Qué falta de respeto, qué atropello a la razón!
¡Cualquiera es un señor! ¡Cualquiera es un ladrón!
—Enrique Santos Discépolo, *Cambalache* (1934)

During the interwar period, "armed robbery" became the most talked about form of crime. It was the *prototype* of crime, a standard format that connected a wide variety of phenomena with various objectives, levels of ambition, and planning. When it came time to diagnose the rise in violence and criminality, certain operational coincidences—use of firearms, means of transport, daytime strikes—lumped together a range of practices whose logic and timing were actually quite varied.

The most typical operation was the ambush of a truck transporting a company payroll or bank deposits. Access to automobiles made it possible for gangs to intercept these vehicles mid-transport, far simpler and less risky than holding up the bank itself, and more lucrative than robbing stores. The proliferation of this daytime crime inspired a host of new security measures: companies began to transport cash in armored trucks and pay armed guards to oversee the loading and unloading of cargo. Heists involving public monies came to be seen as the highest form of economic organized crime, lavishly covered in the printed press. Examples abound, though the first memorable operation occurred on May 2, 1921. In the middle of the day, two blocks from the Plaza de Mayo (and the Casa Rosada, seat of the executive branch of the national government), a car intercepted a customs agent transporting $620,000.[48] Eleven years later, on December 9, 1932, three men boarded a train transporting railway workers' payrolls during a routine stop. A few minutes later, amid a hail of bullets and carrying a suitcase full of money, they jumped from the train and got away. Such a feat required good information, arms, a hideout, and excellent timing—the appearance of the getaway car coincided perfectly with the arrival of the train, and everything transpired in a matter of minutes after the train reached the stop. Payroll heists, which began appearing in the early 1920s and expanded over the next two decades, made some reputations. Mate Cosido, the most socially minded of the modern rail bandits, organized high-profile attacks on large companies like Bunge & Born, counting on an efficient network of informants and a thorough knowledge of national highways, shortcuts, and secret paths—not to mention the railway grid, which he resorted to when the highways were too well protected.[49] If the heist took place in the city, the automobile was used only to flee the immediate scene of the crime, as traffic often impeded a clear getaway. In that case, one or two members of the band would get out of the car a few blocks from the scene (with the money) and calmly board a trolley, then blend with the crowd by pretending to read the paper.

Payroll robbery required some organization. On the other end of the spectrum were amateur holdups of pharmacies, butchers, or garages. After emptying the register, thieves would often attempt to get away in a car or a trolley. A third variant, which required little or no planning, was a carjacking, for which one needed nothing more than a gun and sufficient skill behind the wheel to make a getaway.

Not every *pistolero* fit this description, however. After all, firearms and automobiles were adopted by groups one would be hard-pressed to categorize as assailants, but who were nevertheless closely associated with this brand of thieves. Such was the case with the Sicilian mafias established in the province of Santa Fe at the end of the nineteenth century. As in other places with similar immigration patterns, ancestral practices of kidnapping, extortion, and threats were imported to the Santa Fe *pampa,* sowing terror among small- and medium-sized merchants. By 1930 these practices had become endemic to the area. Due to a combination of factors, including greater ease of mobility as well as concentration of power in the hands of certain leaders, the mafia's territory began to expand beyond the port city of Rosario, and its operations grew in complexity and visibility. As we will see in the next chapter, this expansion led to rising panic. Some high-profile kidnappings, like the case of young Abel Ayerza, who was captured and killed in the summer of '32–33, brought the figure of the powerful organized crime boss to the national stage. At the end of the 1930s, however, the age of mafias appeared to be over.[50]

October 1, 1927. Three men with bandaged heads were waiting in the hallway of Rawson Hospital with other patients. When employees transporting salaries arrived, the "patients" suddenly took control of the bagged money and shot their guns in the air, fleeing with $141,000. A getaway car waited outside.[51] "Unheard of, a spectacular holdup, cinematic," gushed *La Nación*. That one of the most prototypical and famous criminal episodes of the era was not the work of common criminals but that of political activists—in this case, anarchists—speaks to the degree of operational uniformity in crimes against property.

Historians of anarchism have shown the problematic relationship between these "anarcho-criminals" and the old libertarian tradition, as well as the heated internal debates over the use of violence during the early decades of the century. They have illustrated the degree of concern over the precarious distinction between anarchist violence and criminal violence, a confusion resulting from poorly defined targets.[52] Even though it was condemned by central figures of the libertarian world, the *pistolero* turn within anarchism (part of the same repertoire that produced a marked rise in bombings during the 1920s) was a subject of great importance in Argentina, as it occurred within a context of growing radicalization and internal conflicts among anarchists, with more than a few internal battles settled with large fires, explosions, and armed conflicts.[53] The relationship between the anarchist assailants and the doctrine of direct action—which defended the use of *all* strategies leading to revolution—also presented important variants. Severino Di Giovanni and Miguel Roscigna, for example, embodied the most ideological expression of this kind of activism. Their "expropriations," which did not exclude direct links with the world of crime, served the broader aim of the great anti-bourgeois revolution: financing *comités pro-presos* (committees that sought the release of political prisoners and raised money for their families), counterfeiting, funding their own publishing house, and so on. At the other end of the spectrum, the assailant Bruno Antonelli Debella ("Facha Bruta") cultivated a more instrumental relationship with expropriative anarchism and, despite his libertarian connections, his criminal rationale was indistinguishable from that of other gangsters.[54] Although highly visible, expropriative anarchism had a relatively short run: it peaked at the end of the 1920s and underwent brutal repression following the 1930 military coup. By the end of that decade, its moment had passed.

Setting aside the question of the role of violence in the path toward revolution or its legitimacy within the anarchist tradition, what is most relevant here are the similarities between the methods of "expropriative" robbery and those of bands who intended to use their loot in a very different fashion. The links between anarchism and criminality were nothing new, but at the beginning of the century the figure of the "dangerous" anarchist was associated with a very specific kind of violence (bombings). By the 1920s and 1930s, this relationship had unraveled, allowing for a new hybrid figure to emerge: the "anarcho-criminal." The relationship between criminal and anarchist methodologies, which was made clear in photographic reconstructions of anarchist holdups, fed into a larger perception of organized crime. In police reports the term *"pistoleros"* was reserved for anarchist expropriators. From the point of view of the material history of illegal practices, these bands were far from being an anomaly: in their public performance against the law, they belonged to their time.

It is difficult to determine how political violence was understood within the context of perceptions of a crime wave in the 1930s, but it was undoubtedly an important component of its interpretation. Moreover, the confusion between political violence and common crime was deliberately exploited, as uprisings against political fraud were narrated using the vocabulary reserved for common criminality. During the Radical revolts of January 1933, for example, the Conservative paper *La Opinión* announced that headlines "inform the government about the *gang robberies* conducted in Buenos Aires and other parts of the nation."[55]

Other expressions of "tough politics," however, more than justified the kind of language that would conflate *pistolerismo* with the struggle for power. Such was the case with the *matón de comité,* a type of street thug who embodied the era of fraud, weapons, and gambling. With the heightening of confrontations between Radicals and Conservatives, some *caudillos* of Greater Buenos Aires made alliances with known *pistoleros* to reinforce their territorial control and eliminate the Radical Party's threat in the streets. The partnership between Conservative *caudillo* Barceló and the thug "Ruggierito" is one of the best-known examples. On the borders of legality, where politics and police action intersected, gambling and prostitution served as a source of wealth on both large and small scales. The *pistolero* on the outskirts of Buenos Aires emerged as a player in this fight for political and territorial control. We will return to this subject in chapter 5.

The figure of the *pistolero* was the product of a convergence of factors in 1920s and 1930s Argentina. His rise, like his decline, can be located at the intersection of histories of modernization, consumption, and political life. Though scoffed at by traffickers, the regulation of the arms market placed limits on a model of masculinity associated with the mass circulation of pistols. The violent defeat of "expropriative" anarchism at the beginning of the 1930s eliminated some of the most visible practitioners of *pistolerismo.* The long road to the end of this period of political fraud marked, in turn, the marginalization of a way of doing politics that was rapidly losing legitimacy. During the Peronist period, further efforts to reform the Buenos Aires Province police would circumscribe the links between police and *caudillo* politics. There would also be changes at the representational level. In the thousands of newspapers that continued to relay stories of the *pistolero,* a new figure appeared: the modern police officer, summoned by radio and arriving at the scene of the crime in his new patrol car. To do them both justice, the languages of science and naturalist literature would have to yield to those of cinema and comic strips. This is the transformation explored in the next chapter.

CHAPTER 2

Languages of Crime

Twelve readers are engrossed in a photographic storyboard reconstruction of the Rawson Hospital robbery, published in *Caras y Caretas* in October 1927. A woman on the trolley, a guard on a crowded street corner, a chauffeur, a doorman, a butcher, a shoe shiner in the plaza, a government official with his feet on his desk, a family working at a market stall, a gentleman getting ready for a shave at the barbershop, workers at a meatpacking plant: all read the news of the robbery, each "believing that they've found a clue that could lead to the criminals' capture." The chronicle connects widely dispersed readers, entwining them in one of the most irresistible spectacles of the metropolitan press.[1]

Narrating crime is an ancient and demanding practice. The discursive repertoire for describing homicide, fraud, robbery, and kidnapping reflects traditions with diverse origins, ideological implications, and aesthetic qualities. Taken as a whole, these tools have changed as they have adapted to the nature of specific crimes and reflected a particular era's frameworks of attributing causes and assigning blame, as well as the narrative and technical tools available. This chapter describes a period in which the most important national media outlets in Argentina began to alter the established language they used to describe crime, a moment when journalists, photographers, and illustrators began to deploy a wider set of resources to represent homicides, robberies, and kidnappings in the Buenos Aires press.

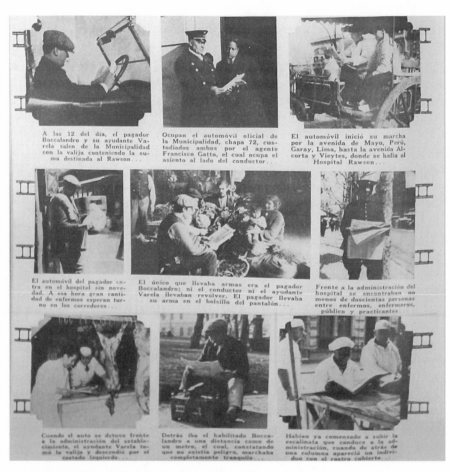

FIGURE 5. *Caras y Caretas*, October 15, 1927.

Studies have shown that transgression and the breaking of the law constitute key thematic elements in the origins of Argentine literature, particularly in the transition from publication in the commercial presses to the national novel. In the late nineteenth century, writers used police reports to produce realist, naturalist gaucho literature and paperback novels.[2] Beyond its literary traditions, Buenos Aires also has a long history of crime reporting. Though this history is still not well known, we can trace it back to the newspaper *Tribuna* (1860s) and then into the 1870s with *La Revista Criminal* and *La Patria Argentina*. Major newspapers replicated French journalists' crime reporting and, at the turn of

El individuo, dirigiéndose al ayudante, le gritó: "¡Arriba las manos!" Empuñando una pistola se arrimó rápidamente al ordenanza Varela...

Colocándole la pistola junto al lado izquierdo del cuerpo, el enmascarado le exigía silencio, sin ¢uda para que la amenaza pasara desapercibida al público...

En ese momento sonaron varias detonaciones y surgieron otros individuos, viéndose caer heridos al agente Gatto y al habilitado Boccalandro...

Los asaltantes, dueños del terreno y de la valija, huyeron, disparando sus revólvers, ante el terror y la confusión de las personas que lo presenciaban...

'arela, ileso, entró al hospital ¿ara relatar lo acontecido, pero los delincuentes habían desaparecido rápidamente, consumando la trágica obra...

"Caras y Caretas" reconstruye en todos sus pormenores el vandálico suceso, obteniendo con ello un verdadero triunfo informativo de palpitante actualidad...

Cuatro principales testigos

Santiago Peláez, el anciano que dió importantes detalles sobre la filiación de los asaltantes, coincidiendo con la del chofer Blanco, detenido en los primeros momentos.

Manuel Castro, que al regresar a su casa, después de ser asistido en el hospital, fué transportado en un automóvil dirigido por el chofer Blanco.

José Baliño, quien en unión de Castro fué también conducido en el mismo automóvil hasta su domicilio pocos minutos antes del asalto.

Enfermero del Hospital Rawson, Indalecio Pérez, cuya declaración aportó datos interesantes por no estar de acuerdo con la del chofer Blanco y la de los pasajeros.

the century, crime stories became prevalent in the new illustrated magazines. The most important of these, *Caras y Caretas,* reserved print space for crime stories throughout its forty years of life, which began in 1898.[3]

At the close of the nineteenth century, terminology taken from medicine, criminal anthropology, and psychiatry solidified a new "criminological common sense," providing a baseline of ideas regarding crime's causes that came to be shared by thousands of lay criminologists in living rooms, cafés, and trolleys. The enshrining of the fashionable genre of "the great case" meant, among other things, that ways of describing the transgressor centered more and more around one specific type of reasoning—the etiological, seeking to account for the causes of criminality (biological, environmental, psychological, or combinations thereof) by investigating each subject's past. This emphasis on personal history—for example, measurements of facial traits, a father's alcoholism, a mother's pathologies—opened the door to the kind of sensationalist voyeurism that came to characterize turn-of-the century police and crime reporting.

Three decades later, the themes and methods of crime stories had evolved, incorporating a new protagonist, the *pistolero*. Reporting popularized this figure to such a degree that it became difficult to separate the social phenomenon of *"pistolerismo"* from the advancements in the very graphic media that brought him to life: the expansion of their ability to reproduce images, the indulgent heterogeneity of their sources, and their commercial logic. The key to understanding the rise of the *pistolero*'s visibility resides in the affinity between the new languages of mass entertainment and certain criminal practices.

"A CRIME OF CINEMATIC PROPORTIONS"

The animated crime stories of the 1920s and '30s produced a shock to the senses. The repertoire of graphic and textual tools, mixing fiction and documentary, produced a cacophony in the reader. Indeed, this could also be said of all of the sensationalistic press since its early appearances in the late nineteenth century in Buenos Aires (and in other large cities). Its hyperstimulating power, which amplified the physical and perceptual stresses of the urban milieu, was a central aspect of the neurological ecology that enveloped the modern subject. It modified the texture of daily experience, emphasizing its velocity, fragmentation, and disorienting potential.[4] During the 1920s and '30s, these qualities could be found within an ever more varied collage of text and iconography replicated in the hundreds of thousands of copies of printed media.

In the 1920s, major papers like *La Nación* and *La Prensa* (pioneers of crime writing at the turn of the century) continued to report on the most important criminal cases. However, popular newspapers like *La Razón, Última Hora,* and (especially) *Crítica* emerged as new voices in the genre, taking up confrontation and melodrama as a trademark style. A decade later, *Noticias Gráficas* and *Ahora* took these excesses even further, consolidating the new expressive economy of the genre.

Their editors quickly came to understand that the entertainment value of crime reporting increased when accompanied by images. This was particularly evident when photographic technologies improved: the flash permitted a higher film velocity and more sensitive emulsions, and smaller cameras allowed a series of photographs to be taken in rapid succession. Combined with the newer, faster optics, all of these advances led to higher quality images.[5]

The tabloid format, which originated in New York, defined the symbolic vocabulary of crime in the 1920s. "The impact of the tabloid newspapers in their first three or four decades—dating from the birth of the *Daily News* of 1919," writes Luc Sante, "is something we can now imagine only with difficulty."[6] U.S. tabloids introduced a new model of press coverage that had an enormous influence on the Argentine press. Joseph Pulitzer, owner of the immensely popular *New York World* and a pioneer of the expansion of the penny press at the beginning of the century, argued that photographs helped him accomplish the true objective of his newspaper: to speak to the nation instead of to a small select audience.[7] Photographers began competing with each other, achieving celebrity status as they chased after the biggest "scoop" of the day. Arthur Fellig ("Weegee"), the first journalist granted access to a police radio, often boasted about arriving at the scene of a crime before any of his competitors. Weegee was so obsessed about being "in the right place at the right time" that he dreamed of taking photographs of a crime as it happened: "Some day I'll follow one of these guys with a 'pearl-gray hat,' have my camera all set and get the actual killing," he proclaimed in his self-celebratory book, *Naked City*.[8] Colleagues as far away as Buenos Aires shared in his fantasy, going to great lengths to capture images of crime.

Photography of *porteño* crime can be traced all the way back to the city's illustrated magazines, beginning with the pioneering *Caras y Caretas*. There, images of the latest murder story were juxtaposed with accounts of child beauty pageants, the "society" pages, articles celebrating scientific discoveries, political satire, and travel notes. And the photographers shot every aspect of the investigation: suspects, witnesses, the murder weapon, the cadaver, bloodstains, and the official and unofficial crime scene investigators. The most ordinary artifacts of city life—the front of a house "where the crime was committed," a tree, a hallway, a back garden "where the murderers entered"—became charged with ominous meaning.

The only picture the photographers at *Caras y Caretas* were missing was the one that Weegee dreamed of: that of the crime itself. When the cycle of robberies (described in chapter 1) began, magazines overcame this obstacle by publishing openly fictionalized reconstructions of crimes. It bears noting that these images were not mere inventions of a sensationalist press: photographic reconstructions of crime were already being used in police and judicial investigations. With the help of internal contacts, journalists could obtain this material, passing it directly from a judge's filing cabinet to the newspaper. The editor's captions, however, tended to be more spectacular and imaginative than those written by his judicial counterpart.

The nineteenth-century crime story structured the evidence around a retrospective investigation based on the detection and interpretation of clues and traces, resulting in a profusion of images of objects at the scene of the crime. The protagonists were "the official investigator," "the heroic journalist," and the victims. Whenever possible, a cadaver was produced. In the 1920s, journalists moved away from focusing on the investigation to a story line that centered on the crime itself. The trend was part of a larger change, as papers began to include photographic staging in their narrations, images that offered urban violence as spectacle. The photos that told the story of the assassination attempt on President Yrigoyen, those that showed the exact moment when a train collided with a car that had crossed the tracks, or for that matter any photo showing a public incident in mid-action: all were geared toward enhancing shock value through the sense of immediacy provided by the image.

Fictional photos of urban violence married the old journalistic need to entertain with new languages of spectacle, especially cinema, the medium that best exemplified the modern atmosphere of speed and change. Masked figures, crowds of extras, and scenic montages of banks, homes, and downtown city streets were all used to reconstruct for the readers the sensational crimes of the big city. One typical example was *Caras y Careta's* narration of the anarchist payroll robbery of Rawson Hospital described in the previous chapter.

The assault was reconstructed in four scenes inserted between two celluloid tapes—a format that recalled the excitement of the silver screen. The sequence was flanked by two small portraits: one of a corpse, and the other of a wounded man. Yet, the focus of the piece was not the suffering of the victims, but the dizzying action. Since the primary targets of these *pistolero*-like robberies were the coffers of faceless

FIGURE 6. Staging of a street incident for *Caras y Caretas*. AGN, Department of Photographic Documents. The arrow indicates the magazine photographer's location.

institutions, the victims became indistinct, commanding little emotional connection. Moreover, it was made explicit that the actions of the *pistolero*-star were fictional. This was made clear not only in the captions, which described an "exacting" reconstruction and "actors, immersed in their task, working deliberately," but also in descriptions of the crowd that gathered to watch the reconstruction, "enjoying [it] immensely."

The subject of the article was the *pistolero*—his weapons, his cars, and his performance. One did not need to scour the extravagant examples of sensationalist media to understand why the *Revista de Policía* called for controlling a press that seemed to delight in paying homage to criminals' "courage" and "valor." Even a police-friendly publication like *Caras y Caretas* (a longstanding advocate of "law and order") enticed readers with alluring crime reenactments. Photographs of criminals leaning out of cars, pointing their guns at the camera, did more to evoke the delights of crime than decry its moral and penal risks. The only police officer visible in the scene depicted in figure 8 looks ineffective, like a bystander. He's been left flatfooted, already several steps behind the criminals.

Whereas turn-of-the-century accounts described the delinquent as pathological, using scientificist language, the media of the 1920s

El sensacional asalto al habilitado

Las reconstrucciones del vandálico suceso hechas

El agente Gat-
to, muerto por
los foragidos. **1** La reconstrucción del asalto hecha por los redactores de "Caras y Caretas". Primera escena. **2** Otra vista de la reconstrucción hecha por nosotros y que tanto éxito tuvo en el público. Segunda escena.

Las noticias del atentado son leídas ávidamente y cada lector cree hallar una pista segura

FIGURE 7. "*Caras y Caretas*' Reconstructions of the Loutish Act Were a Great Success," *Caras y Caretas,* October 15, 1927.

characterized the *pistolero* in terms that were more technical than scientific, more attentive to present actions than to complex retrospective questions of personal history and causation. The question underlying these descriptions was no longer *why* the criminal committed his crime but rather *how* he did it: what weapons he used, what kind of car, if he had accomplices, where his hideouts were located. As the conceptual etiological matrix slid toward a morphological form of description, representations could group several criminal types (the anarchist "expropriator," the mafioso, and the common thief) with distinct genealogies and objectives into the single category of *pistolero*. In this framework, the biological, psychological, and socioeconomic history of the criminal was no longer important, and reference was no longer made to social class, nationality, or race—with the notable exception of ethnic mafias. The *pistolero*'s individuality became defined less by his mysterious pathology than by the form (and the notoriety) of his crime—in other words, by the performative quality of his actions. Therein lay the nucleus of his celebrity, bringing him into the fold of *pistolero* cult that so characterized the epoch.

"The '*pistolero*' is a man who brags of having accomplished great feats," observed Commissioner Cortés Conde. "After a holdup, one of his first tasks the next day is to collect all the newspapers that feature his crime, often exaggerating the danger and precision of his methods."[9] Some criminals even intervened to help shape their own public images. The bandit Mate Cosido, from Chaco Province, "fascinates the coun-

ıdo pagador del Hospital Rawson

ıchas por "Caras y Caretas" obtuvieron un gran éxito

3 Los redactores reconstruyen el hecho ante un público numerosísimo. Tercera escena.

4 Los actores, en plena tarea, trabajan concienzudamente para dar una exacta versión gráfica. Cuarta escena.

El habilitado que resultó herido en el asalto.

. seǵura

try," declared *Ahora*, analyzing his popularity. A series of articles promising the "true story" behind the outlaw described him as a combination of a socially minded bandit and a *pistolero*. He was the victim of police injustice who stole from the rich and gave to the poor; but he was also "audacious" and possessed an extraordinary talent for escaping after each assault. He used his weapons aggressively, but with discernment. Mate Cosido also took care to shape how the media narrated his most famous crimes: he ordered his crew to avoid killing. If he and his gang kidnapped a young woman for ransom, *Ahora* noted, she was treated "with care." "All witnesses agree . . . Mate Cosido and his men attempt to make the kidnapping tolerable for their victims," commented a special *Ahora* envoy to Chaco Province.[10]

Ahora was the publication that most contributed to delineating the figure of the interwar *pistolero*. Not that the magazine's representational strategies were particularly original. Its extravagant coverage combined visual codes of the cinema with the journalistic spectacle of true crime, drawing from a history of crime coverage that harkened back to *Caras y Caretas, Crítica,* and *Noticias Gráficas.* It was also deliberately retrospective: well into the mid-1930s and continuing for more than two decades, *Ahora* would revisit old *pistolero* stories and provide updates on famous cases, helping to create a popular memory of crime. For some time the magazine published a lot of re-creations of old crime reports from the "tough" years—the 1920s and '30s. In 1940, for example, it launched "A History of *Porteño* Crime," which featured

FIGURE 8. Reenactment of a robbery for *Caras y Caretas*, circa 1927. AGN, Department of Photographic Documents.

cases from the previous two decades: kidnappings, mafia wars, payroll robberies, the fall of a notorious gang. Lavishly and luridly illustrated, these recycled cases formed an archive of local crime.

Ahora's story on Mate Cosido was part of a larger trend in which organized crime bosses received the kind of attention usually bestowed upon movie stars: sentimental gossip, observations on the criminals' fashion choices, and the fabrication of legends.

As an early archive of the collective memory of crime, *Ahora* was also a factory of myths and celebrity. More importantly, perhaps, the magazine became a clearinghouse for a broad range of resources. Let's look at the threads—from cinema, literature, and journalism—that formed this rich narrative repertoire.

With its emphasis on the photographic essay, *Ahora* continued a tendency first developed in *Caras y Caretas*, although its more obvious template was the more sensationalist *Crítica*, a newspaper that exemplified the transition from a model of storytelling focused on clues and evidence to one that echoed the expressive economy of the entertainment industry.[11] With a daily circulation that surpassed one hundred thousand newspapers in the 1930s, *Crítica* published pictures of the

Así lo Mataron

DON PEDRO DE ROJAS ha reconstruido la es-Feliciano Albornoz. Los agresores descargaron una cena del asesinato de Pigüé, en que perdió su vida verdadera lluvia de balas sobre aquél, que a pesar un conocido periodista radical de la localidad, don de pretender defenderse cayó herido de muerte

FIGURE 9. *Crítica*, September 24, 1932.

cadaver of a butcher who committed suicide (by hanging himself like a side of beef), of an old woman murdered by means of asphyxiation, and of another woman whose face had been slashed by her lover. When the magazine could not find a suitable image, it turned to artists, counting among its regular illustrators the political caricaturist Diógenes "Mono" Taborda (known for his drawings of Radical president Yrigoyen) and the renowned Spanish artist Pedro de Rojas, who provided a bridge between the European tradition of press illustration and that of southern South America. In her analysis of his work, Marcela Gené notes that in *Crítica*'s pages, "tragedy often took the form given to it by [de Rojas]."[12] The magazine also published complex collages that mixed illustrations with photographs.

In the 1930s, this graphic toolbox was expanded to include the comic strip, which was used to relate those stages of the action that had escaped the photographers. Railway disasters, a prison break at the Cárcel de Encausados, or a "Dramatic Progression of Astonishing Scenes" were narrated in a series of sequential images.[13] Argentine comics (as well as translations of U.S. comics) had recently entered into mass circulation. *El Tony*, the first magazine dedicated completely to the genre, won over audiences in 1928, and the comic strip soon fed into the growing spectacle of crime.

The nineteenth-century case study, whether medical or detective, followed the models of English and French chronicles, which had, thanks to ever-faster communications, found their way to editorial offices in Buenos Aires. Thirty years later, crime reporting looked more to the United States. If the high-profile North American cases now occupied so many pages, if the adventures of Al Capone now unseated those of a Parisian poisoner, it was because Argentine editors were receiving more and more information about those cases. This change was connected to the increased power of the United States in South American, especially the United Press and the Associated Press, which had displaced the French news agency Havas at the beginning of the century.[14]

Meanwhile, police magazines—written by police officers and read in police quarters—began to complain that local crime writing was mimicking U.S.-style "sensationalist" reporting. They were not wrong. Local stories were chosen for their similarity to the most modern criminal practices of the U.S. (which were highly stylized by journalists and Hollywood screenwriters), and narrated using techniques associated with the U.S. corporate-dominated entertainment industry. These styles of writing became popularized in comic strips as well as in hard-boiled crime and pulp fiction.

Lafforgue and Rivera have shown that at the beginning of the 1930s, Buenos Aires developed a mass consumer audience for detective and crime novels. *Magazine Sexton Blake,* published biweekly by Editorial Tor beginning in 1929, was followed by *Colección Misterio,* which later became *Series Wallace.* These collections provided local readers with translations of the genre's latest authors. Among the most popular was British writer Edgar Wallace, whose works departed from the sophisticated puzzle plot, the ingeniously solved riddle so typical of the English genre: "Crime and blood, and three murders per chapter; such is the insanity of the age that I do not doubt for one moment the success of my venture," said Wallace.[15]

Pervading the world of comic strips and crime literature was Hollywood's long shadow. In the 1920s, '30s, and '40s a lot of crime fiction was brought to the big screen. Like the scriptwriters who based their work on press stories and crime fiction, reporters (and more than a few writers) also adopted the tools of cinema. The "cinematization" of crime reporting was one part of the vertiginous globalization of film and, along with it, Hollywood culture.

A vehicle for strong emotions, as well as the maximum expression of the quick-paced life of the modern subject, the cinema was feared even by its own producers. A quick glance at the newspapers would show the extent to which newspapers and journalists would aggrandize cases of actual crime by comparing them to the exciting films shown in *porteño* theaters. "A Crime of Cinematic Proportions," "True Motive for a Dramatic Film," "An Audacious Assault, Worthy of the Cinema" read the headlines, while the facts and characters of those stories were modeled on those of the big screen. One comic strip in *Crítica,* telling the story of a criminal's escape from prison, began with the headline: "Filmmakers Lost Out When They Missed Filming the Escape of Mr. Claps."[16] The story lines of some cases (the disappearance of two girls, the kidnapping and failed rescue of one Dr. Favelukes, and the above-mentioned Rawson Hospital robbery) were captured—"just like a film"—in a sequence of small drawings presented as if mounted on celluloid tape.

The poor, pathetic, pathological, time-honored figures of traditional crime reporting—a woman defending her honor, an immigrant who killed his concubine in a tenement house (*conventillo)*—continued to delight readers of *Crítica, Noticias Gráficas,* and *Ahora.* But alongside them also appeared a new kind of criminal. His elegant dress, membership in a gang, and access to the latest in weapons and automobiles all gave him an air of professionalism. He resembled the gangsters of the silver screen.

As we have seen, the very modernity of the *pistolero* impeded his integration into a local tradition, with its own models of masculine violence. While he may have borne some resemblance to the scruffy neighborhood *compadrito,* "with a kerchief around his neck," and was in many senses his successor, the *pistolero* shared a more visible parentage with characters imported from abroad. His most identifiable forebears were to be found not so much among gauchos or Borgesian fictions about the margins of the city, but in translation from comic strips and, most of all, Hollywood cinema.

Tracing the Hollywood origins of the *"pistolero criollo"* is an unavoidable but perilous exercise. From a twenty-first-century perspective, it is impossible not to see these newspaper images through the filters and associations that several decades of gangster movies have imposed upon us: the dark glamour of the clothing, the weapons, the cars of the '20s and '30s. Then again, contemporary readers were not immune to this patina of

FIGURE 10A. (Left) "Like a Film," *Crítica*, September 28, 1932.

FIGURE 10B. (Right) "The Grotesque Film of the Delta Investigation," *Crítica*, October 7, 1932.

associations. Their encounter with a photograph of a recent robbery, for example, occurred in close proximity to the latest Hollywood movie, with its scenes of car chases and gunplay in the streets of Chicago.

Filmmakers have been interested in crime since the genre's beginnings, when the subject was used to explore the medium's narrative possibilities. The climactic rise of the gangster film, however, was linked to the innovation of sound. Between the late 1920s and the early 1930s, sound injected raw authenticity into films—the screeching of speeding cars and the rat-a-tat of machine guns destroying everything in their path. Newspapermen and movie producers took the urban, Depression-era gangster and further developed his appeal. He was a modern character, the protagonist of the folklore of the era: business-minded and glamorous, he was a consumer of sophisticated goods, elegantly dressed, and surrounded by beautiful women with whom he would steal away in luxury cars. Al Capone was the most prominent real-life example. His fame certainly derived from his reign in Prohibition-era Chicago, but it was also the result of good timing: his criminal escapades concluded just as the largely unregulated production of sound film took off during the early 1930s. The *pistoleros* and mafia bosses who came after Capone would not receive the same attention from a film industry now forced to operate under the more serious moral scrutiny of the Hays Code.[17]

When sound technology appeared, Hollywood films accounted for 90 percent of films shown in Argentina, and were already deeply influential in the country's mass culture. The United States led both in film production and in the supply of film technology. By 1922, Argentina was the world's third largest consumer of U.S. films. According to the U.S. Department of Commerce, total exports of U.S. film products that year was valued at $465,328, with Argentina accounting for $40,253. In 1927, there were almost 24 million feet of filmed material exported to Argentina (as compared to 16 million feet exported to Brazil).[18]

In Buenos Aires, the city with the most movie theaters in Latin America and the first to equip its theaters with sound technology, gangster films were a remarkable success. *El Heraldo del Cinematografista,* a cinema trade publication, recommended that they be shown in popular movie houses: the visually striking final machine gun battle scene that crowned *Bad Company,* for example, added to its commercial appeal.[19] In 1931, more than fifty crime movies were shown locally, including more than a few gangster films. Among them, *porteños* got to see future classics like *The Public Enemy, Little Caesar,* and *Scarface,* which found their way to theaters in Buenos Aires not long after their premieres in the U.S. Growing criticism and concern were quick to follow.

In Argentina, it was taken as a given that real-life criminals took inspiration from the new gangster films: "*Criollo* criminals tend to imitate the North Americans, carrying out bold robberies and crimes just like them," offered *Crítica,* the newspaper that most exaggerated these parallels. In a more serious and preoccupied tone, *La Prensa* worried that the cinematic fascination with Chicago crime was dangerous, as it projected the arts of banditry onto a public that included families with women and children, while *La Nación* described one bank robbery in the Buenos Aires neighborhood of Flores as "like those popularized by the North American film industry."[20] In police stations, where officers read the same papers as the general public, no one doubted the contagious effect that U.S. crime movies were having on local viewers. In fact, police files noted that accused criminals openly acknowledged the inspiration.

Of all the U.S. gangsters, none was as celebrated in Buenos Aires as Al Capone. He became the archetype of the gangster imaginary, projecting its attributes upon local *pistoleros*. Capone was an international celebrity, and his name extended far beyond the crime pages of daily newspapers: the leaders of the new media met regularly at a restaurant bearing his name. Natalio Botana, founder of *Crítica*, was even called "the Al Capone of journalism." In 1933, *Carrying a Gun for Al Capone*, written by Capone's bodyguard, was translated and published in Buenos Aires as *Memorias de un pistolero*.[21] Forever obsessed by the world of crime, technology, and utopian get-rich-quick schemes, the writer Roberto Arlt was not immune to the movie gangster's spell. By the end of the 1930s, his reviews of North American crimes were littered with English words and underworld characters—with names like "Tony Berman" and "Frank Lombardo"—wielding machine guns, sporting silk ties, and smoking cigars. Al Capone appeared in a number of Arlt's vignettes, which were printed in *El Mundo*. In these essays, the Chicago gangster was depicted as a celebrity who was quite solicitous of his public image, friendly with judges and the political elite, the object of every photographer's attention, and the host of sumptuous parties. Arlt's Capone even took time to consider the plight of the less fortunate.[22]

Meanwhile, the Argentine press's "al-caponization" generated a new model of representation for the local criminal. Papers referred to the well-known thug and bodyguard "Ruggierito" as "Capone's little brother in Avellaneda." The anarchist Di Giovanni was said to "imitate Al Capone," while Juan Galiffi ("Chicho Grande") was known as "our Al Capone." English words were used to describe how Galiffi, like the archetypal U.S. gangster, had moved from Sicily to America as a poor peasant, becoming a "self-made man," triumphant in the "business" of modern crime in Rosario (which was dubbed "the Chicago of Argentina").[23] The U.S. category of "public enemy" was also adopted into the local lexicon. The Chicago Crime Commission used the phrase in 1930, and the following year it was popularized in the U.S. by an (excellent) movie of the same name. Back in Buenos Aires, the press identified Chicho Grande as Argentina's "public enemy" and then bestowed the same title upon Pibe Cabeza. Media descriptions added that the latter combined elements of the urban *pistolero* with those of the fugitive gaucho, drawing comparisons to John Dillinger, the leader of the Depression-era bank-robbing "Dillinger Band."[24]

Reenactments, comic strips, movie references: the press and their reading publics constructed a represented "truth" that extended beyond the scope of regular reporting on criminal activity (important in and of itself). The images distanced the reader from the personal plight of the criminal: his history (criminological or clinical) became far less relevant than his performance and his common genealogy with figures from the entertainment industry. In these reports, the detailed description of a criminal's face was pertinent not because it served to explain his deviance but because it added to his celebrity. Trivialization at the service of spectacle? There is little doubt that these dramatizations inspired far less indignation than stories that focused on the victims of a crime or those that highlighted the assailants' troubled life stories. Compared with the sinister portraits of murderers peppered with anthropometric data and pathologies, the "crime of cinematic proportions" did little to provoke moral outrage. In the 1930s, however, a new form of crime renewed criminal storytelling's emotional impact.

KIDNAPPINGS

The Argentine summer of 1932–'33 was the summer of the Ayerza case. Of all the crimes and robberies that the papers had covered in the preceding years, none captured the public's attention as much as the story of a young aristocrat who was kidnapped and murdered by the Sicilian mafia's descendents in Rosario. Every newspaper in Buenos Aires, the sensationalist and "serious" alike, followed the story closely. The outcome prompted mass protests. When Congress began to debate the most severe penal code ever proposed in Argentina, the case loomed over the proceedings. High-profile crimes serve as touchstones within a collective memory, and the Ayerza case was no exception. Those who were adults during those years would always remember—against a backdrop of political scandals and the rise of Nazism—the case that made history.[25]

In the 1930s, a series of high-profile crimes—Favelukes (1932), Ayerza (1932), Martin (1933), Pereyra Iraola (1937), and Stutz (1938), among others—made kidnapping the subject of regular discussion in Argentina.[26] The phenomenon was not new. During the first decades of the century, the Sicilian mafia was known for extortion kidnapping in Santa Fe, and police reports tell us that the practice gradually spread far beyond. Stories of kidnapped children intensified the threat. The impressionistic evidence is difficult to quantify (police statistics are scarce), but kidnapping was clearly seen as a symptom of an overall increase in organized crime. Police located it within the continuum of armed robberies, human trafficking, and the kinds of coordinated, complex crimes previously analyzed here. Kidnapping's newfound visibility was not a measure of its novelty, but rather its sudden discovery by the press when, in 1932, members of Buenos Aires's high society became targets for the first time.

On October 4, an esteemed Jewish doctor, Jaime Favelukes, made a scheduled house call to an unknown patient in downtown Buenos Aires. He then mysteriously disappeared. A few hours later, his young wife received a letter demanding a ransom of 100,000 pesos. Since there were few clues as to who his kidnappers were, and the official investigation lacked direction, a range of theories began to circulate in a context of doubt regarding the reality of the threat. "Is it possible—the city asks itself—that they would really kill a man if his family was unwilling to pay the money?"[27]

In the face of authorities' disoriented silence, the public speculated about who the kidnappers were, considering the gamut of criminal archetypes. First among them were the anarchists. The recent execution of Severino Di Giovanni and Paulino Scarfó in February 1931 had revived in the public's imagination the old idea of the "dangerous anarchist." That the anarchists' crusade to "expropriate" the bourgeoisie's wealth had been restricted to bank robberies and counterfeiting operations, not kidnapping, did nothing to prevent the theory of an anarchist link from flourishing.[28]

Another hypothesis took interest in the fact that the subjects, as *La Prensa* said, "appeared to be Rusos," suggesting another kind of criminality, as well as taking on xenophobic (and anti-Semitic) undertones. In 1930, Favelukes, who was director of the Hospital Israelita, served as a witness in the trials against the Zwi Migdal—a Jewish organization charged with trafficking women for prostitution. Some saw a potential connection between the mysterious kidnapping and the ethnic crime networks, suggesting that the case might reflect a "settling of scores" within the Jewish community. Elsewhere in the same newspapers, a completely different scenario was put forward: the philanthropist doctor orchestrated his own kidnapping. This hypothesis circulated in the days immediately following Faveluke's reappearance on October 9.[29]

A crowd gathered outside the doctor's home, hoping to catch a glimpse of him up close, celebrate the happy resolution of the mysterious case, and hear the family address its supporters. For some, the media frenzy that followed was awkward. "The Happily Kidnapped Man"— as he was dubbed by Roberto Arlt in *El Mundo*—became a celebrity on the radio and in the press: "So happy was the outcome of the crime that it makes kidnappings look more like jovial sprees, in which even the victim, with the help of the newspapers and radio programs, communicates his satisfied impressions to the entire country, just like in an Edgar Wallace novel."[30]

While the doctor was posing for photographers and giving interviews, news broke that Silvio Alzogaray, a *Crítica* correspondent from Rosario, had been murdered. His death bolstered suspicions that the Sicilian mafias were involved in the Favelukes case. Alzogaray had insisted from the start that there was a Sicilian connection. The reasons for his murder were never fully brought to light, but mafia involvement became an unavoidable conclusion for any reporter familiar with Rosario, where organized gangs had been extorting ransoms and committing murder for over two decades.[31] And while *porteño* papers had covered some of those crimes, including victim profiles (coachmen, shopkeepers from small communities), these stories never made the headlines, thus escaping the attention of the wider public. The murder of an investigative journalist working for an important publication suggested a change in the scale of mafia operations. All fingers pointed to Juan Galiffi ("Chicho Grande"), whose identity Alzogaray had revealed shortly before he was killed. On October 15, after investigating the possible mafia connection, newspapers presented photographs of the members of a Sicilian mafia network responsible for Dr. Favelukes's strange kidnapping. But this resolution of the case was immediately overshadowed by breaking news of yet another kidnapping. Between October 25, 1932, and February 21, 1933, the public held its breath as it awaited news of a young man named Abel Ayerza, abducted while vacationing in the countryside.

Abel Ayerza was born into a traditional Catholic family from Buenos Aires. His father was a highly respected doctor. Abel himself was a medical student and member of the Legión Cívica, a paramilitary organization associated with former de facto president Uriburu. Ayerza's disappearance lasted for over four months. Of the three people who were with him when he was abducted (two friends and a farmhand), only one, Santiago Hueyo (the son of the minister of the economy), was also captured. He was released hours later on the outskirts of Rosario. The precedent set by the

Favelukes and Alzogaray cases, together with information provided by Hueyo, meant that from the outset the press's attention centered on a mafia kidnapping, putting pressure on the (much questioned) Santa Fe police force. Battling a reputation for being corrupt and ineffective, police authorities began to conduct raids on mafia-connected homes. A spectacular show of force ensued, featuring machine guns and an arsenal of long-barrel weapons positioned conspicuously on the roofs of their trucks. Three planes from El Palomar air base overflew the area. Many arrests were made, as roads in and out of Rosario were subjected to intense police scrutiny. All drivers were required to present identification. All for naught: days, weeks, and months went by without any news of Ayerza. After countless false leads and mutual accusations, there were no significant developments in the investigation. Initial sensationalist press reports gave way to more modest updates, far removed from the front page.

That summer, young Ayerza's fate became the topic of countless conversations. Radio announcements of his appearance inspired premature celebrations, complete with sirens and fireworks. Bottles with messages from the young man were found in public, left by pranksters. The figure of the kidnap victim became a metaphor for political shortcomings: the opposition decried that fraudulent Conservative politicians had "kidnapped" Argentine democracy by binding the hands of that great hostage of politics, the Sáenz Peña Law of universal suffrage. Meanwhile, there was no trace of Ayerza, despite mounting rumors that the ransom had been paid. Once more, the hypothesis of a self-kidnapping insinuated itself into the public debate. Perhaps he was in hiding in Europe, laughing at all the concern being shown. Or maybe the whole thing was a joke made by idle young men.[32]

When Abel Ayerza's body was finally found on February 21, the news detonated like a social bomb. As a train transported his remains from Córdoba, where his body was found, crowds gathered all along the route in spontaneous demonstrations of sympathy and grief. Arriving at Retiro Station in Buenos Aires, the train was met by "official representatives, figures from our social, university, and sporting organizations, higher-ups from the military, friends of the deceased, women and men from the community."[33] The car carrying the coffin moved slowly through the crowd. As it passed, the mourners threw flowers, swore vengeance, wept, and cursed. Some fainted; others broke down.

"On sidewalks, balconies, in doorways along the street, along the sides of the avenues, families and groups of people from the community formed a cordon for the cortege," read one account of the funeral procession. Uniformed members of the Legión Cívica watched over the coffin. One of the speakers, overcome with emotion, could only manage to raise his fists and cry out, "Abel Ayerza, you will be avenged!" Other speeches combined pious reflections with denouncements of unrestricted immigration and diatribes against the leniency of the new penal code. Speaking for the Ayerza family, Juan Antonio Bourdieu accused the state of being complicit in the crime and issued a call to arms.[34] Another figure from the pro-Uriburu shock troops, Alfredo Villegas Oromí, ended the ceremony by demanding that the law take a harder line against crime. Taking up the call, the crowd marched to the Plaza de Mayo.

Ayerza's kidnappers, who were indeed connected to mafia leader Juan Galiffi, were detained and jailed in April of the same year. In July 1939, the Cámara de Apelaciones (Court of Appeals) issued the sentence: life in prison for the five principal actors, and terms of ten, nine, and seven years for the co-conspirators. Galiffi was deported on April 17, 1935, though some insisted that he secretly returned to the country. The arrest in 1939 of his daughter Ágata—made into a *noir* celebrity by the media—symbolized the decline of Argentina's Sicilian mafia.

MELODRAMA AND THE MORPHOLOGY OF A CRIME

SPEAKER:—And he walked calmly over to his newspaper
delivering the stunning news of the victory over the terrifying
gang of mafiosos and the return of the child to the Vally couple.
The papers that day sold out.

—*Ronda Policial* (Police Round, radio drama)

A paradigm of commercial journalism—that of the unscrupulous reporter, eager to exploit any sign of melodrama—was an archetype found in films, crime literature, and radio soap operas. In his merciless, competitive world, a kidnapping was a good story, a "beautiful crime." The abduction of a common citizen introduced an unfamiliar fear and therefore had shock value.

That such a violation of the rules of social coexistence might happen in the most respectable areas, and in the most unexpected of situations, had an inhibiting effect, sowing doubt about the nature of even the most innocuous of social interactions. Ideas about the relationship between crime and territory had to be revised now that the automobile had freed gangs from being bound to one place, imagined or real. The Ayerza saga showed that danger could migrate from province to province, from the city to the countryside. While much of organized crime possessed this kind of geographical flexibility, the time frame of this "new" crime was unique—a kidnapping might take months to be resolved. A new morphology maintained the public's attention throughout the horrifying duration of the story and engendered new kinds of reactions. Prior to the final outcome, there was no choice but to wait, creating a dynamic in which a reader participated in an imagined collective experience of public suspense. At the same time, the extended chronology of a kidnapping made it possible for the press and the public to scrutinize victims in a melodramatic staging of their suffering.

Sociological literature has shown that certain crimes receive, and have always received, disproportionate attention from the press. This is particularly true of homicide.[35] The story of a murder begins after the crime has been committed, and journalists must reconstruct the sequence of events retrospectively, weaving together different elements that connect the murder to the cause, and the body of the victim to the body of the criminal. Kidnappings, by contrast, are made public before the outcome is known. The events occur over an extended period and the story develops, day after day, in real time, as it is narrated. Thus, a kidnapping story is one of the first crime stories to allow for the possibility of a "happy" ending, inviting readers to become more personally involved. In this way, the crowd that gathered to welcome Favelukes—a man transformed by his kidnapping into both a victim and a celebrity—or the throngs that gathered to view Ayerza's coffin as it traveled from Córdoba to the Recoleta Cemetery, were visible signs of a collective anticipation conditioned by graphic media.

The open-ended nature of kidnapping connected it to another form of popular culture: the occult, which still possessed a remarkable vitality.[36] The story of a kidnapping is essentially that of an odyssey, the anxious uncertainty of a desperate search for the victim, the rumors of his whereabouts and fate. Crime writers at *Crítica* (and many newspapers in the interior of the country) called upon astrologers, mediums, and clairvoyants to use their gifts of divination and long-distance communication. Ascertaining the hostage's destiny by means of astrological charts and horoscopes might have been entertaining to some, but it horrified others.

Kidnappings turned into national melodramas, happening in real time with living protagonists. The story focused on the dramatis personae. In the Favelukes case—the first collective vigil in a major kidnapping—the public participated in order to express its solidarity with the victims. To depict the scene, *Crítica*'s illustrators drew an anguished family in their living room overlaid on a photograph of their home, showing a suffering wife in her bed and the couple's children sleeping innocently nearby.

Suspense focused the public's attention on both the unfolding of the crime and the victim's ongoing suffering. The potential for melodrama and suspense was emphasized by reporters themselves: "The kidnapping has already taken place. The police work diligently to clear up the situation. The family of the victim endures the profound unease that comes from contemplating the possible fate of Dr. Favelukes. They rely on emotional support: the parents, the children and the wife of the victim all united in the same concern, in the same pain, in the same uncertainty."[37] This was not a story of clues, witnesses, and experts. Even when those elements appeared, what drove the plot was still the agony of the victim's father, mother, friends, and neighbors, all of whom maintained their vigil. It was a story of emotion, not of rational, objective reconstructions. The impersonal authorities in charge of the case were depicted as flat characters, as distinct from those who suffered, who seemed to have stepped right out of a melodramatic novel.

As the story of kidnapping became a story about family, its emotional power grew. Even if their contact with the press was scarce, the victim's mother, father, wife, and children were its primary characters. The crime's actual victim was never considered independently from the suffering of his loved ones awaiting at home: the nervous breakdown and fainting spells of Favelukes's young wife, his children's innocent inquiries about their father, his mother's anguish. The crime of abduction activated timeless images of maternity, brotherly love, and the bonds of marriage.

In the Favelukes case, the family was young and respectable. As we have seen, the doctor gave many interviews upon his release and participated in reconstructions of his kidnapping. When the story was printed, the photographs of the reenactment included an additional sequence depicting Favelukes reuniting with his family. The most aberrant aspect of this crime—the victim's disappearance and removal from his home—was now publicly rectified, brought to a close in scenes acted out for the community of readers and mediated by press photographers: Favelukes seated in his comfortable home, with his father, wife, and small children close by. The headline reads, "Breakfast on a Joyous Day." Thus concludes the melodrama of the first major national kidnapping. "Dr. Jaime Favelukes, his father, his wife, and his son appear in the affectionate tranquility of the home. The anguish of so many days is now over." A photo of the couple going to temple on Yom Kippur offers the final image of a crime resolved.[38]

There was little talk of punishing the kidnappers in the happily resolved Favelukes case. Abel Ayerza, by contrast, never returned home. The press turned Adela Arning de Ayerza, the *mater dolorosa,* into the story's central protagonist and the representative of Abel's suffering. Her austere and pious portrait appeared next to images of Ayerza's funeral, where angry calls for tougher laws resounded. It was this visible suffering—maternal, feminine, and full of religious resonance—that so enflamed the public's demands for justice. Standing next to Abel Ayerza's coffin, Carlos Silveyra addressed those gathered: "If our sadness is great, greater still is the indignation felt before the spectacle that paints an image of this savage moral torture: while a man is rendered powerless by the ferocious appetite of the lowest of people, the heart of a mother, the inner depths of an innocent mother bleed, clawed out by the paws of beasts."[39] The open wound to the moral order produced by Ayerza's kidnapping and murder would never be healed. Or rather: its healing was possible only in terms of the weak symbolic tools of a written justice (and as such inscrutable from the public's point of view) guided by a penal code that had recently abolished the death penalty.

KIDNAPPING AND PENAL IDEOLOGY, OR THE RESURRECTION OF THE DEATH PENALTY

In his essay "Martita Ofelia: Romances para ciegos" (Martita Ofelia: Ballads for the Blind), the anti-liberal Jesuit Leonardo Castellani, referring to the kidnapping of a young girl named Marta Stutz, denounced the press for using fortune-telling, astrology, and "psychometric" practices in its coverage of the case, as well as for depicting atrocious crimes in animated drawings. According to him, they were signs of the decline of Argentine culture at the hands of liberalism. Gustavo Franceschi, another leader of Catholic reactionary thought, concurred.[40]

These arguments were hardly surprising. Castellani and Franceschi's disgust was in line with long-standing criticisms of the sensationalist press, which extended beyond the confines of reactionary ideologies and was shared by leftist and avant-garde intellectuals as well. However, rising crime is an old theme in the critique of modern society, an unmistakable symptom of its descending spiral. For those critics at the heart of the anti-liberal reaction, front-page kidnappings—and the tabloid carnival surrounding them—were reflections of the immorality of a society with godless schools, an ultra-liberal press, and a cinema all too eager to place its machinery at the service of the latest seductive trends. In this view, crime was a consequence of an irresponsible policy that welcomed *evil* foreigners into the country, while authorities' inability to resolve cases was the result of political corruption. Kidnapping victims were considered martyrs of a democratic system in full-blown decadence.

Central to this vision was the perceived connection between secularism, liberal democracy, and the penal system. "Our penal code rides the trolley while criminals use automobiles," declared the nationalistic newspaper *Bandera Argentina*.[41] The old Catholic argument against positivist criminology as having abandoned the idea of assigning blame in favor of addressing the sociobiological causes of criminality now gained steam: "We must once again allow the great notions of blame, responsibility, penitence, social vindication, human individuality and human conscience back into positivim's frail judicial-political system."[42] The Senate debated these ideas before passing the 1933 penal code.

The Ayerza case represented a critical moment in the history of the relationship between public opinion and the law. The restoration of the death penalty was once again thinkable in large part due to the climate of opinion left in the wake of that episode. Two months after the kidnapping (and before the outcome of the case became known), the executive branch sent a new penal code to Congress for consideration. It included regulations that would allow for institutionalization *prior* to an offense being committed, and the expulsion of those foreigners deemed "dangerous." The legislative commission added the death penalty to the list of reforms.[43] In the days leading up to the debate, innumerable editorials demanded that Congress dissolve the old code, which had been founded on nineteenth-century classical (liberal) punitive thought and positivist criminology. "The terrible lesson," stated *La Razón*, is that we must end, for once and for all, the "absurd sentimentalism of the excessively scientific criminologists" and eradicate the lax sentencing laws of turn-of-the-century penal reform. *Bandera Argentina* also campaigned for more severe punishments: the paper called Rodolfo Moreno, the author of the 1922 code, and Eusebio Gómez, an eminent jurist and positivist criminologist, "dangerous ideologues," including in that category anyone else the paper saw as being even remotely responsible for the "Trojan horse" of the "spineless" penal code as it now existed.[44] *La Nación* and *La Prensa* editorialized in favor of harsher sentences and joined in the challenge to excessively "scientific" legislation.

FIGURE 11. "What Congress Doesn't Want to see: The Law of Social Defense," *Caras y Caretas,* January 14, 1933.

Although less given to grandiose editorial statements, *Caras y Caretas* did not let the issue pass unremarked. It opted for a graphic campaign composed of photographs and illustrations depicting scenes of armed robbery. The magazine's use of the entertainment value of crime gave way to warning its readers of threats, and from there to the issue of penal law: stripped of their more romantic qualities, the gunmen pointed their weapons directly at the reader, while the paper noted that Congress was reluctant to pass stronger sentencing laws. The death penalty appeared as a spectral force, one capable of stopping abductions and murders.[45]

Social pressure to modify the penal code was a well-known (and much criticized) phenomenon among jurists and legislators.[46] The public had

FIGURE 12. "Death penalty," *Caras y Caretas,* July 29, 1933.

clamored for harsher legislation before—for example, when emotional crowds rallied in favor of the new Law of Social Defense following the June 1910 anarchist attack in the Teatro Colón. Nevertheless, the role of common crime in political and social foment has been largely ignored in Argentine historiography. Here, for example, the anti-crime movement allows us to look at the circulation of anti-liberal discourse well beyond the narrow channels of warring newspapers—that is, in areas where the most strident variants of an anti-Semitic, anti-immigration, anti-communist, and anti-democratic credo took form. The broader treatment of crime (and of kidnapping in particular) sheds light on how typically anti-liberal topics filtered into conversations that were devoid of explicit political articulation or a clear crusading spirit. Embedded in discussions about the details of crime, ideological principles became quite concrete.

Newspaper readers discovered that Ayerza had been kidnapped at the hands of the Di Grado family, Sicilian owners of a vegetable market in Rosario. In the photographs published in the papers, the family looked nothing like the celebrity gangsters of the silver screen. These portraits were mug shots: the faces accosted by the flash, the men unshaven, wearing caps and clothing typical of rural immigrants. These images signaled a broader shift in the language of the crime story.

These were faces that gave substance to the notion of a direct danger to the community, until then glimpsed only confusedly in a sea of representational stimuli. These photos served as a counterpoint to the widely circulated, iconic photograph of the victim. Ayerza's fine features stood as a permanent reminder of the horrendous acts perpetrated by his now-visible killers. This contrast between his face and theirs fed into the opposition of "us" and "them," etching the attack deeply into the national psyche and structuring the outcome of the case as well as its ideological interpretations. Few nationalist arguments offered the public a more convincing synthesis of the dangers of liberal cosmopolitanism and its threat to the Argentine soul than the oppositions to which Ayerza's kidnapping gave rise.

The Ayerza case revitalized a debate that had, ever since the 1922 penal code was signed into law, focused on that document's virtues and defects. In a book written at the time, Rodolfo Moreno Jr., author of the much reviled code, denounced the brutal pressure of public opinion in favor of sanctioning the new laws. Any appearance of a causal relationship between the abolition of capital punishment and the cases that the readers followed in the paper was an illusion, he said. The public's arguments for the death penalty were not based on direct observation of the judicial process, but rather a barrage of repetitive messages that it received from sources far removed from the legal system.[47]

Even if the initiative to reform the code came as a political response to the recent wave of kidnappings, its origins can be traced back further, and its motivations were more complex. In fact, the effort represented only the latest in a series of attempts to reform a document that had been the object of criticism since the day it was enacted—for the tepidness with which it incorporated the juridical precepts of positivism (contrary to what was reported, there were many difficulties in translating scientific prescriptions into penal law), and for the lack of provisions for dealing with the new brand of professional criminality. After many failed

FIGURE 13. "The Faces and Tragic Eyes of Abel Ayerza's Assassins," *Crítica,*
February 23, 1933.

attempts at reform, said Arancibia Rodriguez, a leader of the Senate
commission dedicated to the issue, senators found themselves besieged
by the urgent demands of public opinion, which blamed Ayerza's death
on the inadequacy of the reforms and on liberals, whom they viewed as
having opened the door to the forces that now threatened society. The
debate quickly got mixed up with previous discussions regarding the
fear of social revolution, in which the Sicilian kidnappers were lumped
into the same category as communists, anarchists, and other "enemies of
the nation."[48]

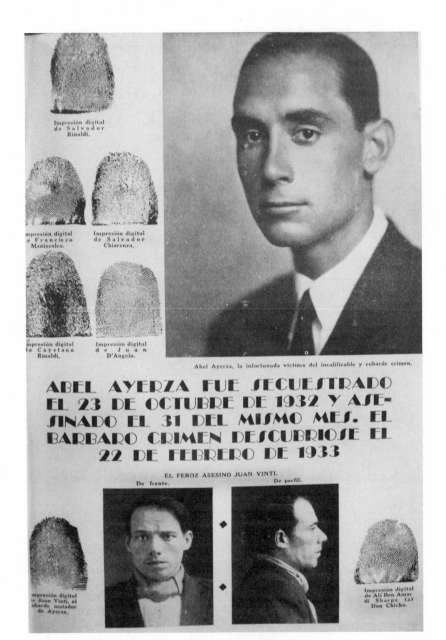

Impresión digital de Salvador Rinaldi.

Impresión digital e Francisco Maniscalco.

Impresión digital de Salvador Chiarenza.

Impresión digital e Cayetano Rinaldi.

Impresión digital de Juan D'Angelo.

Abel Ayerza, la infortunada víctima del incalificable y cobarde crimen.

ABEL AYERZA FUE SECUESTRADO EL 23 DE OCTUBRE DE 1932 Y ASESINADO EL 31 DEL MISMO MES. EL BARBARO CRIMEN DESCUBRIOSE EL 22 DE FEBRERO DE 1933

EL FEROZ ASESINO JUAN VINTI.
De frente.   De perfil.

Impresión digital e Juan Vinti, el obarde matador de Ayerza.

Impresión digital de Alí Ben Amar di Sharpe (a) Don Chicho.

FIGURE 14. Ayerza and Juan Vinti. *Caras y Caretas*, March 4, 1933.

Although the death penalty had almost no practical importance and was rarely applied even when the option existed, it did serve a metaphorical function by maximizing punishment. Its reinstatement was proposed by Manuel Iriondo, then minister of justice, and was supported by the majority of the Senate, which had never favored its abolition.

The Academy of Law and Social Sciences, along with other legal associations, also came out in support of the measure. The 1933 bill was approved by the Senate, but, as had been the case for previous efforts, the reform never made it into the penal code. Once the debate moved out of the newspapers and into the Chamber of Deputies, the potent effect of public opinion gave way to practical and doctrinal debates about the death penalty and pre-criminal institutionalization, reviving the kinds of old alliances and practical objections that ultimately prevented its ratification.[49]

The kidnapping saga created a climate of public hostility toward nineteenth-century penal reform that went far beyond its usual detractors in the tight circle of Catholic ideologues, and led to a growing association between such reform and political decadence.

Kidnapping, that prolonged violation of moral order, produced an emotional tension that journalists sought out for commercial reasons, and it unleashed deep fears in the greater society, as the victims—fathers, children, wives, and, above all, mothers—were construed as models of the Argentine family. An image of a weak and heterogeneous state lurked beneath these melodramas of suffering. To the catalogue of immorality on display in all narratives of crime, kidnapping added a slow-motion exposé of the state's deficiencies, blind spots, and contradictions, where intense emotions juxtaposed with all the ups and downs of the investigation (technical, jurisdictional, political) amounted to a daily exhibition of the impotence of the ruling classes and their institutions. Kidnapping proved to do more to expose these weaknesses than any of the usual outcries against corruption and electoral fraud. The suspicion that surrounded the police, whose well-known complicity in crime and fraud had already brought it into disrepute, appeared to be confirmed by its inability to resolve a case of parents and sons, life and death, on the national stage. With its highly symbolic power, the death penalty embodied an expiatory view of punishment and atonement, replacing a penal logic that—in the name of science—rejected Christian notions of blame, responsibility, and penitence in exchange for a reform program of prolonged criminal institutionalization.

Read alongside the urgencies and drama caused by these high-profile cases, the proposals of criminology (long-term imprisonment) became associated with the impotence and moral weaknesses of democracy. Behind the excess of stimuli and the aesthetic and narrative incoherencies of the sensational press, the logic of this story activated an impulse toward retribution. Calls for the reinstatement of the death penalty became a metaphor for atonement and found support in a united front made up of both the nationalist right and a wider public, normally reviled by anti-liberal aristocratic leaders. Medical and psychiatric rationales lost the battle with "common sense" as the spectacle of kidnapping revived old notions of crime, blame, and the necessity of punishment.

CHAPTER 3

Order and the City

The effects of the 1930 global economic crisis on everyday life in Buenos Aires are difficult to measure. Depending on one's perspective, two very different scenarios emerge. Some historians have viewed the 1929 crash as a watershed moment; others have seen its repercussions as relatively mild—a momentary stumble with no real long-term consequences. Historians who take one perspective or the other also draw very different conclusions about the subsequent years. They paint divergent pictures of *porteño* society and the political and economic turbulence that played out over the decades that followed. Our story must therefore contend with two distinct (and rather disconnected) methods of periodization that yield two very different narratives.

The first perspective views 1930 as a year of structural change, the passage between a relatively worry-free decade and one of unprecedented drama and complexity. In this conceptual framework, the "difference" of the 1930s has allowed for the emergence of long-standing models of periodization, including one that identifies it as a unit (corrupted, "infamous") that illuminates, by contrast, the rise of Peronism in the 1940s.[1] Numerous political and economic histories have positioned 1930 as a watershed, a period of transition marked by two major events that roughly coincide: the global economic crisis, which, in Argentina, prompted a reevaluation of the agro-export model that had dominated for half a century, and the coup of September 1930, the first in a long series of institutional disruptions led by the military.

The second narrative, largely centered in the city of Buenos Aires, works around the notion of an "interwar" period. Even if Argentina did not participate as a combatant in either world war, the decisive consequences of these global conflicts in local politics and economy have yielded an alternative conceptualization, one that takes into consideration other changes. In this view, the period from 1920 to 1945 is bookended by two major transformations: the rise of the demographic and agro-exportation boom on the one hand, and Peronism on the other. In examining the period between these two processes, these historians largely look beyond macro-scale political and economic clashes and focus instead on the lived experiences of the city's residents.[2] If the scale of analysis is reduced—this interpretation argues—a more tranquil tale of continuity between the 1920s and the 1930s emerges. It's the history of the rather quiet development of city neighborhoods and suburbs of Buenos Aires, where the global economic crisis had a relatively moderate impact. The easing of social conflict—specifically, the decline of anarchism and its more radicalized forms of protest—is paired with the emergence of an upwardly mobile group of "popular sectors" with rather diffuse class boundaries. This crowd of upwardly mobile *porteños* is represented in an iconic image: residents of the once packed *conventillos* (tenement houses) moving out of the city center and into less turbulent, outlying neighborhoods. There, they organized themselves into clubs and political reformist groups, establishing public libraries and development societies (*sociedades de fomento*), as Catholic parishes (*parroquias*) multiplied. Thus emerged a new city of neighborhoods, as thousands of immigrants (and children of immigrants) transformed social life. This historical perspective, developed in the 1980s, became a framework for examining political practices, forms of religiosity, the rise of the entertainment industry, and the emergence of sports and consumer culture.[3] Subsequent work zeroed in on the everyday experience of life in the city and considered the continuities between the 1920s and the 1930s to be an established fact rather than merely a hypothesis.

The following three chapters are written in a similar register, paying greater attention to the public and everyday spaces of Buenos Aires than to major political and economic institutions. I follow a line of inquiry that focuses on everyday life in the city's neighborhoods and provincial suburbs, mining the more marginal corners of the press (local gazettes, newsletters, police publications, bulletins) and the more marginal sections of the mainstream newspapers (police notices, municipal reports, local news from surrounding towns). Yet these chapters also seek to find intersections between the two prevailing narratives rather than fixating on their disjunctions. They consider the question of the "change" of the 1930s not by casting doubt on the evidence clearly showing that the global depression had a relatively mild local effect, but by contextualizing that evidence. The perception of crisis does not always coincide with the comparative data usually consulted for this assessment, and we still lack a deeper understanding of what impact the downturn had on different sectors of the *porteño* population. We can imagine, meanwhile, that a society with unstable class divisions might measure the threat of crisis differently than a society with a more established class structure. And, of course, experiences of economic decline were not uniform. The direct victims of the crash—many of whom were destitute and forced to migrate to Buenos Aires from their provinces—had a very different experience from those who were economically protected from its fallout. Likewise, individuals who identified strongly with a certain class would have perceived change in a manner that was quite distinct from those who saw their position shift in the years approaching the 1930s. In Buenos Aires, the crisis interrupted several years of growth in which income had become better distributed and the standard of living had improved for a large segment of society.[4] It is thus worth observing the impact the crisis had on those *porteños* who, prior to 1930, had experienced unprecedented social ascent—in other words, the thousands of men and women whose recently acquired social status could not yet be taken for granted.

Newspaper and police archives reveal the challenges faced by the police as they sought to maintain order amid remarkable social instability in a rapidly expanding city. The issue of urban order appears and reappears in multiple contexts—politics, civil society, journalism— weaving together macroeconomic and political problems in a framework grounded in the "everyday."

Ideological slogans, news of European fascism, and the drama of political crises coexisted with daily routines and the more immediate context of social life, including street-corner gossip. In this analysis, the "difference" of the 1930s is not found in political fraud or grand nationalist speeches, but rather in a more generic and widespread concern with social order and police vigilance. By examining grassroots calls for order we find a turn toward greater regulation of behavior in the streets of Buenos Aires, a change that plays out in the everyday drama of urban living.

REPRESSION AND THE COUP

The gloomiest accounts of Buenos Aires during the 1930s see the decade as caught between the violent challenges of the economic crisis and the period of repression that began with the political coup of September 6, 1930, when a military faction ousted democratically elected President Hipólito Yrigoyen. These accounts often point out that the Ministry of the Interior, under the direction of Matías Sánchez Sorondo, drastically expanded the political power of the Capital Police during the de facto Uriburu presidency (1930–32). This continued under the ministry of Leopoldo Melo, during General Justo's presidency (1932–38), in the context of political fraud and the banishment of the Radical Party. When the executive branch declared a "state of siege," the police were given (with very little oversight) greater repressive power. This state of affairs would last for six years.[5] Uriburu's government marked the beginning of this era by executing the leaders of the "expropriative" anarchist movement who had carried out some of the prominent armed operations described in chapter 1. Soon after, reports of the persecution and torture of dissidents—particularly Radicals and communists—began to multiply. The personal and political ties between the *porteño* police and the Unión Cívica Radical can be traced back to former president Hipólito Yrigoyen (1916–22 and 1928–30), who as a younger man had served as police commissioner.[6] The 1930s escalation of political violence revealed considerable tension within the force. As was the case at other moments of shifting power, the rupture of 1930 gave way to an interminable series of animosities and accusations: "black lists" to identify dissenters, officers fired for defying requests that they abandon Radical committee affiliations, and high-ranking officials discovered to be "subversively conspiring" with figures that "have fanatical ties to the ousted government." The signs of an internal purge were unmistakable.[7] Meanwhile, the creation of the Sección Especial—so named due to its "special" attention to communism—became emblematic of a new, emboldened police force.

Police intervention in politics, though greatly expanded in this period, was not entirely new. In 1906, Orden Social, a branch of the Division of Investigation, was created to control anarchism.[8] Its activities (feverish in its early days) waned amid the rise of Radicalism, but the unit was never fully dismantled. In the years directly before and after 1930, Orden Social was revived. Records show that its agents spied on thousands of meetings and assemblies per year. By then, this agency had begun to work side by side with another unit, Orden Público (founded in 1910), later renamed Orden Político. These officers infiltrated first anarchist and then communist gatherings, collecting an immense amount of information. By the time the police created the Sección Especial to monitor and repress communist activities, this political entity had become deeply embedded in the world of labor.[9] In 1932, the Sección Especial absorbed part of the sixty-eight thousand individual records already gathered by Orden Social. Thus, the most notorious epicenter of 1930s repression had, in fact, thirty years of formal institutional history.

In the aftermath of the 1930 coup, Leopoldo Lugones Jr. was made the new head of this sinister branch of the police force. His ascension was not well received. One should not underestimate the bitterness generated by the naming of an outsider as Commissioner Inspector in an institution with well-defined hierarchies and a consolidated system of promotion. President Uriburu appointed Lugones at the suggestion of his father, the famous poet (and ally of the new regime), Leopoldo Lugones.[10] As head of the Sección Especial, Lugones Jr. would make ample use of various methods of torture, including the electric prod. Indeed, Lugones's office has frequently been depicted as the precursor to the *danse macabre* of the 1976 dictatorship. Throughout the 1930s, human rights organizations brought together lawyers with socialist, communist, and Radical backgrounds to defend political detainees, gather victims' testimonies, and describe the methodologies that the unit employed.

I've detailed elsewhere the experience of political imprisonment during this period and shown its close connection to the expansion of police power in penitentiary spaces.[11] Here I am interested in a lesser-known dimension of the Sección Especial: the unit's large-scale practice of espionage, which embedded informants in party meetings and newspapers. This strategy expanded the reach of the Capital Police beyond city limits, into Greater Buenos Aires and more distant provinces.

The Sección Especial was founded in an undisclosed office in early 1931. When it began, it was staffed with only a handful of employees, most of them foreigners hired to translate communications confiscated by the postal censor.[12] In April 1932, the Capital Police converted the Sección into an official division and placed it in a permanent office. As it expanded, the division exerted an unprecedented level of coercive pressure on militant communists. Officers who monitored the area around the headquarters of the newspaper *Bandera Roja*, for example, began to detain "many communists at its exit and, among them, militants who had not yet been identified." Between 1931 and 1934, the

Sección Especial intensified its raids on small businesses, schools, and homes, summarily detaining upper- and lower-level leaders.

Far from being secret, the espionage activities of the Sección Especial were routinely recorded in published annual reports that noted the number of assemblies infiltrated, activists arrested, pamphlets seized, and presses confiscated. The evidence suggests that any communist gathering—no matter how small—would have at least one police informant standing in a corner. As its vigilance expanded, the Sección Especial also found itself in constant need of new employees, particularly officers skilled in shorthand, who could clearly and concisely "transcribe the speeches of public speakers." Meanwhile, confiscated materials became so abundant that the office assembled a "red library," stocked with books obtained in daily raids. They accumulated "130 volumes in only a few months."[13] Record keepers also read the newspapers each day, archiving relevant information.

Meanwhile, General Justo's regime had put together a rather motley wiretapping system to track its adversaries.[14] Despite successive purges of documentation, Justo's personal papers preserve traces of the kind of police information that powered his backroom political strategy. A team of informants followed his main targets, pro-Yrigoyen Radicals. These employees were meticulous in transcribing their conversations with unhappy *yrigoyenistas*, which were copied down on official letterhead paper, while moles infiltrated Radical groups and delivered information about upcoming insurrections. Through these efforts, the regime sought out internal Radical dissidents: large numbers of public employees were dismissed for their affiliation with "certain committees."

The Sección Especial's notoriety in the annals of repression is well deserved. Nonetheless, the "hardened" police of the 1930s surfaced as a response to ideas that were far more widespread and complex than can be deduced from this unit's activity alone. The significance of the Sección Especial can only be understood through a deeper examination of interconnected transformations during the same period.

GOVERNABILITY CRISIS AND POLICE LAW

In July 1932, the chief of the Capital Police, Col. Luis J. García, approved a list of misdemeanor edicts (*edictos contravencionales*) intended to impose order in the city.[15] Considered as a whole, these edicts constituted a powerful reinforcement of the police mandate to monitor urban order in Buenos Aires, introducing a definition of this power that extended its boundaries into political and social life in a crusade that would last through the end of the decade.

It has often been said that police power is built upon rather hybrid and murky legal foundations. The regulations governing police authority are not grounded in openly debated legal codes. Rather, they reflect a collection of "minor" legal precedents born of heterogeneous norms. The corpuses that make up the legal framework of the police thus combine laws and decrees with seemingly modest and fragmentary edicts, orders, and low-grade police penalties that fall in a legal zone somewhere between the penal and the administrative. In the case of the Buenos Aires City Police in the 1930s, infraction edicts existed in a gray zone between law and de facto power. Their hybrid nature could be traced back to the diverse areas of intervention of the nineteenth-century police, from which modern police regulations inherited a vague mission to create "good government and public prosperity." In contrast with other institutions associated with maintaining order (penal justice, for example), police power was derived from a multiplicity of sources. Its conceptual roots were "impure."[16]

By the 1930s, the edicts represented an assortment of rules and directives that mapped out the wide range of spaces and situations open to police intervention. The aspects of social life subject to regulation were as varied as life itself: the list of edicts included public dances, drunkenness, carnivals, scandalous behaviors, vagrancy, begging, card games, the owning and transporting of weapons, loud noise, rights of assembly, public security, and so on. Some regulations deemed of particular importance were expanded and transformed into law. Clandestine gambling, for example, saw such a rapid rise in popularity that it inspired a sizable public morality movement; calls for regulation eventually led to the illegal gambling act, the Ley de Represión del Juego (1902). The law granted the police the power of "forceful entry" without any judicial mediation, or better put, it allowed the chief of police to act as a de facto judge.[17] This authority also held the legislative power to create new edicts and, according to the Infraction Code of 1888 (Código Contravencional), the (judicial) power to determine punishment: he could impose fines and up to thirty days of incarceration.

In July 1932, chief of police Col. García revived these powers in the face of judicial and legislative attempts to limit his agency's reach. He found this loophole thanks to the work of the minister of the interior, Leopoldo Melo, who had been trying (unsuccessfully) to strengthen police power though parliamentary channels. In so doing, Melo discovered the edict's potential: it enabled the police to apply a sanctioned authority "to maintain urban order" (police law) to the maintenance of *political* order. To justify his inventive application of the old police mandate, García pointed to the scarcity of legislation in place capable of aiding the institution in its mission. His arguments were not new. By this time, the police had developed a long history of discursive antagonism with the courts. Conflicts arose especially in reference to guarantees of rights, often viewed as an obstacle to the police's mission of maintaining "order." In trade magazines, for example, one finds abundant critiques of the lenient penal system and judges' unwillingness to uphold criminal punishment. García was thus joining a chorus of existing calls for increased police authority when he requested that Congress pass an *"estado peligroso pre-delictual"* or "pre-criminal threat" law: the mandate would allow police to apprehend individuals who were deemed dangerous even though they had not yet committed a crime. When Congress and legal scholars rejected the law, García turned to the power of the edict, explaining that it would at least temporarily compensate for the judges' and legislators' inaction. As a result, political use of a seemingly modest set of regulations allowed for a series of major legal exceptions to flourish. The edicts opened up a range of possibilities of police action with repercussions that extended well beyond the (already vague) temporal limits of the state of siege.

García's justifications resonated with the simultaneous news of the high-profile kidnapping cases described in the previous chapter. As we have seen, these stories generated a growing climate of concern and pushed public opinion toward emergency measures. One *Caras y Caretas* cartoon, for example, contrasted a bland, sleepy image of Congress against the executive energy of the chief of police. García turns to Minister Melo and rolls up his sleeves; they both hold brooms adorned with the words "Against the Undesirables" and "Against the Criminals."

So began a period in which the police added a list of new, unilaterally issued regulations. The first edict targeted public gatherings and was couched in the broader mandate of maintaining public order. The directive outlined "incorrect uses" of the street and invoked as justification the "uncivilized" ("noisy," "violent," "overcrowded") methods of assembly used by the opposition during political campaigns in the late 1920s—a topic heavily covered in the major papers. It strictly regulated the right of assembly, declaring that any gathering had to be scheduled in advance, and that the date and the names of speakers and participating organizations had to be provided to authorities. It further stated that the police could attend all gatherings and that any individual convicted of disor-

FIGURE 15. "Now That Congress Is Sleeping, We'll Take the Initiative to Clean up Our Country," *Caras y Caretas*, March 18, 1933.

derly conduct would be given the "maximum penalty" (thirty days in jail). The edict opened the way for hundreds of political detentions.[18]

Other edicts spoke more directly to the influx of migrants moving into the city in the aftermath of the 1930 economic crisis. Following the crash, thousands of men and women abandoned the hard-hit grain-producing regions of central and northern Argentina in search of work in cities. One report at the beginning of the 1930s recorded the phenomenon thus: "In the vicinity of the border between the Capital and the Province of Buenos Aires, there are numerous *desocupados* [unemployed] pushed by provincial authorities in nearby towns to come to this city."[19] The police quickly declared that the numbers of displaced people far exceeded the municipality's capacities; an improvised camp-site on Canning Street and the emergency shantytown ("Villa Deso-cupación") in Puerto Nuevo quickly filled to capacity. Reports explained that the *desocupados* were arriving from the north and the west, pushed out by the downturn in the agricultural economy. They traveled follow-ing the north-south train line, stopping in small towns, where they were pushed away and ordered to continue to the capital. The *porteño* authorities resented their provincial counterparts for urging the col-umns of poor onward with promises of hospitality that were impossible to fulfill. "If it is confirmed that the neighboring towns are pushing out the unemployed and, on top of this, counseling them to go into the Fed-eral Capital, the city will soon have to bear a moral and social burden that is extremely heavy, to make no mention of the danger, hunger, and extremism that may arise as well."[20]

The new "small city of grime" (Puerto Nuevo) awakened considera-ble embarrassment among *porteños*. Socialists in the Concejo Deliber-ante (the city's governing council) denounced the camp as a "spectacle of misery and filth" at "the doorstep" of the first city of the Republic.[21] In June 1932, Roberto Arlt (who at the time had very close ties to the intellectual base of the Communist Party) visited what he described as a "dark stain" of demoralized men, dirty blankets, and garbage.[22] He found three thousand unemployed persons living five blocks away from the glamorous Florida Street, "that box of bonbons, our city's path of gold and crystal." The "stain" extended far past the formal boundaries of the camp, crossing the train tracks and reaching Dock Sud, the city's southern port. Arlt described the men and women who took shelter there: European immigrants who had fought in wars, *criollos* who had worked in the countryside; one group had arrived by foot, another by sneaking onto cargo trains after the corn harvest in Santa Fe. In his essay, he describes seeing a man who had been driven mad. His mad-ness, a witness explained, "is fixed [on a single] idea, in which he reim-agines his own destitution as the result of someone having closed off the city, preventing him from moving through its streets."

A second witness told Arlt that during the day, many left the camp in search of food and work. Before long, these groups of roaming "*desocu-pados*" became a new subject of focus in the crime pages of local papers. News columns often echoed police reports, informing the public that "[the *desocupados*] annoy the city's inhabitants with their continuous incursions in pursuit of handouts and swindles, [constituting] a decid-edly unattractive stain on the progressive Capital." *El Mundo* offered similar headlines: "Various *Desocupados* Attempt to Rob Businesses," "Attacking Several Businesses, *Desocupados* Provoke Another Serious Scandal," "One *Desocupado* Kills Another with a Knife," "Many *Desocupados* of Puerto Nuevo and Canning Are Registered Criminals," "The *Desocupados* Once Again Commit Bold Robberies in Palermo."[23] Located near the central train station at Retiro, the camp was described as an underworld (*bajo fondo*) of the 1930s, where communism, contraband, anarchism, gambling, and begging intermingled. Very soon, the Sección Especial sent out its network of informants. They patrolled the camp, raided and burned dwellings, and summarily arrested inhabitants. In 1932, the police established a new station to patrol the settlement.[24]

The new edicts on "Vagrancy and Begging" and "Public Security" cannot be understood apart from this context. The regulations allowed police to preemptively detain individuals "found with anything that could be used for a criminal act" (such as a crowbar or other objects used in robberies). Persons who had a history of "loitering by the docks, railway or tram stations, banks, bus stops, theaters, hotels, movie houses, or any other public place or gathering, without a justified cause" became targets. Individuals found "loitering" were marked as criminals, as were "chronic vagrants" (posing as vendors while "imploring the public for charity") and people keeping company with beggars. The context of economic crisis revived the old trope of the "dangerous" riverbank, *the bajo fondo orillero,* now associated with the spectre of impending revolution.

Framed within the old logic of maintaining order in the street, the edicts produced a legal tool enabling police to make preemptive arrests. In fact, the notion of "preventive seizure" was a central component of the late nineteenth-century positivist-criminological program, which had advocated making this judgment the legal prerogative of experts. Legislators, however, were persistent in their rejection of the idea of "preventative seizure," taking a principled stance based on the Constitution. As a result, the penal code that was passed and approved by Congress in 1922 excluded this cornerstone of the positivist agenda. The police protested against the omission, calling legislators and jurists "weak." Several subsequent chiefs of police pressed Congress to pass a law that would expand their powers of incarceration. In 1932, by way of police regulations, the ruling entered into use without any debate. The edicts thus laid the groundwork for a new legal standard: the principle of a "state of potential crime."[25]

The edict that was perhaps most closely tied to political repression was a regulation that restricted the use of firearms. It established that "those who carry weapons of any kind in the streets, in businesses, or public spaces" and "those who make use of firearms—without committing a crime—with any motive or in any situation, within the city, even in private domiciles, public by-ways, gardens, or enclosures" would be subject to a fine or fifteen to thirty days in jail.[26] As we have seen, firearm restrictions had been demanded in the press for some time, with many seeing such a measure as an invaluable tool to stem the rising tide of violence—namely, *pistolerismo*. Regulation, they presumed, could restore the state's monopoly over arms control, as well as its power of pacification. Nevertheless, within this framework, authorities showed greater interest in certain gun owners than others. Indeed, all reports of illegal weapons possession were sent straight to the Orden Político branch, a protocol that neatly expresses the kinds of criteria guiding the edict's application.

Police edicts also reactivated the Ley de Residencia (Residential Law), a judicial tool for expelling "undesirable" foreigners, which went in and out of use over the course of its five and a half decades of existence (1902–58). The Capital Police was the agency charged with applying the law, and it made effective use of it in the turbulent context of the 1930s. Although we have no precise data, we know that there was a sudden rise in the deportation of foreigners during this era, many of whom were charged with committing both political and civil offenses. A comparison of police reports, press reports, and President Justo's declassified papers reveals that between 1932 and 1936 the police expelled hundreds of "undesirables" accused of communist and anarchist activism or participation in organized crime. Members of sex-trafficking rings and the Italian mafia were targeted and often charged with kidnapping and extortion. The deportations continued throughout the decade, used regularly as tools against communist and anti-fascist militancy.[27] Criminal charges were often grounded in a simple edict related to public gatherings, disorderly conduct, or weapons possession. The new toolbox of edicts was behind the rise in political incarceration as well.

As multidimensional tools in a continuum between different types of patrolling, the edicts established a link between the "soft" policing of neighborhood streets and the more hardline approach to political activity. Their operational manual allowed the police to use the basic rationale and techniques of maintaining order as part of a broader political agenda. Was this merely window dressing for political repression? While such an interpretation might explain the executive branch's sudden enthusiasm for a set of modest city regulations, it does not help us to understand how those regulations appealed to the real urban concerns that continued to shape the police agenda. In the 1930s, the question of order in the streets was a phenomenon in and of itself, with roots in both the state and broader society. If the demand for order *extended* its logic to a counterrevolutionary escalation, to the violent subtext of political fraud and social discipline that were part of the crisis, this does not mean that this logic did not in its own right correspond to a broader social consensus of the era.

THE GREAT PUBLIC SECURITY COLLECTION

Between 1932 and 1935, citizens of Buenos Aires organized a series of campaigns (Colectas por la Seguridad Pública) to gather funds to arm the police. Through these fund-raisers, the police acquired pistols and patrol cars, built perimeter outposts, and set up a radio network. In 1933, residents also organized neighborhood petitions demanding that the state put "more police" on the street. Large businesses, *sociedades de fomento* (development associations), and local clubs joined together in a call for a stronger police presence across the urban grid.

These efforts reflected a widespread outcry that had been gaining momentum over the course of the 1920s. As we have seen, headlines alerted readers to large-scale organized robberies while smaller, everyday crimes filled police reports. "A New Record: 10 Robberies" read one headline in *Crítica;* "Muggings in Every Neighborhood of the Metropolis," read another.[28] Even in less sensationalistic newspapers, crime became part of regular coverage. In *El Mundo,* the paper most widely read by the vast and diverse middle sectors of society, news of armed attacks made headlines several times a week, occasionally a few times a day. They painted a vivid picture of *pistolero* outrages: "They robbed him, bound his hands and feet and took him away in his own automobile"; "It's a daily occurrence: yesterday another driver was robbed"; "After a young thug was arrested, his friends shot at the two policemen"; "Three assailants of pedestrians arrested in the 43rd Precinct"; "Opportunistic thieves gagged a businessman and looted his store"; "After terrorizing him with revolvers, they took his nickel watch and his money"; "Twelve pesos and a vehicle were taken by the audacious thief"; "The assailant left him penniless and standing in the street."

Now and again editorials echoed worries about too few police on patrol, unruliness in the streets, the need for regulation of firearms, or the weakness of penal law, sundry anxieties that finally led people to take collective action in the form of fund drives. This was not the first time that the police had counted on civil society for financial support: they had long depended on donations (of money and property) to make up for their chronic material shortfalls. In 1919, the police created Police Homes (Hogares Policiales) to raise and earmark funds for officers who struggled to pay rent. Soon, these "homes" became centers for development, charity work, patriotic ceremonies, and discussions about neighborhood planning. An executive commission, the Comisión Directiva Pro-Hogar, "made up of the most prominent neighbors," ran each center and often awarded a monthly prize to the officer who best served the neighborhood. These commissions also led votes on proposals for smaller acts of solidarity, like providing night watchmen with a thermos of hot coffee during the colder months of the year.[29] As we will see, the police struggled to keep up with city growth. But while finding officers to patrol the new neighborhoods was difficult, those who did sign on were given many opportunities to integrate themselves into the fabric of the new communities. Walking the beat, they got to know the stores, churches, bars, clubs, and development societies, and the neighbors that frequented them.

The Great Collection for Public Security (Gran Colecta por la Seguridad Pública) operated on a different scale than these smaller, local exercises in solidarity. It was initially organized by groups from the economic elite and wealthiest business sectors who had sought to take action against the wave of robberies on cash registers and armored trucks that had begun a decade earlier. In February 1931, representatives from the Unión Industrial Argentina, the Bolsa de Cereales, the Unión Mayoristas, the Asociación de Propietarios de Bienes Raíces, and the Sociedad Rural (all entities with a vested interest in ensuring the safe transport of goods) gathered at the stock market building. Compared to the amounts donated by these organizations, official state donations were negligible. The municipality contributed $20,000, but beyond this, official aid was limited. The national government's contribution consisted of allowing the Colecta to import weapons for the police duty free.[30]

The press and radio promoted a "Day of Public Security" on July 7, 1931, to raise more funds. Police ties to the country's major radio station (Radio Belgrano) pushed the campaign onto the national airwaves. In living rooms across the city, where the rhythms of domestic life had already been transformed by radio, residents heard repeated calls for police solidarity.[31] Meanwhile, a number of entertainment companies organized events and, in each neighborhood, commissions solicited support from local businesses and industries.

The public display of support was visible throughout the city. Police-men on the beat carried books of one-peso coupons that were sold "at the public's request." Two planes dropped leaflets explaining the drive.[32] "In the busiest parts of the city—subway stations, theaters, movie houses, prominent commercial centers, streets with high volumes of pedestrians, etc.—one-hundred-and-ninety tables have been set up to receive public contributions." The image of the sacrificial "fallen" police officer—very important in institutional symbology, as we will see—was featured in public appeals for empathy and responsibility. Some fund-raising tables were manned by the children of police agents killed in the line of duty, while two banner-flying carriages paraded the downtown streets, with the orphans of fallen officers Sarmiento and Perna riding in front.[33]

Small-scale donations came in quickly. Caught up in a competition between police stations, neighborhood groups distant from the down-town area gathered extraordinary sums of money. The forty-six pre-cincts of the city created commissions that they called "Pro-Arms for the Police," and a substantial number of citizens from upper, middle, and lower-middle sectors aided in the modernization campaign. Meanwhile, these smaller donations put pressure on the so-called first section, the banks and businesses whose owners had begun the Colecta movement, to increase their donations. Although the economic heavyweights even-tually collected the largest sums, police fund-raising remained an impor-tant neighborhood-level project. Collection committee records show that neighborhoods repeated their generosity in similar drives in 1932, 1933, and 1934. Overall, the results were substantial: funds were used to buy new weapons, artillery, patrol cars, a police broadcasting and telephone service, and a network of perimeter police outposts.[34]

After the 1931 fund-raiser, the public began to mobilize around demands for more police on the streets. "The resources so generously and enthusiastically raised by the people on Public Security Day, and also in the current campaign to arm the police, will both be for naught," read one petition, if the state does not deploy more police officers to patrol the streets.[35] The most powerful called for a police force that could maintain public order, control crime, and end the threats to major businesses, port warehouses, large factories, transport vehicles, and train stations, where hundreds of thousands of people circulated every day.[36] Many others demanded a heightened role for the state in guaran-teeing order, maintaining personal security, establishing a monopoly on violence, and protecting private property.

Historians have convincingly shown that during the 1920s and 1930s, civil associations improved the conditions of *porteño* neighborhoods.[37] The clubs, libraries, and development associations (*sociedades de fomento*) were instrumental in securing many improvements to infrastructure: roads were paved, sanitation was improved, electricity was installed. By the mid-1930s, neighbors were using these same organizations to demand that the city deploy more police. "Our delegates, men from all neighborhoods, men from the development associations, where the demands and desires of the population are heard, have unanimously proclaimed that the [existing] police force is insufficient," states one letter.[38] Collection tables sprang up all over the city: the Sociedad de Fomento and Bibliotecas Populares de Liniers, the Asociación Vecinal de Fomento "Los Amigos de Villa Luro," the Asociación de Fomento y Cultura "Flores Sud," the Asociación "Los Amigos de la Ciudad," the Junta Cultural de San José de Flores, the Sociedad de Fomento "Villa Ortúzar," businessmen, industrialists, and neighbors of section 22a, "Los Amigos de la Avenida General Paz," Liga de Fomento Federico Lacroze, Sociedades de Fomento San Cristóbal Sud, Comisión Edilicia Nueva Pompeya, El Pilar de Nueva Pompeya, El Despertar, El Progreso de Villa Lugano, El Sol de Villa Riachuelo, and so forth.[39] The movement was a concerted, well-organized effort.

The petitioners' concerns were consistently articulated: too few police patrolling the neighborhoods (a point that will be explored further in the next chapter); an increase in robberies and other crimes against property as a result of the economic crisis; the danger to the public posed by traffic accidents; inappropriate or violent behavior by young people in the streets, and so on. One association called for a stricter penal code. Another (clearly influenced by the press) mentioned the danger of children being kidnapped as they left school. Most alluded to common problems that resulted from the insufficient police presence. One letter with a long list of signatures and endorsements from small business (from hat makers, hardware stores, perfumers, etc.) read: "Honest men want to live in a peaceful, calm environment, and there will neither peace nor tranquility as long as criminals rule the streets, make other people's possessions their own, and turn the lives of their fellows into cannon fodder."[40]

They did not attack police methods. Rather, they lauded the efforts of the overburdened policemen, patrolling the streets in isolation, outnumbered by the population they served and spread too thinly across the city. These petitions did not demand a more repressive police force: they simply asked for more officers to help guarantee peace, order, and public morality. They longed for a patrolman who "knows all of the neighbors, their ways of life and customs, and can recognize both the thief and the night stalker." One letter stated: "The uniformed silhouette of the policeman scares the criminal into the shadows. In the heart of the thief, the feeling of being watched . . . can usually prevent a crime from ever taking place."[41]

The grassroots character of these initiatives invites us to reexamine explanations of changes in *porteño* police in the 1930s that emphasize political urgency or the repression of workers' organizations. As we have seen, anti-democratic banners, the well-known voices of authoritarianism, military and religious leagues, and nationalist intellectuals were all marginal to this call for order and street policing.

To the fragile, everyday neighborhood order, the threats were not so much ominous as disruptive. Some were new, some recurring. The petitions mentioned beggars (on the rise since the economic crisis) provoking incidents in plazas and on sidewalks; thieves (alone or in gangs, amateur or professional) with easy access to cheap weapons bursting into businesses or homes to steal what others had worked so hard for; they also mentioned careless drivers who brought more and more noise and violence to the streets. Some threats were well known but had acquired new meaning as the *barrios* expanded and became "civilized": crowds of noisy kids, mischievous boys ringing doorbells and hunting birds with slingshots and rocks; men who posted flyers on the walls of houses and businesses, damaging property and disrupting the visual ecology; "inappropriately dressed" individuals "bothering everyone with their lack of culture," *invertidos* (gay men) and drug users. These "dregs of modernity," less tolerated in the 1930s than during the previous decade, prowled around the newly mortgaged houses, standing between the city and its march to decency, threatening "the peace and security of homes and workplaces," and violating the sense of respectability that the signers of these documents were so carefully constructing.

These concerns about everyday disorder were not dissociated from the economic and political earthquakes of 1930. The economic crisis and a clear increase in violence became intertwined with a kind of retraction, above all in the newly settled neighborhoods, where there appeared a generic call for order, a diffuse spirit of self-defense. While it may have touched upon some of the great formal ideologies, it did so without necessarily identifying with any of them. Certainly, there was an affinity between these complaints and the more hierarchical premises of nationalism—the ideological tradition usually invoked to refer to

1930s reactionary thought. They were, however, more closely linked to the growing culture of middle-class Catholicism flourishing in these neighborhoods.[42] They also cannot be completely separated from the most civilizing strands within the very popular Socialist Party.

Rather than subscribing to particular political identities, public outcry reflected a broader preoccupation with order, personal security, and material preservation. There were several demands within this outcry: for a social order that eschewed extreme expressions of conflict, for an "ecological" order that decried the irresponsible use of public space (where excess and strident outbursts were becoming increasingly intolerable), and for a moral order that abhorred modernity's frenzied indulgences.

What was needed was "more police" and "more state" across the urban grid: more cops on the beat in the maze of streets, more state presence to take custody of the emerging urban order, more *imperium* for the application of edicts and municipal regulations. The kind of police officers that *porteños* wanted to see on those street corners were those that fulfilled the traditional role of maintaining order. They were not agents of political enforcement, but guarantors of the "eliasian" tradition. They were shoring up what Norbert Elias called the "civilizing" function of society, where the source of control (and self-control) resides in the collective pressure of one's neighbors. The policeman's silhouette, cast against the light of the electric streetlamp, emerged as a symbol of protection against disorder and illegality. *Omnes et singulatim:* beyond keeping watch over the general order, neighborhood petitions imagined the neighborhood officer as someone who, through his firsthand knowledge, could distinguish, *one by one,* the honest worker from the prowler and the felon.[43]

This explains the anxious attempts on the part of the police hierarchy to draw a clear line between the moral position of the street policeman and that of the people he watched over. Disciplinary logs suggest that increasing pressure was brought to bear on neighborhood policemen, who were now deemed to be too friendly and indulgent with the drunks, numbers runners, and other dissolute individuals they were expected to monitor. In order to properly exercise authority out of doors, the officer had to carefully monitor his own behavior behind closed doors, as it were. As we'll see later, there were challenges involved in this effort. First, however, we should turn to certain aspects of this renewed emphasis on street surveillance.

Noise patrol. Police were granted the power to fine or arrest individuals for three to fifteen days for making noise: if they "fight within their homes or in private spaces, and [if] these acts ... *cause alarm and disturb the neighbors"*; "shout or [make] other noises or *cause alarm or perturb the work or rest of the neighbors"*; "play music or sing in the street *disrupting public tranquility"*; or *"cause annoyance* through the loud hawking of newspapers, magazines, or other goods for sale."[44] Although noise is an aspect of urban life so ubiquitous as to have been registered in the complaints of citizens of ancient Rome, it's safe to say that noise in the great cities of the industrial age was more varied and more grating.[45] Not all sound meant the same thing, however. The songs and proclamations that once formed part of street life began to lose their place in the industrial city, while the sounds of marital disputes and "uncivil" expressions of passion that escaped through windows became intolerable. During political campaigns in the 1930s, the *porteño* press denounced noisy street protests, the sounds of partisan passion being equally intolerable in the "civilized" city. Gamblers' "excessive outbursts" further added to the list of "bothersome" noises, as games spilled out into public spaces. As threshholds of sound were surpassed, tolerance for them increased as well. Technological advances such as the radio and the gramophone allowed *porteños* to play music at all hours and at unprecedented volumes, while poorly regulated auto traffic resulted in a cacophony of roaring motor engines and car horns.[46] Innumerable editorials deplored the din produced by cars without mufflers.[47]

In this growing, modern city, the rules that governed noise were still ill-defined. A range of regulations promised consequences for sound disruption, from small fines to corporal punishment. These regulations were "patrolled" collectively insofar as a violation was issued when a sound was determined to be "bothersome"—that is, when it broke the tolerance level of those living nearby. The enforcement of regulations thus depended directly on one's neighbors' idea of tranquility; ultimately, they were the ones to determine the level of sound that did not permit them "to work or rest." Police, of course, were in charge of enforcing the law, but public demands structured that enforcement. Perceptions of what constituted a noise violation came from opinions editorialized in *La Razón, La Prensa, El Mundo,* and *La Nación.* These perceptions also came from neighborhood complaints—that is, from those incidents where one neighbor demanded moderation on the part of another and ended up seeking out local police to arbitrate the conflict.

Edicts and ordinances dealing with moderation intersected and overlapped with the patrolling of morality. Drunkenness "in the streets, plazas, cafés, 'cabarets,' stores, taverns and other places that offer drinks, or public stalls" became another target of scrutiny. The public dance, an ancient type of social gathering known for immoderation and monitored regularly by the police, reemerged as a subject of discussion. Mentioned in the edicts as "immoral or obscene dances" and associated with prostitution, they were usually held downtown in the port neighborhood of La Boca (home to thousands of Italian immigrants) and on streets near the riverbanks, traditionally sites of illicit activity. Now they were made targets of increased police regulation. At the beginning of the 1930s, calls for intervention reached an all-time high, with many decrying that Buenos Aires could no longer be, and *should* no longer be, the infamous southern "Sodom" that it had been in the late 1800s.[48]

The legal rubric of "scandalous acts" was subject to another set of norms. Historically associated with prostitution, it included a wide range of acts and gestures deemed indecent: uttering obscene (or "graceless") words that offended sensibilities or breached good manners, urinating in public, bathing in places that "broke the laws of decency and decorum," wearing attire deemed socially inappropriate, and so on. An edict restricting specific behaviors at carnivals (a kind of street festival that had always been surveilled) prohibited adult men from using masks without obtaining prior permission, as well as from cross-dressing, playing games involving water, or throwing objects from balconies. The regulations also included a more vague prohibition against "all uncultured acts," including "rude language or improper attitudes that in any form bother other people."[49]

What do we know about the enforcement of these rules? The statistics reveal a near 100 percent rise in violations, suggesting a spike in police enforcement that was broadly maintained throughout the decade.

Of course, the accuracy of these figures should not be taken at face value: police who are under pressure to raise enforcement statistics are likely to exaggerate their numbers when they report to their superiors. It's also difficult to determine if there was a clear logic behind the application of the edicts. As ethnographies of police street behavior have suggested, enforcement is highly selective. Since police could not (and never have been able to) completely accomplish their mission, and as the spectrum of potential tasks is infinitely greater than their effective capacity, each officer has (and has always had) wide latitude in deciding when to intervene: the enforcement of edicts has a high level of autonomy. Beyond the gaze of their superiors, the street cop could decide which edicts to apply and how to apply them, when to apply them, and when to ignore them.[50] Police commissioners were aware of this selective autonomy and

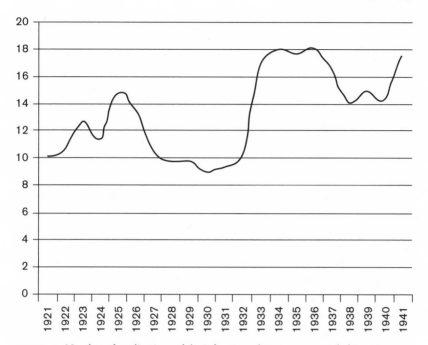

GRAPH 5. Number of applications of the infraction edicts (per 1,000 inhabitants), Buenos Aires, 1921–41. Source: Author's graphic using data from Policía de la Capital, *Memorias de la Policía, 1921–1941.*

independence and, for this reason, each station worked on prioritizing certain edicts over others. Officers were instructed to strictly enforce some regulations, "moderately" enforce others, and in some cases, abstain. As a result, edicts were applied unevenly.

The opacity of this system (and the lack of more specific documentation) prevents us from acquiring a better understanding of how these norms were policed. Still, we can make several informed conjectures. On the one hand, the publication and diffusion of an operational manual for the edicts set priorities and informed officers' daily micro-decisions: what was important was so by virtue of being included in the manual. At times, the manual highlighted new norms. At others times, the guide resurrected long-dormant laws, reinforcing the mandate to effectively apply certain regulations from an immense body of police edicts built up over the course of decades.

So: why was there such an upward curve in the number of registered violations? And what kinds of edicts were enforced? First, those pertaining to customs and morals: "drunkenness" saw the biggest jump (to some 19,000 violations per year, compared with an average of between 8,000 and 9,000 per year during the previous decade), followed next by "scandalous behavior" (which rose to about 5,000, compared with averages ranging from 2,500 to 4,000 in the mid-1920s).[51] Next came those edicts having to do with social order: "disorder" (6,600 per year, compared with about 4,000 in the previous years) and two categories that saw a sudden increase: "panhandling" and "vagrancy" (2,500 and 1,300, respectively). Finally, nearly 1,000 people were punished every year for "carrying weapons," an edict that was often used, as we will see in chapter 5, for political repression.[52]

Classic narratives of police history, beginning with those originating with the institution itself, have characterized police modernization as a gradual shift from the generic to the specific—in other words, from a colonial, nineteenth-century institution that applied a broad definition of order (management of trash and noise, transportation, and violence) to a police force specializing in certain tasks (most particularly, catching criminals). In this progression, a greater focus on criminality would indicate a greater degree of modernization. In Buenos Aires, those who denounced political policing as well as those who demanded the incarceration of more criminals assumed this evolutionist narrative, ignoring the dimension of policing concerned with maintaining public order.

Regardless, distinct projects began to converge around the "harder" police agenda of the 1930s. We can identify three. The first related to modernization and professionalization adopted by police leaders, which took the form of recruitment reforms, adjustments in training, and technical advances (more on this below). A second direction of the 1930s police agenda had a strong counter-insurgency element, which found its source in a political leadership (*uriburista* first, and *justista* later) that sought to use the police to eliminate threats to the status quo after the 1930 military coup. This led directly to espionage and the use of police edicts against dissident populations, to the repression of Radicals and communists, and to the creation of Orden Social and the Sección Especial. In turn, it also precipitated the downfall of "expropriative" anarchism and the most highly organized instances of *pistolerismo*. Finally, there was a third, less notorious, dimension to 1930s policing: the reinforcement of its most traditional institutional mission, that of monitoring the circulation of people throughout the city and safeguarding their coexistence. It would be an error to minimize the weight of this logic: tens of thousands of police interventions per year speak to the expansion of a type of urban policing that was serial and ubiquitous, and closely associated with a rising demand for order.

Clearly, these were not new issues. They had dominated the agenda many times before, as is shown by statistics on arrests for the decades preceding and following 1900, with their emphasis on controlling "scandalous" behavior, alcoholism, and street violence. Like other port cities transformed by a wave of immigration, Buenos Aires posed enormous challenges to its authorities' ability to maintain order and make the urban grid legible. Moreover, the diagnosis of the problem came from a police force that was completely overwhelmed by the magnitude and rate of change, and lacking in social and political support. Julia Blackwelder has shown that at the turn of the century, the number of policemen per capita declined in Buenos Aires, while increasing in port cities of North America. She attributes this difference to the weak relationship between the *porteño* police force and its political parties. Despite nearly constant calls for greater order and the systematic use of the police for political and social repression, no political group created any lasting bond with the institution. The police, thus, did not benefit from any particular party's success and could not count on the state's generosity to fund their operations.[53]

By the 1930s, this situation had changed. After the great demographic revolution, expectations of beautification and public health were increasing, and transportation infrastructure was in place. As many *porteños* were able to acquire their own places to live, and many more engaged in long-term plans to do the same, an idea of order emerged within a larger set of newly modified social expectations, expectations that were more strongly articulated in civil-society organizations than in political groups, boosting urban police intervention. In European and North American narratives, the figure of the street police officer is set against the industrializing city at the end of the nineteenth century. In Buenos Aires, this figure belongs to the 1930s, at the close of a period of mass immigration. By then, the search for a more serene outcome of this great experiment had, for many, become common sense. The nationalist elite, who had criticized the modernizing project for two decades, were not the only ones calling for urban order. So too were the immigrants and children of immigrants, the primary protagonists of modernization and change.

CHAPTER 4

Detecting Disorder

One hardly notices the intimate relationship between the
police and the city, because they've both changed so much,
even if they have remained in their place. Adapting himself in
order to stay relevant, the street cop watches over the life in
the city and its circulation the way he used to watch over the
lives of neighbors. Little by little, he stopped serving one
patron to serve another, and if he used to relate to human
order, he now relates to urban disorder.

—Ezequiel Martínez Estrada, *La cabeza de Goliat,* 1940

Keeping order in the city is the oldest of police duties.[1] On guard by day
and by night, the colonial watchmen dispersed throughout the city
undertook a mission that was modest only in appearance. They were
part of a more extensive project of constructing a (modern) image of an
omni-perceptive state. In the 1820s, the Policía de Buenos Aires adopted
the image of a watchful eye as their emblem, placing the symbol on their
medallions, badges, and letterhead. This institution "never slept." Set
against a symbol of the sun (which irradiated light on the darkened city)
and a rooster ("the bird of daybreak"), the eye symbolized the homogeneous continuity of police control over the territory of its jurisdiction.[2]

Watching the city by day, watching it by night, the police attempted
to give the appeance of being the ubiquitous eyes of authority. From the
dark, muddy village of the nineteenth century to the great metropolis of
the present day, the same utopian ideal of omniscience has guided the
use of vast human and technical resources. The following pages focus
on the crisis and subsequent resurrection of this ideal during the first
decades of the twentieth century. It traces this history into the 1930s,
when the police began using the new technologies—radios and patrol

FIGURE 16. The official seal
of the Buenos Aires Police,
1822.

cars—that fundamentally altered methods of perceiving and collecting
information on urban life.

IN SEARCH OF THE METROPOLITAN POLICEMAN

When *porteños* called their police force "the best in the world," they
were turning a propaganda slogan into a common joke, since these supposed "agents of order" were an easy target for public mockery. In comic
strips, the early twentieth-century policeman was a classic buffoon, criticized for his inefficiency and his inability to impose authority. Ridicule
was what prompted Colonel Ramón Falcón to request that city authorities restrict actors from donning police uniforms, because they always
portrayed policemen as "awful characters, nearly odious, that discredit
[the police] in the popular imagination, [and encourage] mockery and
ridicule by the majority of the public . . . [leading to] disrespect for
authority."[3] In the 1920s, the popular and populist newspaper *Crítica*
also capitalized on the poor reputation of the police by mounting a series
of staged "robberies" designed to ridicule the force. Staging a fake crime
in front of photographers and bystanders, the paper illustrated the pow-
erlessness of the police, reducing the myth of ubiquity to ridicule.[4] These
campaigns also ridiculed the police declaration of "total war" on organized crime as mere talk. Every day—in articles and editorials, as well as

photos, comics, and caricatures in tens of thousands of copies—the state's ability to stop crime was doubted.

For the police, this crisis in public opinion reintroduced a classic issue of modernization and reform: the murky division between the police and the public, between those being watched and those doing the watching. In some public representations the *yuta* (derogative slang for cop) appeared as an enemy, and in others he was just another poorly respected, easily mocked neighborhood character. In his poem "El bailongo," for example, Héctor Gagliardi described a police officer passing by a *milonga* in a *conventillo:*

El botón de aquella esquina	The cop on the corner
hasta la puerta se acerca	arrives at the doorway
a controlar si la fiesta	to make sure the party
transcurre seria y tranquila	is calm and orderly
El encargado lo adivina	The host guesses well
lo invita a "tomar un trago"	and offers him "a drink"
y al rato sale "cargado"	and in a moment he leaves, "loaded"
a efectuar la recorrida.	and ready to walk his beat.[5]

Gagliardi knew something about how and where the exercise of control slid into idle chit-chat and drinking wine. He worked as a police officer for six years (1933–39) before becoming a poet and tango lyricist.

The police chiefs were even more keenly aware of the easily blurred line between policing and breaking the law, and saw the task of marking a boundary of professionalism between police officers and the communities they patrolled as a priority and major challenge. The main target of their professionalizing reforms were (and had always been) street cops, the lowest-ranking officers. And they were not alone in this preoccupation: in most major cities of the continent, modern police authorities shared similar concerns.[6]

From his post on the urban grid, the neighborhood police officer was also struggling to comply with the long list of duties outlined in his police manual. In fact, given the high levels of illiteracy on the force, it was likely that many could not read the manual at all. At the beginning of the century, the lowest (and the most numerous) ranks of the Capital Police had little professional training. Salaries were low, and the job came with very little in the way of social prestige. Retention rates were poor. Police work was so unpopular that some low-ranking officers even tried to conceal their profession by changing quickly out of their uniforms after work or hiding their occupation from public view altogether. For many, police work was little more than a means to an end.[7] In the 1930s, when

societal demands for "more police" were on the rise, and when the introduction of the automobile had transformed the skill set required for control of the street, the salary for rank-and-file police officers remained
low, despite rising significantly as compared to previous decades, putting
it on par with that of other manual laborers. At higher ranks, police
leaders could earn almost ten times as much as entry-level officers, a
wage gap that underlined stark class divisions within the force.

Of course, apart from the similarity in pay, the work of a police officer
was nothing like other kinds of manual labor. The poet Federico Gutiérrez, who at the turn of the century worked at the *depósito de contraven-
tores* (the police jail, for small-time offenders), described this difference
with particular lucidity. Gutiérrez was a singular case: he became an anarchist while working as a bureaucrat in the police department and was fired
when his double identity was discovered (during the administration of the
famously anti-anarchist Chief Ramón Falcón). After he left the force,
Gutiérrez published a book, *Noticias de policía* (Police News), describing
his experience.[8] In his account, he underlined the status of the police officer
as an *authority*, something that disinguished him from a dockworker—
who might earn more, but who didn't have any authority. Perhaps without realizing it, Gutiérrez had tapped into a central debate about the status
of police work. His uniform and his gun were not the only tools at the
officer's command: he was also the sole state functionary with the power
to arrest and impose force directly upon other citizens. This status was not
clear in the early recruitment drives, however, and establishing it as central
to the policeman's professional identity was the goal of a long and deliberate process of reform, one that experienced some of its more decisive
moments in the early decades of the twentieth century.

One part of this process involved a larger effort to provide more generous social benefits within the force. Officers began to see professional stability as compensation for their relatively low wages, a much-appreciated
guarantee given that job security was nonexistent for other workers, so
many of whom were dependent on the highly unpredictable agricultural
industry. The department's pension plan acknowledged the physical risks
of working the streets by providing benefits after only twenty-five years of
service (as opposed to thirty years for other government workers). Meanwhile, neighborhood businesses financed an additional fund (the Caja de
Socorros) for police officers and their families. All of these measures were
geared toward embellishing what looked like a rather unappealing option
for those at the bottom of the labor market. The idea was to build a platform for sustainable recruitment.[9]

These networks of support were in place when the turbulent 1930s began. However, professionalization required more than just improvements in salaries and pensions. It was also necessary to change certain habits of the beat cop, including his relationship to gambling. The many rulings and directives issued to regulate this practice suggest that it took place within a rather wide margin between prohibition and tolerance. Police officers not only played but also received *"mensualidades"*—a monthly payoff in exchange for turning a blind eye, which served to offset their meager salaries. Furthermore, authorities interested in restricting gambling understood that when it came to betting, the police could not be easily separated from the policed. The policeman's love for the racetrack was well known: "All of the commissioners were *burreros* [horse racing fans]," observed Esteban Habiague, who was himself commissioner of the Avellaneda police force during the long tenure of the Conservative *caudillo* Barceló.[10] The same could be said of Habiague's *porteño* colleagues: a popular radio commentator and print columnist on horse racing who went by the name of "Last Reason" was just as celebrated in the police press as he was in the more popular media.[11] The police force's notorious penchant for horse racing posed a disciplinary problem. Although police authorities could prohibit officers from betting during working hours, they could only request that they refrain from doing so while off duty. And if this was not possible, officers were encouraged to not wear their uniforms or otherwise exhibit their status at the track.[12]

The line between state prohibition and social practice was even murkier when it came to the dense culture of illegal gambling. In underground haunts and speakeasies, illegal card games and the *quiniela* (the "numbers game"—the illegal counterpart to the legal lottery) were popular pastimes. Police officers were known as avid participants at these establishments. One report noted that the employees of the Sección Leyes Especiales "are colluding with individuals who play prohibited games, giving them advanced notice of [police] raids." Another reported: "The friendship between Officer Joaquín Pedro Jacinto González and José María Barrero, the Boedo theater ticketer who runs the phones for the bookie Francisco Saccomano, is well documented." A third stated that a block away from a police station, "a subject named Delfino ran a gambling den that was not reported to authorities" and that "his sudden disappearance on the day he was to be turned in to Inspector Iglesias" was suspicious. Also suspicious was the delay of one "Officer González . . . in arriving at the intersection of Boedo and Carlos Calvo, where he had been summoned by Subcommissioner Payba to report an infraction of anti-gambling law 4097. Before his arrival, one of the persons he was ordered to arrest suddenly disappeared."[13]

The repeated calls to put an end to police collusion in illegal gambling suggest that the practice persisted. Among the standard set of local characters connected to the *quiniela*, like the "numbers runner" and the *capo*, or kingpin who ran the game in each district, we also find the police *quinielero*, the officer who played the numbers and received a monthly commission to look the other way or alert the kingpins to an upcoming raid. The *quinielero* was regularly denounced in the police press. There, he appeared as an object of admonishment, but could also be described with smug complicity. Any record of these indulgent behaviors disappeared in the 1930s, however, and evidence suggests that police chiefs made moves to crack down on the practice.[14]

Police disciplinary records show the contours of everyday neighborhood corruption. These texts can be read as bearing witness to the objectionable practices of *porteño* police—evidence of the ways in which abuses of power were tolerated (a phenomenon that still resonates today). To what extent should this be considered a real discovery? Only when approached under the sway of a nostalgic myth of the "pure" police of the past, the notion that there was once an original, ideal police officer whose dedication to community service was untainted by corruption do such findings acquire shock value. However, the evidence of corruption is so overwhelming that extensive archival research hardly seems necessary. Neither is this evidence a universal exception to the rule—given the nature of police work, *all* police must work alongside the "inviting edges of corruption" emanating from the street. It is within the nature of police work to walk a tacit line of negotiation, one that tenuously separates the legal from the illegal.[15] In this case, the evidence pointing to a system of favors and exchanges on the edge of legality describes a historically specific phenomenon: the ways in which the police put down roots in the rapidly expanding neighborhoods of Buenos Aires in the 1920s and 1930s.

The acts of complicity that could earn a police officer friends engendered a kind of closeness that compromised his authority. "Agents should not chat with the public," read a headline in *La Nación,* summarizing the results of a meeting of law enforcement administrators on "instructing street personnel [on how] to abstain from engaging in unnecessary conversation."[16] Among police administrators, minor acts of corruption by street officers were reframed as a problem that put the entire institution's credibility at risk. The officers were the "eyes of their superiors," and as such they were asked to represent and insist on the rule of law in every circumstance. Like many other police chiefs dedicated to modernizing the police force, Colonel Luis J. García (1932–35) found that during the 1930s, street-corner socializing was one of the police pastimes most resistant to change. He discovered that a recently disciplined officer would only days later be found chatting away with the neighbors living along his beat: "good and honorable people, but all too entertaining." Officers accepted drinks, asked for "contributions" from neighborhood stores, collected money from illegal gambling houses in exchange for protection, and put their badges at the service of personal agendas.

The advent of the patrol car opened up new avenues on the slippery slope. As we have seen, the automobile brought temptations for all of society, and the police were no exception. In one case, an inspector was found bringing home a load of wood (a gift from a neighbor) in one of the Twenty-Eighth Precinct's brand new *voiturettes*.[17] As these practices were so common and well tolerated in the unwritten codes of behavior, officers were not always expected to denounce violations of the written rule. A subcommissioner of section 31, for example, very imprudently decided to call attention to the abuses of power of his superior. This officer, he claimed, had accepted gifts from neighbors, filled his gas tank for free, and was a nonpaying customer at a restaurant in the *barrio*. His report was not well received. He was accused of slander and reprimanded for confusing innocent practices like "the acceptance of donations common . . . among friends" with abuse of authority.[18]

The chiefs of the Capital Police saw the blurred line between officers and society as a recruitment issue. Since the very creation of the police force, its leaders had promoted professionalization and modernization as part of a reformist agenda seeking to elevate professional standards, especially among the lowest ranks. Doing justice to this complex process would require a long-term intra-institutional study, beyond the scope of this book. However, it should be noted here that policy changes of the 1920s and 1930s were part of a much longer cycle of reform.[19] Initial steps geared toward raising the status of the profession emphasized the importance of elementary education. In 1907, in an effort to eradicate illiteracy in the police force, a curriculum of basic reading skills was put in place, and soon followed by efforts to provide technical education for agents and cadets. In the 1930s, the criteria for recruitment and training were solidified, as were formal mechanisms to construct police identity. Following the main questions guiding this book, we'll focus on those aspects of reform that concerned the larger mission of police control of the city.

For the late nineteenth-century *porteño* police (as for their colleagues in 1910, mounted on horseback and in full-dress uniform at the centennial), the authority to arrest citizens was granted after only a short and superficial training period. Such power, both modest and monstrous, was constantly denounced by its political victims. With the exception of specialized forces (like the Guardias de Seguridad), street agents, who were the most visible representatives of state order, were recruited sporadically and unsystematically, often in last-minute excursions into the provinces. Police authorities routinely ventured to the northern (poorer) provinces in search of men willing to fill posts abandoned during the harvest season.[20] One can imagine the stark cultural barriers that separated this motley police force from the residents of the cosmopolitan city. In certain contexts, this could be considered an asset: rural recruits typically had little in common with the urban workers—many of them highly confrontational anarchists—they were charged with controlling, which no doubt reduced the chances of policemen identifying with protesters.

Travel narratives during the 1910 centennial celebrations called attention to this contrast. In a city of immigrants, the police were mostly *criolla,* or native born. In the 1920s, the image of the policeman still fit this profile. For leftist groups, the ethnic and racial makeup of the police was viewed as an added insult to injury. The violation of their constitutional rights, as they saw it, was compounded by the indignity of being policed by their inferiors. "The minds of police employees are in embryo; they are at a middle stage somewhere between an idiot and a *picapedrero* [stonecutter]," observed the anarchist/dissident police officer Gutiérrez.[21] The socialist paper *La Vanguardia* went further: the city police was comprised of "an element that had not yet emerged from the atavistic influences of patronage, brutality, and ignorance—[characteristics] that the civilizing influence has sought to overcome since the beginning of the century. Their incorrigible attachment to their thuggish habits is an embarrassment to this city's culture at every level, [and] their ethnic inferiority contrasts unhappily against the European character of our metropolis." In the anarchist paper *La Protesta,* the street cop was described as the "Indian on the corner"— a copper-skinned aborigine daring to arrest workers who were "far less drunk and violent" than he was.[22] Many accounts described the officer's short stature, "rustic" brain, rudimentary intellectual capabilities, and base attitudes—all reflections of the "barbarous *pampa*" from whence he came. He was said to be "incapable of civilizing himself." Indeed, in these characterizations, the police officer looked more like a criminal than the workers who were being arrested and charged.

"Young, tall, agile, awake and educated": the portrait of the ideal street officer that emerged from the reform projects of the 1930s speaks to a keen awareness of the widespread negative stereotypes that circulated in civil society. This new policeman was expected to sign a conditional contract for one year, with a previous period of instruction that might extend from fifteen days to a month, and then to a year. Applicants also had to pass minimum aptitude requirements, including completion of primary school and training at the Police Academy, where they learned the basics of police theory and practice, penal and procedural law, national history and geography, reading and writing, military instruction, physical education, and boxing and jiujitsu. They were also required to have a clean record, and to be at least five feet five inches tall for members of the cavalry and firefighting units and five feet seven inches tall for the infantry. Notably, these height requirements coincided with the median for working-class men between twenty and twenty-four years of age in the rich *pampa* area, but would have been above the average height in poorer provinces, where men were shorter as a result of nutritional deficencies.[23] Taken alongside other new requirements for a more "civilized" police corps, the insistence on height requirements suggested a thinly veiled effort to "whiten" the force.

DETECTING DISORDER

"Is the teeming city of Buenos Aires adequately surveilled by the police?" asked an officer in 1933. The question made sense, of course, because the answer was obviously negative, as was made plain by the chorus of voices openly disputing the state's ability to combat crime. In *El Mundo*, a number of editorials stoked concerns about crime and somberly questioned the abilities of the police.[24] To what extent were these complaints well founded? They certainly reflected the kinds of exaggerations that regularly appeared in commercial journalism, but as Buenos Aires grew and changed, traditional methods of controlling public space were indeed proving insufficient, and the failures had become impossible to conceal. Two decades of unbridled growth and the rise of the automobile made problems even more acute than in other cities that underwent similar changes in surveillance techniques.[25] These problems began with the perception of disorder, which was itself a function of police presence on the city's streets.

In 1912, an issue of *Sherlock Holmes*, a magazine that was usually sympathetic to the police, included a reader-submitted joke that alluded to the infamous ineptitude of street cops when circumstances required their intervention. The joke was accompanied by an image of an immovable, rotund officer, apparently incapable of responding to an incident transpiring only a few yards from his post.

A street cop's assigned duties had changed little since the period of mass immigration, when policing had been structured around the idea of an even and exhaustive state gaze, applied from strictly equidistant control posts.[26] Records kept by commanding officers reveal that poor funding was a permanent obstacle to keeping up with police vigilance. Yet the police were also employing a type of visual control that had largely fallen out of favor, a problem that went well beyond material limitations. The nineteenth-century model of posting officers in eight-hour shifts at fixed points, a practice that had long been widely criticized, became even more untenable when the speed of motorized vehicles transformed the ecology of public space.

Countless stories described crimes being committed within a block of a police control post, pointing out that street cops who were assigned to stand at a fixed point were incapable of intervening in events occurring just beyond the scope of their field of vision. The supposed "ubiquity" of police vigilance was clearly a delusion, and their "authority" became an object of mockery.

In a city of more than 2 million, four to five thousand rank-and-file officers worked the beat (out of seventy-five hundred on the force). What do these figures tell us? When the Capital Police was created in 1880, it was made up of a relatively high proportion of agents per inhabitant. But as the city's population boomed, police numbers did not keep up. By around the time of the centennial (1910), and in the midst of the demographic boom, the population had risen by nearly 250 percent, while the police force had grown by only 20 percent. At the beginning of the automobile age, the proportion of officers per ten thousand inhabitants was continuing its decline. With its peak in 1880, the proportion gradually decreased, reaching its nadir during the interwar period and then beginning a slow ascent in the mid-1930s—a reflection of a concerted effort on the part of neighbors and city residents to petition authorities for more police, as we have seen. Only when population growth had largely stabilized were these pleas finally heeded.

The public presence of the police is an important indicator of the state's ability to exercise its authority. As unspoken reaffirmation, police presence is the institution's most essential and persuasive grammar. Beyond recruitment requirements or technical resources, the public

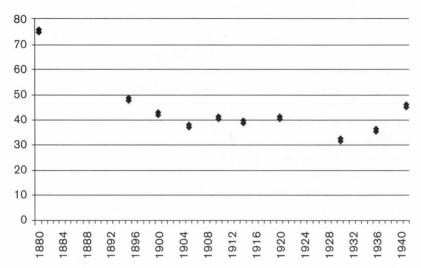

GRAPH 6. Number of street police per 10,000 residents, 1880–1940. Source: Policía de la Capital, *Memoria de la Policía de la Capital*; Anuario Estadístico de la Ciudad de Buenos Aires; Rodríguez, *Historia de la policía*, vol. 6.

presence of uniformed police suggests territorial control, even when (or, especially when) the agents are merely walking the streets, simply *permitting* passersby to circulate. Their power stems from the implicit connection between the policeman on foot and the patrol car stationed at the door of the station or the van slowly cruising the street. The less this force is applied, the more effective is its sovereign function; conversely, the persecution of delinquents or the repression of workers exposes the reactive and violent nature of the police, its tenuous control, and its raw methods of coercion. Like all forms of power, police violence is more persuasive as a threat than as a practice.[27]

In Buenos Aires, efforts to maintain the illusion of the "sovereign presence" of the police were disrupted when a series of acts seemed to confirm the public sentiment that there were "too few police." The first occurred in the wake of the 1930 coup, amid electoral fraud, political crisis, and the Praetorian turn of the police. To make up for a lack of personnel, a decree created the "Police Reserves"—a unit to be deployed in the event of "serious disruptions of order." The expression itself exemplified the state's preoccupation with an uprising led by supporters of the recently ousted Radical Party. The Police Reserves were composed of two contingents "to assure the unquestionable reputation of these reservists and their independence from police activity": police who had recently left the force (in the previous five years) and respected civilians from each precinct. There is no record of the reservists ever having been used.[28]

These types of initiatives should be interpreted in the context of more traditional, everyday challenges, including that of delimiting police responsibilities in the city and the many "distractions" the police force faced in the form of services it was called upon to provide for other state agencies. Indeed, circumscribing these boundaries was the cause of an ongoing tension between the police, the municipal government, and the justice system. At the same time, the automotive revolution—and the regulation of street traffic that it entailed—had redefined the role of the police in relation to the very life of the city, as Martínez Estrada noted in his famous *La cabeza de Goliat*. The annual reports submitted by the Capital Police to the Ministry of the Interior repeated this diagnosis, one that can be read as a somber reverse image of those powerful (omnipresent and omniscient) icons of police order, the rooster and the eye (*el gallo y el ojo*). In a fragile and litigious arrangement, the city dictated the regulations for the flow of traffic, and the police used its *imperium* to enforce the prescribed order. This additional duty required significant energy and resources, as it involved managing the flow of vehicles and handling thousands of cases of traffic violations (among other incidents). The new level of activity kept the police trapped within a web of bureaucratic red tape, "distracting" them from their "true mission": to guard the streets and pursue criminals.[29] The number of infractions perceived and punished by the police rose dramatically during the 1930s.

As the graphic shows, enforcement per capita increased from about 15 per thousand to almost 50 per thousand (a change that should be read in tandem with the parallel rise in the application of infraction edicts analyzed in chapter 3). In absolute terms, this meant that the police went from enforcing tens of thousands of regulations in the 1920s to over a hundred thousand in the late 1930s. Additional statistics show that more than 90 percent of these thousands of incidents were for speeding, obstructing traffic, parking violations, jaywalking, and moving against the flow of traffic. Twenty-two categories of traffic violations put transit at the center of police activity. Nineteenth-century regulations that attempted to set aside paths for animals and humans, as well as spaces for waste, had, in the 1930s, mutated into an exercise in separating horse-drawn carts from motor vehicles, buses from bicycles, and pedestrians from everything else. More than anything, newer regulations sought to monitor the incivility of speed and to mitigate the kinetic heterogeneity of public space.[30] Police manuals printed during these years

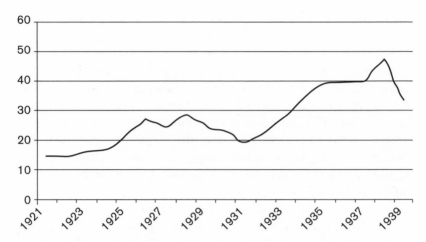

GRAPH 7. Number of infractions per 1,000 inhabitants, Buenos Aires, 1921–39.
Source: Anuario Estadístico de la Ciudad de Buenos Aires; Policía de la Capital,
Memoria de la Policía, 1921–1939.

are filled with micro-regulations attempting to adapt to the ever-changing modes of transportation. Soon, the slow coach that so delighted the young Borges could no longer legally drive down Las Heras Avenue. In no district were the regulations tighter than in the commercial and financial center of the city, where the narrow streets were host to a wild parade of trolleys, buses, old cars, new cars, bicycles, and pedestrians.

The business of managing this traffic presented new challenges to police authority. The upper classes—often driving the most modern and expensive automobiles—were not accustomed to accepting police authority, and often willfully ignored it. As automobile ownership became more accessible, police engaged in more and more confrontations with individuals who were not in the habit of submitting to the gaze of the police. It is telling that the greatest number of traffic tickets written up during this period were issued for "disobedience," a label that speaks to the challenges of exercising police power in busy traffic. In these situations, the police acted as state representatives who exercised a position of authority "from below" on drivers who usually had far more social capital than they did and whose power in public space had been sharply increased by motorized speed.[31] As one officer recalled, drivers did not necessarily behave contemptuously, "but nor were they fully compliant with the officer doing his duty." Some neighborhoods, too, were more difficult to police; for example, the area around Corrientes and Esmeralda, filled with cinemas and theaters, had a bad reputation among street policemen because it was frequented by well-dressed, affluent citizens who, when they violated the law, were especially reluctant to submit to authority.[32]

Meanwhile, the expansion of urban neighborhoods obliged the police to stretch their limited human resources across an ever larger area. From the beginning of the twentieth century, the cartographic boundaries of Buenos Aires had begun to blur as urban life expanded and new public transport (trolleys and trains) crossed into new territories. With new access to real estate and the extension of urban public works (electricity, sanitation systems, etc.), the "theoretical radius" of the city grew while the population density per precinct declined.[33]

The record growth experienced by Buenos Aires developed at an uneven pace, with new sections being fully incorporated into the urban grid while others remained only weakly integrated. This uneven fabric generated ever new challenges for police control, as the gaze of order had to adapt to a texture in constant flux. The rhythm of change was so fast paced that police could no longer rely upon the data (sketchy, in any case) from municipal censuses, and had to produce their own cartographic data. Officers went house to house, counting the number of residents in each city section.[34]

Irregular construction, empty lots, temporary buildings, alleys, passageways, and inconsistent lighting: the police had to adapt to an urban landscape that was peppered with dark areas beyond their surveillance. These uncertain spaces didn't last too long, however. As one overwhelmed police chief noted in 1925, "Newly populated sites in previously empty lots that neither had, nor had required, surveillance" generated plenty of new demands on the city police. Even in areas that had long been populated, methods had to change, because the new density of occupied space made old approaches obsolete: "The colonial house, with its immense patios and a few rooms housing only one family, has been replaced with a skyscraper, multiplying the number of inhabitants in the same perimeter . . . and the activity of neighborhood life has intensified by a similar proportion."[35]

Beyond the usual problems of lack of personnel and resources, it was the very ability to perceive disorder that was called into question, at a time when so many barriers blocked the view of the policeman's "ubiquitous eye." The urban fabric that this gaze was able to reconstruct was parceled, heterogeneous, and often barely legible. In petitions and formal complaints, new residents expressed their frustration with irregular police control, contrasting the "privilege" of those whose homes

MAPS 1 (above) AND 2 (right). Neighborhood growth in Buenos Aires, 1910–48. Maps courtesy of Alicia Novick, Graciela Favelukes, and Federico Collado, www. atlasdebuenosaires.gov.ar/ thematic units/urbanization.

happened to be next to a police station with the negligence experienced by those who lived only a few blocks away. It was impossible to satisfactorily answer the complaint.

Police cartography did not ignore the changes taking place in the city, but it reflected a plan that worked better in theory than in practice. While police manuals suggested that there should be one officer for every six or seven city blocks, agents in the street were often given the task of watching over more than forty, fifty, or even sixty blocks on their own. The numbers mentioned in newspaper editorials and neighborhood petitions were as high as one hundred. Neighbors complained that such minimal policing was almost worse than no policing at all. With things as they were, a would-be thief would simply wait patiently

for an officer to walk by on his rounds. As soon as he turned a corner, the thief could be certain that the policeman would not be making another appearance for several hours.[36]

In his biting critique, former policeman Gutiérrez saw in the unequal distribution of police (dense in areas considered rich and powerful, barely perceptible in areas on the periphery) the explanation for the proliferation of firearms among citizens in the frontier *barrios*. "Downtown there is an officer for each house—the Archbishop's palace, the courts, the Congress, all the offices have at least three or four [policemen]—in the suburbs, there is one for an entire section." To illustrate his point, he described an incident at a dance in the recently settled neighborhood of Villa Crespo: a man was shot, in agonizing pain in the middle of the street. It took the police officer assigned to the area (a friend of the dance's organizers) six hours to respond to the call.[37]

Even though the ratio of police per inhabitant in Buenos Aires was not much lower than that in other major cities, North American cities were seeing police numbers rise, keeping better pace with population growth, while Buenos Aires was experiencing a sustained downward trend.[38] The uneven distribution of personnel was the other decisive factor. New neighborhoods did not always have a commissioner, and they often lacked the subordinate officers and auxiliary forces necessary for regular operations. And in these neightborhoods, what was a police station, really? It was often just a small outpost of the state in a rented house built for another purpose, and most likely far removed from the geographic center of its jurisdiction.[39]

Police reforms did seek to correct policemen's sedentary habits. Instead of posting officers to fixed corners, new projects were designed to train them to circulate from one post to the next, thus expanding the radius of surveillance and generating a greater presence within an assigned area. Under these new guidelines, policemen would not act as lighthouses but as patrols, the walking representatives of the state, on the lookout as they moved, maintaining equal distance, but covering the widest possible territory.

These new plans were curtailed by police officers' own opposition and a lack of backup. The question of neighborhood coverage remained critical in the 1930s. In the downtown area (the zone between Callao, Lavalle, 25 de Mayo, and Avenida de Mayo Streets), and in highly trafficked intersections that required constant vigilance, police presence remained significant. Beyond these zones, instructions were not very ambitious: "For ten minutes per hour the officers will go out to the corners closest to their posts [and walk] one block in a straight line."[40]

After considerable trial and error, however, the irregularity of the police gaze was gradually corrected, and the ratio of police per inhabitants slowly increased. A law authorized the construction of thirty-one new police stations and eight other outposts, beginning a broader movement toward the strengthening of police visibility across the city. Posts were reorganized and became more evenly distributed.[41] Meanwhile, the Security Division, which held jurisdiction across the city, began to serve as a backup for more understaffed precincts, "especially in neighborhoods with fewer patrols, where the nature of the population requires the most surveillance."[42] By then, the Public Security fundraisers (Colectas) were making an impact on city streets.

THE RADIO AND THE PATROL CAR:
POLICE FANTASIES OF TECHNICAL MODERNITY

A recent recruitment video for the Argentine Federal Police begins with a series of thrilling images: patrol cars with lights and sirens, a squadron of motorcycles weaving between cars and buses, helicopters in flight above Buenos Aires tracking a car below, modern artillery, a robot disarming a bomb, control rooms outfitted with large flat-screen monitors, digital maps of the city, and microphones for instant communication with street officers. Switching between these images and others that underline a more human dimension, where officers interact with neighborhood children on tricycles, police work is portrayed as a highly technologized profession.[43]

This visual description, reminiscent of an action movie, reflects a long-standing trend whose decisive moment came in the 1930s, when the Capital Police adopted certain technologies that permitted it to reclaim its imagined former status as an omnipresent and omniscient force, as well as an offensive power. In the course of a few years, the institution built a radio network and purchased a fleet of patrol cars, motorcycles, and trucks. Police officers were assigned Colt pistols, and machine guns and tear gas (both products of wartime) were introduced in select operations. Taken as a group, these tools altered police methods of intervention, along with its powers of perception and detection. By comparison, modifications made during later decades would remain marginal.

Let's begin with the weapons that were acquired with the money raised by the Public Security Collections. The details of the purchase are revealing. The police ordered and obtained nearly 9,000 .45 caliber Colt pistols, 25 Thompson machine guns, 7 Monitor rifles, 120 Berretta carbines, 12 Federal pistols for gas and signals, 14 Walter pistols, 154 tear gas masks, 30 masks for other kinds of gas, and 5 armored trucks.[44] Colt, which by that time was providing many city police forces with arms, communicated by cable and through a corporate representative who traveled regularly through Latin America. Nevertheless, because direct acquisition was mired in red tape, the pistols and ammunition were ultimately bought through an intermediary at the Rasetti Armory, which had experience in arms importation. Another local armory, Leon & Bonasegna, provided the machine guns. Seven thousand holsters were acquired through a third office, Butavand y Cía. Thus, at a pivotal moment in the process of police modernization, the state acquired arms and equipment from the same sources as common citizens, a fact that spoke both to the scale of the private arms market and to the previous development of a large importing capacity.

The powerful Colt .45 became standard issue for all city police officers, an indispensable component of the modern metropolitan police corps. Since then, the gun has been a distinguishing and identifying accessory, the palpable sign of an unrivaled coercive power. As many young recruits had little experience managing a firearm, police staff organized target practice, competitions, and a firearms shooting test (Inspección General de Tiro) at the newly renovated shooting range. U.S. police officers even traveled to Buenos Aires to participate in shooting competitions with local officers.[45] In an era of mobile gunfights, it was not enough to practice on a fixed target: a new tool, "acquired in the United States," projected a film about an armed robbery on a screen, allowing officers to practice on silhouettes in movement. "At the precise moment fire breaks out, and in all the panic of people running back and forth, the assailants climb trees and jump into vehicles; one must take careful aim at the shooting robber, and, if possible, [stop] the one with the suitcase. When the bullet . . . touches the screen, the tape stops and one can analyze the target and make corrections."[46]

The second major acquisition, tear gas, was a first in Latin America. Presented as a more humane weapon, tear gas was a prime example of a wartime invention that migrated from the trenches to the city street— a path that reflected the armament industry's newfound peacetime market (as we have seen, the machine gun took a similar path). Gas was used in grenades, rifles, batons, and concealed pens. It was prized for its quick and safe effects. It became a tool for both political and everyday crowd control—used to disperse protesters and evacuate fugitives from buildings. It was also "ideal for police and prison use, and for the protection of banks and institutions."[47]

The police also used the proceeds from the Public Security Collections on a new fleet, equipping the force with patrol cars and motorcycles (some with sidecars). This update was the latest investment in a longer history of police mobile surveillance that could be traced back to the purchase of horses, and continued when the force incorporated bicycles to "fly around" at night and control traffic. Police Chief Ramón Falcón (1906–9) oversaw early additions to the fleet, but, except for the introduction of the first patrol cars during that period, the force went without major updates for some time. Initially, only commissioners and detectives were given vehicles, permitting them to monitor the beat cop's work from their cars.[48] In the 1920s, the relative slowness of police response

FIGURE 17. Armored vans parade. AGN, Department of Photographic Documents.

was more humiliating than ever: "Everything is [about] speed, a near vertigo," read one overwhelmed report. In this urban space revolutionized by motor vehicles, state vigilance continued to depend on flesh and blood getting itself around the city. The time lag between quick-paced crime and the slow reaction of police became all the more apparent and ridiculed amid the surge of "new" crime: when assailants fled in a car, the envious policeman was forced to chase behind on horseback.[49] A sluggish police force in a city of speed: there was no question that the money raised in the Colecta would be used to buy automobiles, since the police were quite literally playing catchup behind their targets. By 1933, each police station was equipped with at least one Ford patrol car.

In order to reverse the reputation for inefficiency, the new tools for combating disorder were put on display, with armored cars and armed personnel making appearances in patriotic parades. Meanwhile, Police Day—a ritual that began in 1926—became a triumphant militarized occasion. In October 1933 (and again in 1934 and 1935), porteños were invited to admire "the martial skills of the police cadets . . . the quick maneuvers of the police motorcyclists and the grandeur of the armored vans."[50]

The arrival of patrol cars represented a milestone in the long search for a way to project police omnipresence and omniscience in the urban grid, which is why it occupies such a central place in the institution's historical narratives. Nevertheless, the impact and capabilities of these vehicles are still widely debated. Research from other cities invites skepticism, suggesting that the acquisition of motorized vehicles did not necessarily advance police awareness or the repression of criminal activity. Indeed, there is no decisive link between crime rates (or rates of detected offenders) and this technological improvement in patroling.[51] Unfortunately, we do not have sufficient data to evaluate the impact of patrol cars in Buenos Aires, although the available evidence suggests some hypotheses. First, the appearance of patrol cars helped to counter the image of a police powerless to keep up with automobiles involved in criminal activity. Patrol cars were a symbolic assertion of authority in the streets, and their appearance affected public opinion. No measure for improving police surveillance, either before or since, had been more visible or been *made* more visible. As we will see, the effect it had can be traced to the role of press and radio in discovering the new spectacle to be made of maintaining order. The story of the modernized police could finally be narrated by means of convincing artefacts with a legible function.

The much-publicized technical modernization of the police marks a chapter in the legitimization of this institution as a guarantor of order, able to fulfill that mission and ward off a deep crisis of public confidence. So even if the patrol car did not improve crime rates in any perceptible way, it nevertheless affirmed the definition of the police as mainly an anticrime agency, precisely at a time when their ability to catch criminals was being called into question, and when other tasks—such as the repression of workers and political dissidents, and maintaining basic order—pointed to a great dispersion of activities, including many jobs that might have been considered beneath the dignity of a "modern" police department.

The consolidation of the image of the police as a force devoted to pursuing criminals was framed in the capital, but went well beyond its city limits. In the next chapter, we will look at how motorization affected the jurisdictional limits of police work, and how the new vehicles contributed to representations of *porteño* police effectiveness by drawing a contrast (in terms of modernity and virtue) with the provincial police. For now, suffice it to say that police trucks, motorcycles, and cars helped patrol officers to demarcate the border between the capital and its suburbs, and to cross that border during routine incursions into surrounding towns of the province of Buenos Aires.

The history of urban police technology is also that of changing modes of presence within the city. As its profile became more impressive, the

Capital Police also became more mediated and distanced in relation to the society being patroled. This is why the sudden modernization of the early 1930s was met with questions about the future relationship between police and society. Some noted the inherent risks in the new methods of patrol: enclosed in their cars, connected to a central radio, the police might lose touch with common citizens. As they lost contact, relationships with local informants might deteriorate. Meanwhile, some of the more hedonistic and exhibitionist dimensions of police culture might become excessive. In short, the technology that expanded the police's territory also isolated it from the community.[52]

Have the Capital Police become more estranged from society? So questioned writer and journalist Roberto Arlt in 1929:

> La cana [Lunfardo for the police] is today a uniformed corps with an academy, decorations, prizes for "units" that don't unite anything. La cana, the legendary cana, semi-accomplice of the scoundrel, street-wise, complex, turbulent, despised, has disappeared. "Today any idiot with a uniform is respected," a former sergeant told me not long ago: before, the uniform didn't matter, what mattered was the man.[53]

In opposition to the bland and professionalized police (now drained of the authority they once derived from their familiarity with the city, earned *outside* institutionalized lines), there emerged a nostalgia for the old "bedraggled officer" and for the old neighborhood that he watched over. The new police officer was mobile, equipped with gear, and ready for action. Nostalgia for his predecessor, remembered as a humane character in service of regular citizens, became another measure of the impoverishment of life in the anonymous city.[54]

This diagnosis had some basis in reality: with all the demands of constant mobility and the risks involved in greater velocity, police presence had indeed changed. When they were not in their patrol cars, traffic cops directed cars from a vantage point above the flow of traffic, separating them from common passersby. Suddenly, their movements seemed like robotic gestures. With their adoption of the codes of a new expertise, interactions became more measured and distant. And as the police modernized, some policemen gave in to their own *tanguero* nostalgia for a bygone era, a nostalgia that was widely expressed in the very institution that embodied the expansion of urban control. As in so many tangos, the street corners they watched day and night were permeated with longing for a lost past.

Uncertain city coordinates and horse-drawn carriages had given way to electric light, crisp jurisdictional boundaries, traffic noise, and violent shootings. No longer was there any room for the shrewd craftiness of the *criollo* officer in this métier of high-tech equipment. The old-fashioned, streetwise policeman was doomed, lamented the writer Laurentino Mejías, himself a veteran of the police force.[55]

Meanwhile, police officials took to the airwaves, where they developed a radio program presenting fictional pieces exploring the premodern *criollo* roots of the force.

> *Romulo:* Sergeant Don Martín Venancio! (*guitars strum in the background*). Authentic symbol of the legendary past! . . . Our sergeant crosses the wide *pampas* riding his little *criollo* horse, who knows every plant in the land and the dust of every road . . .
>
> *Prudencio:* His gaze is that of a veteran [of the force], surveying in every direction. He is *macho,* he is hard and rough with the delinquent and the devious, but he is kind with the humble and sweet and paternal with the dames.
>
> *Romualda:* And at his side, always . . . Henry Burke.
>
> *Margarita:* The young patrolman, who with his powerful motorcycle is the genuine offspring of the motorized police force.[56]

La patrulla policial: Aventuras del Sargento Venancio (Police Patrol: Adventures of Sargent Venancio—Radio Belgrano, 9:15 A.M.) was part of a broader initiative to improve the image of the police—a subject to which we will return in chapter 6. Venancio was a gaucho detective who possessed an uncanny talent for tracking. He drew comparisons to the archetypes of national literature, such as Sarmiento's *rastreador,* whose tracking skills enabled him to effortlessly follow invisible traces of criminals. That wise, white bearded sergeant also crossed the *pampa* riding a horse "that knows every plant in the land and the dust of every road." Sergeant Venancio's wide territorial reach resonated with the process of federalization. As the stories of this old *criollo* cop spread in the 1930s, they fed the idea that the Buenos Aires Capital Police was an institution with national authority.

Venancio resembled the shrewd rural detectives who populated the genre of the crime story.[57] But this gaucho detective was more an immediate reflection of police culture than he was a product of crime fiction, in the literary sense. When he solved cases, traveling on horseback, he brought together the institution's past and present. Venancio was the sage veteran, wise to all illegal tricks. His skills were more perceptual than intellectual, and he made up for his lack of technological

FIGURE 18. *Antena*, August 11, 1939.

savvy with experience and intuition. His experience dated back to the nineteenth-century wars: in photographs printed in entertainment magazines he appeared in an old uniform, reminiscent of those worn by army foot soldiers (the same men who were recruited to be police officers during the pre-professional era). He was intuitive, direct, and terse about the perceptive resources that produced his triumphs. His boundless empirical knowledge (by implication, handed down to the contemporary police force) was a secret valued by his companion, a young patrolman named Henry Burke, who rode a powerful motorcycle and donned a city police uniform. Burke "is the genuine offspring of the modern motorized police," the magazine *Antena* commented. Women swooned as he passed. Together, these two characters were clearly "the past, with its merits and its self-sacrifice, and the present, with its marvelous and effective systems of prevention."

COMMUNICATION AT THE SERVICE OF ORDER

Some of the most effective police tools derived their power not from obvious display but rather from their invisibility. While officers drove their motorcycles and autos in the streets, and precinct houses showed off their new patrol cars, a more discrete novelty generated expectations on other fronts. Indeed, the instruments that most transformed police capacity to control territory were not the new cars and vans (which affirmed sovereignty rather than detection, exhibiting power better than they actually exerted it), but the invisible network of cables running through the city, a "nervous system" that shook up traditional principles of visual perception and communication. The radio had multiple applications: it could accumulate information about the city, publicize police activity, follow dissidents, and improve the image of the police in the eyes of the public.

Of all the modernizing initiatives taken up by the city police, those that concerned communication were particularly relevant to one important police activity during the turbulent 1920s and 1930s: spying. Phone tapping, for example, raised questions about the right (and ability) of police to listen in on communications destined for "deviant" ends. The new practice revived old agreements with the Postal and Telegraph Department (Correos y Telégrafos) dating from the late nineteenth century, when this agency agreed to inform authorities whenever agency personnel encountered messages that were "considered a betrayal against the Argentine Republic, . . . contrary to morality and good customs, . . . made with the objective of committing a crime, [or] obstructed justice by impeding [either] the apprehension of criminals or any other aspect of its administration." A half-century later, the regulation was still very much in place, as was evident from the volume of mail confiscated by the Sección Especial and the long list of names added to those under surveillance for "communist conspiracy." The same principle was evoked when authorities requested the right to monitor telephone conversations, noting that the main difference was that it was more difficult to monitor a form of communication that lacked a written record (and, it might have been added, that was run by private companies). A tension was born, then, between the continual police pressure for information and companies' contractual obligation to protect subscribers' right to privacy. In October 1936, regulations were finally established. With judicial authorization, the police could require telephone companies to cooperate in the identification of "suspicious telephone subscribers." The former would provide a list of suspected numbers, and the latter would give information justifying tapping.[58] Nevertheless, the police did not have to wait for these regulations to actually be passed for companies to begin providing information, helping to identify important gangs (including those responsible for the London bank robberies of 1933).

Although phone tapping expanded considerably in the 1930s, the revolution in police information did not really depend on this practice. The real novelty was the radio. As the magazine *Antena* put it, the police first envisioned the use of this technology to improve its public image— since "[through] the microphone the people identify with authority." Everyday at 11:15, a radio station at police headquarters transmitted a short program (simultaneously broadcast on Radio Splendid) that aimed at promoting crime prevention by instructing

> the people about the very serious dangers that law-breakers are constantly exposing them to . . . or those they expose themselves to by their own negligence and . . . carelessness, like traffic accidents . . .; [the bulletin] informs the population of the events of the latest robbery, indicating the license plate of the automobile used by the delinquents and a description of those who escaped.[59]

Beyond solidifying the links between police and citizenry, the program's producers hoped it might have a moralizing effect on criminals. They imagined both big- and small-time offenders sitting beside their radios, taking stock of the consequences of their actions and the disgrace they brought to the city. "Even the '*pistoleros*,' when they're taking a moment's break, listen to the smooth, affable talks of the 'Police Bulletin' and recall their recent crimes, as vulgar as they are odious."[60]

Of course, the bulletin's effect was uncertain. Police authorities debated about program content and engaged in the age-old question of what information should and could be revealed to journalists. If the *whole* community was listening to the voice of the police, the kind of information that was being shared should be carefully considered. A small boy listening with his mother, absorbing lessons on the responsibilities of citizenship, might develop a deep respect and gratitude for the art and profession of the uniformed police. But just as easily could a potential criminal be taking note of what techniques police used to track crimes:

> We should not teach the occasional or first-time delinquent how to be careful in his inevitable escape from the scene of a crime, how to avoid leaving a trace of his path! . . . We should not let slip from the wonderful microphoned platform of the Police Department the intelligent and noble legal methods that security personnel use to discover a crime.[61]

FIGURE 19A. *Magazine Policial*, August 1933.

Other programs followed, featuring officers who participated in semi-fictional accounts of preventative operations: *Ronda policial* (Police Rounds, on Radio Porteña), *Crónica policial* (Police Chronicles, on Radio París, Radio Fénix, and Radio Argentina), and *Noticias de policía dramatizadas* (Dramatized Police News, on Radio Belgrano). Meanwhile, despite the number of radio programs directed at the public, it was becoming clear that the great promise of radio technology lay not in its power of persuasion but in its power to monitor. The technology was most useful as a form of communication rather than as a form of public diffusion. For the first time, the equation between territorial control and visual perception would lose its traditional direct and literal sense.

Even considering the general optimism about radio's potential during this period, the expectations of the police were somewhat grandiose. They hoped that radio would expand their powers of perception in new ways.

The police force had possessed its own telegraph since 1875, and telephone networks were installed at the turn of the century. Both systems served to interconnect police stations as well as to connect the *porteño* police with other cities in the world. They were used to issue orders to detain criminals, ask for instructions, and share information between police stations. The telegraph allowed the Rio and Buenos Aires police to coordinate their efforts and exchange information about elusive anarchists and "mobile" thieves.[62] Initial applications of these technologies were modest, but in 1913 service became more regulated and widely used, as the population of Buenos Aires surged. Half a mil-

FIGURE 19B. *Radiópolis–Magazine Policial,* March 1934.

lion telegrams were sent per year between 1915 and 1918, a million between 1918 and 1925, and 1.7 million by the beginning of the 1930s.[63] For more than three decades, the telegraph had accelerated the circulation of information and helped direct internal police coordination. But the radio magnified these capabilities, allowing communication *from the street,* as an incident was occurring, opening up a range of possibilities as well as projects for combining new and old technology.

Magazine Policial, the colorful monthly publication read by thousands of policemen, provided readers with a variety of images of the city's modern metropolitan police. In the image from *Magazine Policial* (figure 19a), the uniformed agents race to a crime scene in their modern vehicles, guided by information that streams through their radios (placed prominently at the center of the composition). The image from *Radiópolis–Magazine Policial* (figure 19b) shows a *porteño* "radiópolis" (somewhat reminiscent of New York) in which a radio announcer holds sway over a crime scene, his power to subdue emanating in radio waves imagined as concentric circles. Such technological fantasies of order linked radio transmission to police action and encapsulated the great promise of the new technology. In fact, they were two promises: better control of urban territory and tighter ties between police and the public it protected. In 1929, *Revista de Policía* predicted that "selfless" radio aficionados would become the infallible allies of the protectors of order.[64] With their help, and with the gradual extension of wireless technology to the most remote corners of the nation, the eyes of the state would be woven into the fabric of society.

As compared to previous surveillance systems, radio offered several advantages. It multiplied sources of information, it did not require specific codes, and it sped up police responses—whether a car chase across the length and width of the nation or help to the scene of an accident or fire. Instant and absolute control: with the radio, the utopian vision of an omniscient police force reemerged as a real possibility.

The police broadcasting office received and transmitted messages sent by patrols and coordinated action through a series of alarms. In 1934, there were 141 "public alarms" in the streets and 47 in police stations, all installed by the Siemens Company to "control the the entire city, within a few seconds." Through a system of bells, red lights, and handsets connected to a central radio system, a police officer (or an authorized civilian, with a key to the apparatus) could direct patrol cars to the scene.

Seven types of alarms could be sent via this system, which was later extended by telephone technology. Every area was linked to this network of instantaneous communication, centered at the department's headquarters on Moreno Street. Along with this expansion of knowledge came the *centralization* of knowledge: together, they transformed the path of information and altered forever the street cop's historical decision-making autonomy.

The map shown in figure 20 illustrates the distribution of the network, showing its greater density in areas where the system had received more funding (and where there were enough police officers to use it), and a comparatively sparse reach in emerging neighborhoods.[65] The radio network was invisible and uneven, but it was easily translatable into graphic information. In the pages of newspapers and magazines, the tarnished ideal of police ubiquity could recover its symbolic power.

The alarm system was effective in controlling street protests and political manifestations—sources of disorder frequently decried in the media.

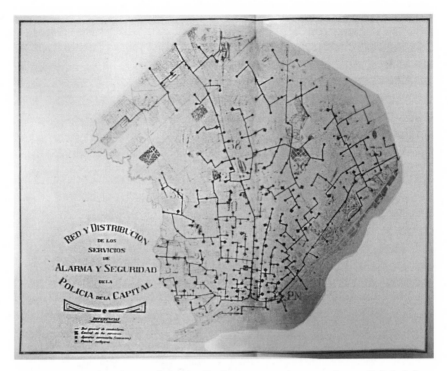

FIGURE 20. Police alarm and security distribution networks, 1934. Source: Policía de la Capital, *Memoria correspondiente al año 1934, 383.*

FIGURE 21. "The Radio in the Service of Public Security," *Micrófono*, July 12, 1934.

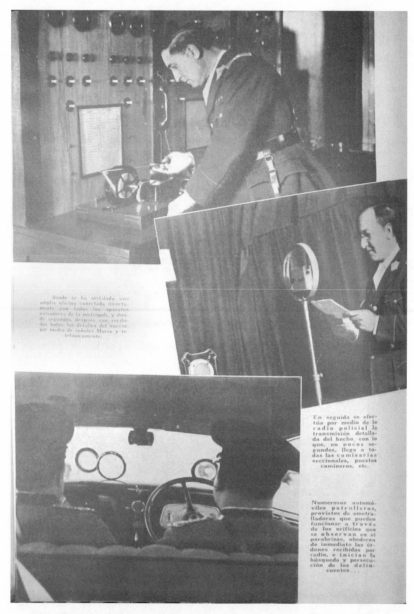

FIGURE 22. "The police network can spread out across the metropolis in a minute." *Caras y Caretas*, August 17, 1933.

Esos son los momentos decisivos, es los que los automóviles patrulleros prestan su colaboración decidida, conjuntamente con las motos policiales. Los oficiales que toman parte en estas persecuciones con verdadero entusiasmo, aun recostados sobre los guardabarros, exponen sus vidas iniciando la lucha...

... hasta que se logra alcanzar y cerrar el camino a los delincuentes, que, una vez cercados y en vista del peligro que corren ante la maravillosa conjunción de elementos policiales...

... deben entregarse, rindiendo sus armas y el fruto logrado en el audaz atraco.

We can observe this in the directives distributed in 1937 to police stations in the days leading up to May 1 (the traditional May Day, or Workers' Day), instructing how to provide surveillance. The Edict of Public Gatherings required the organizers of demonstrations to map out the paths of each column of demonstrators, give the protest's duration and meeting point, and provide a schedule of any speeches that were to be given. Thus, map in hand, the police were able to follow the progress of the demonstration by placing alarm managers along the route in each neighborhood it went through, right up to the socialist headquarters at the Casa del Pueblo, and then throughout the plazas where the closing events were scheduled to take place: "The street alarms communicate all the new information about the columns' movements and [any other developments] from telephones installed by the Communications Department."[66]

Within neighborhoods, wireless communication modified the relationship between police and society by introducing new possibilities for cooperation. For each street alarm there was a neighbor who kept the key and controlled civilian access. The information that could mobilize patrol cars and motorcycles might also come from his calls, reversing the traditional path of stimulus and response. Although we lack detailed data on how these alarms were used in practice, we can consider the ways in which this new setup altered police power: the system certainly did expand police access to information on street incidents, while at the same time increasing the public's expectations regarding police response. Yet, as time went by, the more optimistic projections were frustrated. In order to result in a quick response, the alarm system depended on a number of complementary services that were not always as efficient as the glittering graphics and publicity made them out to be.[67]

Nonetheless, in time the system stabilized. The street alarms continued to function for several decades (the most iconic of these units, at the corner of Corrientes and Esmeralda Streets, was dismantled in 1960). Beyond their more practical application, the system had the immediate effect of being visible; as in the case of the patrol cars, it was no small thing that the public could *see* them. The radio was an invisible power, but these tools were conspicuous, in plain sight.

These new technologies helped the police generate a narrative that easily translated into the languages of the press. The graphic resources of spectacle, already so well developed in earlier media representations of crime, were placed in the service of a new story of the crusade for order, published in the same press outlets that had once depicted the "modern" criminal. In the new reports, technologies granted the police instant powers of perception and speed, providing exciting story lines. The magazines' generous publicity on behalf of the police reflected the fact that the new gadgetry lent itself to good storytelling. Presented to the press as a series of seductive, concrete, and visible improvements, the history of police modernization flowed almost verbatim from the desk of the chief of police to the pages of the most popular weeklies.

This was clearly the case in *Caras y Caretas,* a magazine that had a reputation for being police friendly, but that, as we have seen, prized sensationalism above all else. After a decade of publishing images of shocking *pistolero* crimes, *Caras y Caretas* began to change the focus of its story lines, staging street crimes with actors in a sequence that usually culminated in a police chase and shoot-out on suburban roads.

In this narrative, the criminals were obscured by a crowd of impeccably uniformed "policemen" wielding radios, telephones, armored cars, motorcycles, and the latest weapons; the bandits only reappeared at the end of the sequence, when they were trapped by the authorities on a dusty road while trying to escape via suburban roads.

In "La policía lucha contra el enemigo público" ("The Police Fight against the Public Enemy"—a title echoing similar police propaganda in the U.S.), the magazine *Atlántida* published photographs of new equipment (images provided by the police). The author paired the photos with an anecdote: a merchant on Leandro Alem Street, between Sarmiento and Corrientes, was robbed by three armed assailants who then escaped in an automobile that had been parked in front of the store. A police officer was alerted after the robbery had already occurred; he quickly made use of a telephone on the corner to report descriptions and details to headquarters. The journalist emphasized that the call was received "no more than 25 seconds after the robbery." From headquarters, the information was sent out by radio to patrol cars and officers. The operator relayed the information to the rest of the network by telephone. The thieves were captured in eleven minutes. "A speedier operation would be impossible," he concluded, at least "until we are able to use television."[68]

CHAPTER 5

The Places of Disorder

Order is, above all, a form.

—Hélène L'Heuillet, *Baja política, alta policía*

La Razón, May 1929: "Buenos Aires lives with a legal 'wild west' at its doorstep."[1] *La Libertad,* June 1932: "Police are looking in [the suburb of] Lanús for the men responsible for the shoot-out that took place in [the neighborhood of] Once." *El Mundo,* January 1933: "They hid the arms on a ranch in the district of Avellaneda." *La Nación,* January 1929: "A criminal has been killed in an area of the suburbs." Social Order Report: "The agitators soon realized that they couldn't get away with anything inside the jurisdiction of the capital [so they] moved to nearby towns, mounting their attacks from there."

This chapter delves into the construction of a symbolic opposition between Buenos Aires and its suburbs. Like the city's outskirts themselves, the contrast was born of large-scale demographic and urban changes that were reinforced by a diverse body of documents—expert analysis, fictional narratives, mass media articles, and classified reports. Within this corpus, we will focus on one strand of meaning: that which organized the symbolic location of legality and illegality, safety and danger, order and disorder. Unlike other works on the urban imaginary, here technical, artistic, and literary writings will take a backseat to more widely disseminated discourses: police press releases about security in Buenos Aires, and the stories and images that circulated in both the popular and the "serious" press.

It should not be difficult to justify this selection of documents. As official agents of an order that was defined in territorial terms, the police produced many images and descriptions to symbolically configure the territory of their field of action, whose hubs and peripheries might vary according to institutional agendas and perceptual limitations (both technical and human). In the period analyzed here, the space that police designed and redesigned—the *forms of order*, to borrow L'Heuillet's phrasing—underwent structural reconfiguration.

The police's ultimate mission, as we have seen, was the (utopian) abolition of disorder in the chaotic space of the city. Even if we consider the official definition of this task as one that pertained solely to the detection and repression of crime—a description that elides the importance of other forms of intervention—police agendas acquired a meaning that went beyond that definition—spreading, broadening, and hybridizing. In this process, the role of the commercial press was decisive. There, in the daily papers, we are able to see evidence of the *productive* dimension of the police, one that went well beyond the purely negative aspects of their mission (to *end* crime, to *abolish* disorder) and that developed meaning by way of narratives that could be translated into the language of common sense.

The question of the relationship between the Buenos Aires police and the press is too complex to admit simple generalizations, and a full analysis of its dynamics would not fit within the scope of this work. Still, it is worth noting that as journalists' professional standards were consolidated, reporters adopted a range of autonomous norms related to the use of police sources. In the late nineteenth century, journalists went from being simple recorders of news to being something closer to protagonists, seeking out the "exclusive," the scoop, and trying to "break" the big story. A paper's editorial position vis-à-vis the police depended on its compact with readers, the police chief's political relationship to the editors, and its correspondents' network of confidential informants (which became a form of capital for journalists). The degree to which a paper complacently published the police's account of crime served as a barometer of its relations with the force—during more tense moments, the press erupted into criticism over abuses of power, corruption, or ineffectiveness. In previous work I have examined how the Buenos Aires commercial press of the 1920s antagonized the police.[2] In this chapter, I will retrace those steps and examine press coverage where journalists offered less resistance to the versions of events provided by the police.

Depending on the newspapers or the period considered, the crime pages (known as *"policiales"*) included a set of diverse materials. Beyond the game of headlines and denunciations, reporters structured their agenda around a consensus born of longstanding coexistence and cooperation with members of the police force. One milestone in this relationship was the building of police headquarters in 1888. Correspondents began to spend long hours in the building's press room. The mere fact that the police included in the building's design a room for this boisterous crowd suggests that the importance of press-police relations was well understood as an inevitable part of modern life. Regardless of their motives, in the press room reporters (occasionally with police representatives present) exchanged information, competed for scoops, and stayed in contact with the copy room by phone. More often than not, they waited for confirmation of a rumor, hoped for an exclusive interview, or sought an expert lead or hypothesis. At three or four o'clock in the morning, *mate* was passed around the smoke-filled hall to a background of jokes and stories. These long nights earned their place in the dense mythology of nocturnal police work as an important point of encounter between young men of the press and those of the police force in an atmosphere characterized by a spirit of masculine fraternity. Later, some police memoirs would even boast of early relationships with journalists who would become renowned.

The brief crime reports that these journalists printed in the daily *policiales* sections in *La Nación, La Prensa,* and *La Razón* reflected the language and perspective of their sources.[3] In the previous chapter, we saw how print and radio media helped circulate images of the "modern" police force. It might be added that such a display of bright patrol cars, radios, and armed vehicles fit into a background of commonsense notions about the city's problems: they were part of *ways of seeing* that pertained to the police—or more specifically, to the *porteño* police.

The change described in this chapter might be summarized as follows: beginning in the late 1920s, there appeared a conceptual structuring of space opposing city and suburbs, an opposition that began to coincide with that of legal versus illegal (or perhaps more accurately, high and low legality). Depending on the area being discussed or the perspective adopted, this configuration had two interconnected expressions. The first was embodied by the alarming headlines cited at the beginning of this chapter. It saw the suburbs as a threat to safety, as an "other/outside" space that served as a refuge for criminals. In this view, the suburb was a place where crimes were planned, later to be carried out in the prosperous city. Meanwhile, Orden Social was calling attention to the rise of subversive elements in outlying towns. More diffuse and widespread, the second expression of this urban/suburban duality suggested the kind of permissiveness and lax control that tempted urbanites to *leave* the city. This idea was often expressed as an opposition between a state that was *present* and one that was *absent*, and alluded to a connotation of lawlessness in a suburb that was regulated by *another*, more heterogeneous, and less effective state (that of the province of Buenos Aires).

High and low legality, order and disorder—these dualities operated as symbolic poles indicating a disposition of relativities rather than a literal partition. However, as we have seen, the idea that Buenos Aires was a place of order was merely a fantasy. The control of space is a highly symbolic principle, one that always has an element of the illusory about it. By the middle of the 1930s, however, police authorities sensed that their crisis of credibility vis-à-vis public opinion had largely passed, thanks in part to their having achieved the effect of presence and technical modernity. The triumph of the question of order in public opinion, the application of the infraction edicts, and the remedying of the long-standing reputation of ineffectiveness were all nourished by the favorable contrast with extramural disorder: the orderly city versus the unruly suburbs. Beyond the nebulous horizon of the city limits was a space hospitable to kinds of transgressive possibilities that had been driven out of Buenos Aires.

BAJO FONDO AND THE SUBURBS

The duality of Buenos Aires (city) and Greater Buenos Aires (Gran Buenos Aires) did not emerge in a vacuum. It emerged from a longer standing legal/moral geography that pitted the *bajo fondo* against the modern city. In the last decades of the nineteenth century, this opposition encompassed a range of other oppositions: illegality and legality, dirtiness and cleanliness, opacity and transparency, darkness and light.

Buenos Aires—that suddenly modern port city—had a "dark side," a dense but elusive *bajo fondo* whose precise location was always somewhat vague. What was the *bajo fondo*? According to Francisco De Veyga, a criminologist who spent much of his career studying its components, the *bajo fondo* was a "confusing mass of residual elements of all kinds and of every origin." In its regular usage, the expression alluded to a combination of murky places and people in endless social decline. All of them were associated in one way or another with illegality, due to their own criminal behavior, their association with criminals, or their vices and moral degradation. Frequently, the association with illegality arose from the very illegibility of the *bajo fondo* itself. Where exactly was it? It was not a precise place, but rather a composite of places and scenes in the urban imagination. Some were described in the *policiales* sections in the newspapers, others in criminological studies. Still others came from detective novels and mysteries translated from English and French. Indeed, the local image of the *bajo fondo porteño* was intertwined with the underworld of other cities, as they all shared common traits.[4] Nevertheless, certain singular characteristics can be identified.

As in every major port city, the heart of the circulation of people and goods in the harbor animated the *bajo fondo* of Buenos Aires. The areas surrounding the river were home to shady bars, brothels, and *"peringundines"* (Lunfardo for a dance hall of questionable repute), extending like a stain from the *bajo* (the banks of the river near the city center) to the corners of the La Boca neighborhood. At the turn of the century, the streets near the southern border (where there was a concentration of factories and working-class neighborhoods) received the bulk of police attention. But the *bajo fondo* also filtered into downtown areas like Temple Plaza (at the corner of Suipacha and Viamonte). Buenos Aires, the city of cafés, had any number of notorious establishments; Cassoulet, for example, was a billiards hall with backrooms used for sex work and a backdoor designed to help its clientele escape police raids. The *bajo fondo* thus encompassed spaces like these, as well as places along the border, between the city and the *pampa*, where men drank heavily and dueled at knifepoint.[5] Sometimes these areas were referred to by an older name: the *arrabal,* a term evocative of the vaguely defined city limits of the colonial era and the nineteenth century.

It was a periphery beyond the regulatory politics of the urban grid, where the demarcation of property and obedience to the law were difficult to enforce. In the *arrabal,* optimistic projects of order encountered their limit.[6] During the period that concerns us here, the *arrabal* (setting of the tango) had become an *internal* suburb of Buenos Aires, a city whose enormous perimeter still contained many un-urbanized pockets.

The concept of the *bajo fondo,* like that of the *arrabal,* persists. Today, there are still corners of Buenos Aires that belong to the *bajo fondo,* and nostalgia for the *bajo fondo* continues to permeate the city's musical and literary culture. We find this, above all, in the tourist circuit, where the commercialization of tango repackages the *bajo fondo* nostalgia for crowds of foreigners in the streets, and for the world. The tango musician and *bandoneonista* José Libertella noted that as late as 1981 *Le Monde* publicized one of his shows in Paris as "33 artists from the *bajo fondo* of Buenos Aires."[7] Apparently the evocative draw of those dark, illegible street corners never disappears. But as the *bajo fondo* has moved away from the initial conditions of its birth (the bustling port, massive immigration, the imbalance of the sexes, and the babel-like confusion of the city's composite identities), it has lost its power to threaten. Neighborhood development and the modernizing effect of new urban utilities (which accelerated rapidly during the 1920s) gradually blurred the sense of an "underground," with its prostitutes, troublemakers, and thieves.

The expansion of public electric lighting, for example, pushed the shadowy corners of the city farther and farther away from the downtown area. Between 1920 and 1930, the number of electric lamps went from ten thousand to thirty-eight thousand.[8] The advancing frontline of electrification played into a larger narrative that presented the triumph of light over darkness as part of an ancient saga of order versus chaos and safety versus fear. On the urban frontier, the lightbulb represented the bright light of legality. Its brilliance far exceeded the dim halo of the old kerosene lamps and (for the first time) allowed passersby to clearly discern the unique, identifiable traits of each individual in their path. The streetlight likewise disaggregated confusing crowds and shapes; many perceived it to be an indication that better sanitation and territorial control were on the way. In working-class neighborhoods, well-lit public spaces were also associated with the state's growing capacity to detect disorder. No one understood this better than those who regularly fell subject to this kind of control. During the "Tragic Week" (Semana Trágica) of 1919, a popular uprising began with an assault on public lighting. As soon as protests erupted (on January 9), demonstrators destroyed thousands of gas light posts and electric lamps.[9] The disturbances that took place on that summer night thus occurred in darkness. During less contentious times, these little bulbs were a welcome addition insofar as they were seen as helping to guarantee certain rights considered essential in an era of "progress"—among them, the promise of personal security.

In the 1920s, the feverish subdivision of city terrain into urban lots, along with the extension of public transportation and other services, introduced a new urban imaginary to the frontier spaces at the edges of Buenos Aires. Also, a new economic, moral, and cultural opposition drew a contrast between the city center and the urban residential neighborhoods cropping up on the former frontier. However, this dichotomy (*centro/barrios*) did not raise questions of order, legality, or violence.

MAPS 3 (above) AND 4 (right). Metropolitan growth, 1910–48. Maps courtesy of Alicia Novick, Graciela Favelukes, and Federico Collado, www.atlasdebuenosaires.gov .ar/ thematic units/urbanization.

Rather, is was an economic, moral, and cultural opposition. These meanings were crystallized in tango, fiction, and 1930s Argentine cinema, where the downtown appeared as sophisticated, brilliantly extravagant, full of temptation, and (at times) dangerous for inexperienced women. The neighborhood (the stage for upward mobility) was familiar, inviting, modestly industrious, and fearful of excess—secure and protected in its petit-bourgeois values.

Meanwhile, the *bajo fondo* continued to thrive. The port, Retiro, and the downtown brothels did not disappear, just as the importance of nightlife in this nocturnal city never waned. Small-time clandestine betting survived, as did rumors of "alkaloid" drug trafficking. Yet, the original meaning of the *bajo fondo* was becoming blurry. No longer the counter to the legal city or the locus of threatening criminal networks and practices, the *bajo fondo* lost some of its semantic power as it

became the subject of nostalgia. While residential neighborhoods (with houses and yards, well-lit streets, and civic-minded neighbors) took over the urban landscape, the *malevo de las orillas* (the riverbank thug) and his home in the *arrabal* became the stuff of folklore.[10] By the late 1920s, the dubious byways of the *arrabal* were no longer what they had once been. The sense of greater security gave way to an assortment of representations—popular and cultured, *tanguero* and vanguard—that refashioned these once-feared spaces into legend.

Municipal and provincial censuses for the years 1936 and 1938 indicate that the extraordinary population growth that Buenos Aires had experienced over the previous decades was slowing. The main demographic changes in this city of 4 million occurred in the outlying towns, not in the inside *barrios*. A series of communities near Buenos Aires

(Quilmes-Bernal, Berazategui-Ezpeleta, San Fernando-Las Conchas) were beginning to spring up.

These nearby towns did not yet form an evenly built-up ring around the city, but as time went by, the discontinuities between them were less apparent. Demographers and urban planners began to refer to the "Aglomeración Gran Buenos Aires," raising a central question: should the city extend its administrative authority and its reach?[11] As part of his graduate thesis, Carlos María della Paolera (a founder of urban studies in Argentina) wrote a regulatory plan for the so-called Aglomeración.[12] Inspired by similar projects in European cities, he proposed several methods of incorporating urban settlements that lay beyond the historic city limits. Other plans approached the issue from multiple angles, from landscape to functionality, but paid little attention to the peculiarities of the towns in question. There was a particular concern with sanitation, as the disparity between the premeditated *porteño* grid and the unruly growth taking place outside the city was plain to all observers.

Greater Buenos Aires could only be considered a "place" in opposition to the city. (The inverse was also true: Buenos Aires was an *idea* that effectively bound together very diverse *barrios* by the mere fact that they were "within" the *porteño* city limits.) Not everything that surrounded the city was threatening or unsanitary. In fact, the natural and historical connotation of the suburbs was just the opposite. From the beginning of the nineteenth century, suburban farms were considered bucolic escapes from the busy city. In the great riverfront houses to the north, wealthy families spent their summer months entertaining themselves by cultivating exotic plants and holding garden parties, communing with nature without sacrificing the benefits of civilization. Writer, jurist, and social analyst Carlos Octavio Bunge thought that turn-of-the-century summers in the northern suburb of Tigre were so pleasant that the *porteños* of the *beau monde* "would forget to go to Mass on Sunday or on Holy Days." Instead, they went rowing with friends, painted landscapes, and exchanged trifles as they relaxed on chaises longues on jasmine-lined porches. The heat of summer was allayed by an endless stream of gentile pastimes.[13]

Writing three decades later, the very *porteño* Roberto Arlt described these surrounding towns as edenic sanctuaries where one could escape the chaotic dance of Buenos Aires. The streets, he wrote, were lined with trees so tall that "from every leaf falls a drop of silence," and the villages were "towns to dream in, towns of serenity." There was no shoving about, nor "packs of knuckleheads and cops on the corners." (Arlt being

Arlt, the description soon veered to the disruptions latent in these sleepy towns. The center of operations of the secret society in his novel *Los siete locos* is a peaceful farm set amid flowing honeysuckle vines.)[14]

As in other metropolises, the most attractive attributes of these suburbs—green space, silence, and pure air—served as an antidote for the worst qualities of the city. The outskirts of Buenos Aires offered an idyllic melding of the rural and the urban that in an increasingly mobile society might be conceived of as more complementary than opposite.[15] Extending the logic of expansion from the city center to the *barrios,* following the railway lines outward, prosperous communities sprang up to the south, the west, and the north. They remained dependent on the economy and culture that radiated out from the city center, which, in turn, depended on them. Each workday, thousands of passengers arrived in the capital city by train. At railroad terminals in Once, Retiro, and Constitución, suburbanites joined the bustling crowds of *porteños* of the city center and commercial zones.

This constant flow of people fed the professional and economic life of both the city and the suburbs. In Foucauldian terms, this was a *positive* circulation—economically productive and socially organized. It could be controlled and even directed by the state, but it was never obstructed.[16] The massive scope of these daily displacements nonetheless involved a mix of "positive" and "negative" circulation, and it was not long before the police began deploying officers in railroad stations, considered a choice location for "scammers and tricksters."[17] This mission was assigned to the "Embarcaderos" section of the Division of Investigation.

As the metropolitan area grew (accelerating over the next decades), certain notions of transgression also moved out of the city and into the suburbs—so seductive, and yet so hard for the state to handle. As we have seen, a much talked-about series of organized robberies in the streets of the capital was fueling the public's concern over a crime wave in Buenos Aires. There was a recurring detail in narrations of these crimes: the criminals had come from outside the city. They left the same way they came in: in a fast car. Buenos Aires was the target of crime—robbery, shoot-out, getaway—that had been planned elsewhere, in a territory that was more and more decentralized and extended.

Where did these motorized criminals flee *to?* According to Miguel Viancarlos, the chief investigator of the Capital Police, they fled to a Greater Buenos Aires that was crawling with gangs. They hid in boom towns, blending in with migrants from the interior of the country and immigrants from abroad. "The better-organized robbers have decided to camp out in surrounding towns, where they find impunity for their malevolent actions and the liberty to plot more crimes." Another report noted that the city's neighboring towns had become refuges for men who were "notorious for their antisocial acts": they would come into the city, commit crimes, and then "disappear, leaving [us] without recourse because we have no jurisdiction over them."[18] As the provincial police were unable to control the vast territory surrounding the city (nor did they have any intention of doing so), the motorized bandits did not need to travel very far to find safety, said Viancarlos. "The delinquents who've been operating recently in Buenos Aires," he continued, came out of a constellation of speakeasies, illicit cafes, and front companies chosen for their proximity to the wealthy city. The entire geography of transgression had been altered. It brought with it a new association that was destined to endure: one connecting Greater Buenos Aires with crime and disorder.

Even the most distracted reader of the city's newspapers had a clear picture of the new map of disorder. The street names of this or that corner of the *bajo fondo* had for decades peppered the pages of the *policiales* sections of Buenos Aires papers. Now those same street names lived side by side with the names of towns and jurisdictions increasingly removed from downtown: Avellaneda, Lanús, Valentín Alsina, Morón, Lomas de Zamora, Matanza, Vicente López, San Fernando … The average *porteño* newspaper reader would have first become acquainted with these names in stories of violence or unsanitary conditions: an exchange of fire on a dusty road, a flood, a burst sewer, a police raid on a gambling joint, a whirlwind robbery, an armed conflict between political factions, or a dispute that ended in homicide. Every once in a while, a major robbery downtown (carried out by gangs from some obscure area of the province) reinforced a mounting sense that the city was surrounded by inhospitable suburbs full of *"madrigueras"* (lairs) where many a plot was hatched, a culture-barren landscape fundamentally opposed to the civilized urban order.

VICE IN GREEN SPACES

Vicente López, Florida, Olivos, San Isidro, Tigre, San Fernando: the names of certain towns resonated with the most inviting meaning of the term "suburb," one promising a life free from the kinds of regulations typically found in city neighborhoods, as well from the madness of urban life. *Porteños* knew that this northern corridor offered fresh air, green space, and beaches. They also knew that one did not have to be a wealthy landowner to enjoy what the area had to offer. By the end of the 1920s, the "weekend" had been discovered by many. *Caras y Caretas* described the hot Sundays of 1929 thus: "Everyone escapes to the popular beaches to the north. Picnics, races, sunshine, heat, beer. When a poor man has fun . . . he has *fun!*"[19] The photo of the crammed train platform confirmed that thousands went north to cool off on the banks of the river. And, as often happens when leisure and tourism become accessible to new social sectors, existing users of those spaces reacted critically to the behavior and aesthetic choices of the newcomers.

In 1933, *El Mundo* editorialized that the police should increase their surveillance of these collective outings because "the raucous crowds from the *arrabal*" were prone to lose their moral bearings. In *La cabeza de Goliat*, Ezequiel Martínez Estrada echoed this complaint. He described with disdain the metamorphosis of thousands of otherwise tidy, diligent souls into noisy, poorly dressed brutes, spending the day in bathing suits "drinking and dancing," listening to portable phonographs. Then, on Sunday afternoon, after the picnic, they would return, "overflowing onto the train platforms like lumps of feces spewing from the cars." Where, he wondered, were these men and women during the week? "During workdays they were nowhere to be found. They carefully donned their workclothes and confined themselves to the rhythms and conventions of their jobs and the city." Every Monday, he said, the city "absorbs them like a mother," embracing them in the hallways, desks, trolley cars, cafés, and cinemas that held them in place and concealed their barbarity.[20] In Martínez Estrada's cool, elitist view, the weekend excesses outside of town gave way to Monday's civilizing readjustments.

This northern coast was a thriving, publicly accessible leisure zone. It was also a hotspot for rather thinly disguised (and largely unregulated) illegal activities that benefited from a long tradition of tolerance. As authorities tightened their grip on urban order in Buenos Aires, certain extramural practices flourished. In 1925, for example, Mayor Carlos Noel issued a municipal regulation that halted the construction of brothels. Although many existing businesses carried on (most disguised as "furnished housing" and apartment buildings), the regulations reflected a shift in political and public attitudes on the issue. The movement to abolish prostitution and sex trafficking gained unprecedented support, as municipal regulations, congressional legislation, and the press all fell in behind those causes. In this context, the city police's well-known complicity in these activities erupted into controversy and scandal.[21] Even in the absence of detailed studies on the phenomenon, we know that rather than disappear entirely, some portion of the sex trade simply moved to the outskirts of the city, where much of its business had *always* taken place. And sure enough, the northern suburbs were known for their hospitality toward sex work. Meanwhile, gambling was making a similar journey to the outskirts of town.

Gambling was a strong *porteño* tradition, and the city's most popular form of entertainment. Roberto Arlt, our acid observer of urban life, remarked that in Buenos Aires, everyone was a potential millionaire and every miserable wretch walked around utterly convinced of his latest hunch. Literary critics have made note of Arlt's interest in gambling, but we know much less about the context that gave rise to this common fantasy of "winning big."[22] Certainly, there was no lack of opportunity— legal or illegal—for *porteños* to indulge that impulse. First, there was the racetrack. The Palermo *hipódromo* was a magnet for politicians, high society, entertainment celebrities, the occasional mafia boss, and thousands of anonymous *"burreros"* (horse racing fans).[23] Radiating out from the racetracks themselves, in a series of concentric circles, other forms of underground and illegal betting proliferated. Newspapers and magazines developed regular sections for horse racing news, and the sport became the subject of expert analysis. Fans developed a specialized jargon around horse racing, as illustrated magazines made stars of the jockeys and other personalities. By the 1920s, the racetrack was the brilliant centerpiece of a whole culture of gambling (from the grandest sweepstakes to the most humble numbers racket), one that became indistinguishable from sociability itself.

Whenever the Palermo tracks were closed, an avid horse racing fan would take the train to La Plata, whose own *hipódromo* opened again in 1930, after three years of closure. If a gambler won there on a Saturday afternoon, asked Arlt, how would he celebrate? He "catches his train and returns to Buenos Aires. He rests that night and on Sunday morning, having slept well, he takes the early train (as any virtuous man would) to [the racetrack at] San Martín." Let's compare this description with Last Reason's commentaries in the 1920s. His *"aguatintas hípicas"* described a world centered around the Palermo *hipódromo*. But by the 1930s, when Arlt published his columns in *El Mundo,* the horse racing circuit had become more dispersed, requiring a constant back-and-forth in trains and cars. In the space of one decade, the geography of the races had extended from Buenos Aires to the suburbs.[24]

In fact, suburban racetracks were not even necessary to an underground gambling industry that depended on information transmitted by radio and telephone. Among all of horse racing's satellites, none were quite as profitable as the off-track betting houses in Avellaneda. Despite a ban on live transmissions (which had been prohibited in order to discourage precisely this kind of practice), they received news of every race held at Palermo by means of a rooftop telephone on Avenue Vértiz. In one locale on Pavón Street (run by the famous "Pibe" Ruggiero), gamblers anxiously listened to live reports of the races. "On Saturdays and Sundays on Mitre Avenue, a mini *hipódromo* of nearly 1,000 people gathers," reported *La Prensa*. The journalist was quite shocked by the magnitude and unabashed visibility of illegal gambling, noting that the local police were reduced to managing traffic, making sure that gamblers arrived at the windows in time to place their bets.

The *quiniela* (the "numbers game") was the game of choice for people of lesser means. It was particularly popular among housewives, who found it easy to mix in the small cost of playing the numbers with their other household expenses. For this reason, the numbers runners (known as *levantadores*) could often be found at hair salons, corner stores, and vegetable stands. The *quiniela* was not equally popular everywhere. Runners noted that neighborhoods made up of new homeowners were not as profitable as poorer and older neighborhoods like Boedo, San Juan, Triunvirato, and Concepción Arenal—"that is to say, [places] where each family occupies a floor that they do not own but rent. There, [the *quinieleros*] are found in markets, counting the butcher's clientele among their own, as they are some of the most given to sudden bouts of premonition and hunches."[25]

Even the most invisible gambling operations left behind material traces. A display cabinet at the police museum contains an array of objects confiscated during police raids enforcing law 4097, which prohibited gambling. These objects tell their own stories of duplicity. In the world of illicit gambling, carpentry was a sought-after skill: among the confiscated items were a piece of hardwood from a coal yard carved with secret boreholes, planks with hidden compartments taken from bars "where the gambling law is violated," an armoire "with a secret panel that hid a list of illegal bets," table and chair legs hollowed out "to hide *quiniela* numbers," and a "cigarette tray with a removable panel for hiding bets."

The towns on the outskirts of Buenos Aires offered a more hospitable climate for these practices than did the big city, where business owners who engaged in illegal gambling were required to take greater precautions. In the early 1930s, neighborhood *quinielas* faced more obstacles to survival, while gambling dens and brothels were becoming more scarce. The migration process accelerated when the police began to apply the infraction edicts (with jurisdiction only within the city) and increased their surveillance of a range of practices that had been tolerated previously.

In the province of Buenos Aires, the many practices collectively categorized as *"juego"* (gambling) became a permanent subject of legislative conflict. Provincial lawmakers oscillated between total prohibition and more pragmatic partial regulations—making allowances, for example, for horse racing and the *quinela*. The debate within the Conservative Party—the dominant political force in provincial politics in this period—regarding the legalization of casinos for the purpose of raising funds for social projects ended in a negative vote. As a result, these activities remained clandestine (if in plain sight) for most of the 1930s.[26] The illicit status of gambling allowed it to play an important role in financing local and provincial politics, functioning as the motor of *caudillo* territorial control during the Conservative era.

In February 1932, *La Prensa* pointed out that as long as betting houses continued to appear on the outskirts of Buenos Aires, any initiative designed to eradicate this pernicious custom was destined for failure. "[These houses] in the province's jurisdiction may well be considered extensions of the city's gambling scene." Gambling dens (hidden behind more or less respectable fronts) multiplied, ignoring the prohibition and enjoying the promise of an abundant clientele arriving from the wealthy and populous city.[27] As everyone knew, there was a casino in Tigre that did not even pretend to be anything else. The casino was such an open secret, in fact, that it was often cited as one of the most attractive elements of so-called country life, alongside the fashionable recreational clubs and houses that emerged in the province during the same period.[28] The sheer scale of Tigre's roulette operation raised the ire of authorities in Mar del Plata, who were unable to build their own casinos because of the same legal prohibitions that were so scandalously mocked in Greater Buenos Aires. Meanwhile, the roulette tables and card games, in which entire *estancias* might be lost and won, continued to attract players from the landowning classes. Casino employees on the Atlantic coast knew these illicit circuits well. After the summer season, some put their skills at the service of elite parties in the mansions of northern suburbs like Martínez, Acassuso, and San Isidro.[29]

"From Bahía Blanca to Lincoln, from San Nicolás to Trenque-Lauquen y Pehuajó, and even more so in neighborhoods surrounding the Capital, like Avellaneda, Ciudadela, Florida, Olivos, San Isidro, San Fernando and Quilmes, they gamble from morning to night. Police authorities don't even realize that their complicity and tolerance is assumed."[30] Besides generating these kinds of reflections on the morality of the era, the ubiquity of gambling put the complicity of the Buenos Aires provincial police in the limelight. *La Prensa* reported:

> It would be absurd to feign ignorance of the existence of a roulette wheel, when it attracts a growing number of players who clearly do not live nearby, as they require all manner of transportation, especially automobiles. Hasn't the regular caravan [of cars] every night at the same exact hour—particularly when they return [to the city]—suggested anything to the Tigre police?[31]

Many reports on the subject blamed both police corruption and a diffuse moral permissiveness in the force. The orders that forbade officers from playing roulette, engaging in games of chance (for money), and going to the racetrack had to be reiterated quite regularly, as did prohibitions against bribery and kickbacks. In other words, the provincial police were most certainly engaged both in betting and accepting bribes.[32]

If the casinos and gambling dens of the periphery constituted a problem for the city of Buenos Aires, that problem was more moral than practical. The violent dimension of the suburb found its more precise location along the southern border, the geographic extension of the historic *bajo fondo,* the port areas of Retiro and the Riachuelo. The focal point of scandal and outrage was at the city's doorstep, in the populous town of Avellaneda.

THE OTHER SIDE OF THE BRIDGE

Published first in *Caras y Caretas,* the image and verse in figure 23 contrast "the two sides" of the bridge over the Riachuelo—the river that served as the southern limit between the city and the province. On one side, disorder, grotesque immoderation, rampant vice, and an overly chummy police force; on the other side, the slim silhouette of modern buildings. Avellaneda condensed many notions of the "rough" suburb. The echoes reverberate still, evoking an unstable world varnished with the dark glamour of crime narratives, workers' struggles, popular folklore, key episodes of Peronist resistance, novels about Conservative *caudillos,* and Argentine films of the 1950s.

Disentangling the legend of Avellaneda from the facts of its history is not an easy task. Even if we ignore the most fanciful narratives, there

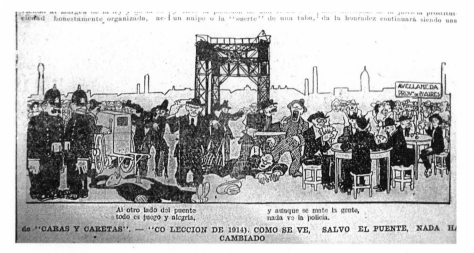

FIGURE 23. "Al otro lado del puente / todo es juego y alegría / y aunque se mate la gente / nada ve la policía" (On the other side of the bridge / it's all fun and games / and though they kill each other / the cops just look away.)

are many reasons why it stands out from other suburban towns. By the 1930s, Avellaneda (which in this period included the district of Lanús) was quite different from the generic semi-rural landscape typical of so much of Greater Buenos Aires. Contrary to the image presented in figure 23, the social and economic profile of the community had more in common with the neighborhoods on the southern boundary of Buenos Aires: Barracas, Constitución, Nueva Pompeya, Parque Patricios, and La Boca.[33]

Avellaneda was, above all else, an urban center. It was the most densely populated city in the province and home to a thriving industrial and commercial zone: tanneries, meatpacking plants, sawmills, dockyard workshops, match factories, and large textile mills filled the city's robust manufacturing sector. Given its industrial character, it is not surprising that Avellaneda was the district outside the capital with the largest proportion of workers—thirty thousand lived there in the 1930s.[34] In time, the town also became known as a stronghold for organized labor and, in particular, for communist activists. The Sección Especial, not surprisingly, devoted great attention and resources there.

This densely populated industrial town shared a border with the capital city. The heavily used Pueyrredón Bridge (renovated in 1931) connected the two sides of the Riachuelo. In the 1930s, Avellaneda was a crossroads for illegal gambling, prostitution, and political and union violence. Gangs were protected by *caudillos* and police-*caudillo* alliances, as well as various strains of *pistolerismo.* "One cannot forget," underlined *La Nación,* while describing one particular shoot-out, "that these events occur at the very doorway of the Capital and in a district that is, without a doubt, the third largest in terms of population as well as in commercial and industrial interests."[35] This hotbed of the workers' movement and "gangsters' paradise" was right next to Buenos Aires.

Newspapers published in both Buenos Aires and Avellaneda in the 1930s gave the impression that every downtown shop in Avellaneda was a mere front for some kind of underground or illicit dealing. Gambling: "It is no exaggeration to say that the majority of the existing storefronts on Mitre Avenue, from the Pueyrredón Bridge to the local plaza, are simply fronts for gambling dens where infractions are committed without any misgivings," reported *La Prensa.* Prostitution: barbershops, cigarette stores, and restaurants "in the downtown area of Avellaneda, not far at all from the 1st Precinct," served as semi-clandestine fronts where innocent bystanders were regularly offered sex, a local paper affirmed.[36] It was common knowledge that social clubs worked as façades for gambling dens, *quinielas,* and roulette wheels. One luxurious clandestine casino, complete with fabulous carpeting, chandeliers, and silverware, functioned inside the Centro de Fomento Avellaneda, the local community development center. Juan Tink—a friend of chief of police Colonel Ramón Falcón and a well-known ally of Conservative leader Marcelino Ugarte—ran the place until the *caudillo* Barceló took it over.

The famous *pistolero* Juan Ruggiero ("Ruggierito") ran a backroom gambling operation from a local office of the Conservative Party. A rather blunt sign announced what was going on inside: "Today! *Escolaso!*"[37] Strategically located next to an exit from the city, this establishment offered its clientele protection against getting robbed on the way home. The ringleader stated his policy thus: "If [a client] gets robbed in the Capital, too bad for him. But in Avellaneda no one will rob one of my clients."[38] The haunt attracted local clientele, but thousands of regulars also arrived from the other side of the river: proximity to the country's wealthiest city and police indulgence explain the steady growth of these (not so) clandestine practices.

The Avellaneda police were not fulfilling their duties: not enough manpower and not enough will—so said newspapers on both sides of the bridge. Conservative governor Manuel Fresco initiated a reform in 1936 (ultimately shot down) that showed the degree to which *caudillos,* fellow officers, and the gambling business had undermined the ability of the police to control their own institution. The authorities of the provincial police who wanted to consolidate their administrative power in La Plata, the capital city of Buenos Aires Province, found it impossible given the degree to which officials in Avellaneda and other towns were already in thrall to local *caudillo* networks (which profited from clandestine gambling and prostitution). Until the rise of Perón, any overt control from La Plata over the police operations in the enormous territory of the province of Buenos Aires was doomed to fail. Even then, vigorous institutional reform yielded only minimal results due to the system's extraordinary resistance to change.[39]

Avellaneda in the 1930s was not just notoriously permissive, but also violent. This is how Borges remembered it in "Death and the Compass" (1944): "South of the city of my story flows a sluggish stream of muddy water, choked with refuse and thick with the runoff of tanneries. On the other side is a suburb filled with factories where, under the protection of a Barcelona gangster, gunmen prosper."[40] Separated from Buenos Aires by a confusion of mud and trash, the looming *pistoleros* of the industrial suburb were an ever-present threat to the city.

The dark glamour of Avellaneda owed much to the abundant 1930s social imagination of crime, but it should be noted that these claims were not altogether unfounded. Although available statistics conflate various types of violence, they allow us to reconstruct a sense of proportion, and indeed they tend to confirm the rather impressionistic views of the press. The data show that the population of Avellaneda grew explosively—by 765 percent—over the first four decades of the century. The rising crime rates were even more remarkable: the disaggregated rate of crimes against persons (homicides, assaults, shootings) rose twice as fast as the population. The clearest jump occurred between 1925 and 1939.[41]

As we have seen in previous chapters, suburban *pistolerismo* was, in part, a product of the conflicts that structured the geography of provincial politics, where open power struggles opposed alternative factions from the Conservative and Radical Parties, as well as unions. The popularity of underground gambling made it a highly lucrative business, and as a result, illegal gaming played a significant role in this turf war. Every once in a while, a battle over gambling and its profits erupted into violence. When the "known operator" "El Pibe Oscar" Modelo died at the hands of his enemies, the news generated major headlines in *porteño* papers.[42] Thuggish "hits" were made on gambling kingpins as well as politicians (who were not always extricable from this underground economy of leisure). "Ruggierito" was taken down in October 1933 in a manner that was typical of the conflicts of these gangs. Not only was he the leader of a network of brothels and gambling houses in the area, but he also headed up the shock troops loyal to Alberto Barceló (the "*caudillo* of Barcelona" to whom Borges alluded). Ruggiero was associated with the bottommost rungs of "low" politics and its populist derivations. Between 1929 and 1930, his conflict with the *pistolero* Julio Valea ("El gallego Julio") spilled out beyond the suburban "*bajo fondo,*" confirming fears that neighboring violence was indeed a threat to the city. The fight "was no longer in Avellaneda nor in Barracas nor in La Boca—the loud racket of automatic weapons broke out on Suipacha Street, just beyond Constitution station and the Avenida de Mayo," *El Mundo* reported in the obituary. Valea was finally killed during a horse race in the Palermo *hipódromo.* "Ruggierito" survived various subsequent attempts on his life, but was murdered in October 1933 in the streets of Avellaneda, his hometown. His death inspired mass displays of grief.[43] Meanwhile, other *pistoleros* carried on: some worked with union leaders, some teamed up with Conservative *caudillos,* and others took up arms in internal union clashes or conflicts between anarchist factions; the latter became visible in a series of fires, shootings, and bombings in bakeries that played out in the local press.[44]

The challenge to the status quo posed by the coup of September 1930 brought this tense scenario to a boiling point. In June 1931, José Rosasco, Avellaneda's police *interventor* (police inspector appointed by the military government) was peppered with bullets while dining at Cecchin, a well-known downtown restaurant. "It was just like in the movies," said one witness who was dining nearby. Dressed as high-class clientele (they left behind one patent leather shoe and a pair of tortoise-shell-framed glasses), the attackers entered the restaurant, approached the elderly Rosasco's table, fired five shots from their brand-new .45 caliber pistols, and then fled the scene in two cars waiting at the door.[45]

President Uriburu appointed Major José Rosasco to the position of police inspector in Avellaneda just after the coup, assigning him the task of "cleaning up" the town. During his brief tenure in the industrial suburb, he had two prisoners linked to Ruggiero executed (at the precinct house, after a swift, improvised court-martial and sentencing, by the police). Rosasco was also behind the brutal persecution of several Communist Party groups and the very hard line taken against "expropriative" anarchism. Just before his death, he arrested Gino Gatti, an activist and member of Di Giovanni and Roscigna's old anarchist band (Di Giovanni had already been executed and Roscigna was in jail). Rosasco also detained more than forty other suspects in the raid. Although Rosasco's murder was never solved, reconstructions of the hit suggested payback on the part of anarchists.[46]

The image of Avellaneda as a "wild" suburb entered the repertoire of commercial journalism. Inevitably, its local thugs were compared with the gangsters on the screens of neighborhood theaters, lending an aura of familiarity, professionalism, and technological prowess to the world of local crime. The appearance of a machine gun in one shoot-out, for example, inspired *Crítica*'s reporters to draw a comparison between Ruggierito and Al Capone, between the *"pistoleros criollos"* and the Chicago mafia.[47] The popular sensationalist magazine *Ahora* offered the same comparison, along with images of pistols, playing cards, and alcohol to illustrate stories of *los gánsteres* on the other side of the river.

In the Avellaneda press, however, sensationalist images and police statistics described a threat against the people of *Avellaneda* rather than the people of Buenos Aires. Indeed, they spoke to a very localized experience of accidents, shootings, assaults, and rival gangs. The local press wrote of this violence throughout the week (sometimes every day).[48] As for the threat to the capital city, the question was hardly ever raised. If it appeared at all, it was to challenge the stigma of the "rough suburb." The Radical paper *La Libertad*, responding to a story that had run in *La Nación*, rejoined: "Avellaneda is not a refuge for delinquents, as is depicted in the metropolitan press." If there were gangs, added the Conservative *La Opinión*, it was only because of the increase in *expulsive* patrolling going on in the capital, which obligated the city's neighbors to share its streets with criminals from Buenos Aires.[49]

The depiction of the ineffectiveness and corruption of the provincial police was shared by the press on both sides of the municipal border. As a rule, such stories were typically linked to calls for improvements in sanitation and other types of infrastructure to complement demographic growth. Legal precariousness and the pact between the political powers-that-be, the police, and illegal gambling, according to this porteño narrative, constituted a threat to the entire population. Such stories were reproduced in the Avellaneda local press to criticize the (Conservative) leadership of the town. At the same time, these critiques resisted the reductive logic of the *porteño* point of view: while the *porteño* press formulated Avellaneda's crime wave in terms of a "siege" against Buenos Aires, the Avellaneda press reconfigured this criticism as evidence of the need for further controls that might benefit the meatpacking and factory workers, who accounted for the main groups of residents and their families, arguing that they were the main victims of local crime and that they nourished the social and commercial fabric of the entire community.[50]

The recurring calls for "more police" were embedded in a host of micro-communal stories about school parties, costume soirées, dances, and beauty contests—that is, in the soil of a growing community. In this Avellaneda was no different from other city suburbs: here and there, scarce police presence inspired fund-raisers and social efforts to demand better security.[51]

Implicit in the (now more widespread and urgent) complaints that came from suburban towns was an ideal image of law enforcement in which honest police officers were distinguished from corrupt cops entangled in webs of vice and factious politics. The police who were lauded at neighborhood fund-raisers and in local newspaper editorials were represented as a pacifying, civilizing force. Their mission was to guarantee a social and territorial order, and to protect the society that had drawn so many thousands of immigrants from faraway towns and (closer to home) from towns in the interior of the country.

During the Peronist years, Avellaneda, a city of workers, was portrayed on the silver screen as the victim rather than the perpetrator of violence and illegality. Carlos Rinaldi's 1953 film *Del otro lado del puente* (The Other Side of the Bridge), for example, reversed the riverbanks of vice and virtue. Set in the 1930s, the film sought to undo Avellaneda's image as a "wild" suburb, one that posed a threat to the orderly capital. Though the film did present Avellaneda as a place with a strong nocturnal and underground character, the bulk of the narrative focused on the daily lives of a thriving community of workers. *That* Avellaneda was contrasted with an opulent and proud Buenos Aires, a vainglorious city that was overwhelmingly nocturnal and rife with depraved parasitism, luxury, and duplicity. In this narrative, crime took root in the urban center, and hardworking suburbanites were left to deal with its repercussions. All that was productive and morally legible could be found in that genuine community of workers, free of cosmopolitan leanings. The real dangers were on the *other* side of the bridge.

PROTECTING ONESELF FROM THE SUBURB

[There was once] a good man who lived on the edge of this city. He lived a quiet life. The years passed without notice. He spent his days working at his job downtown and taking care of his small garden behind his house. There, a harmonious abundance of all types and species of flowers and plants would have continued to grow, had there not arrived a persistent and growing army of ants that began to transform that minuscule garden in the *porteño arrabal* into a wasteland.

In 1933, *El Mundo* used this parable of neighborly frustration to illustrate the plight of residents living alongside the poorly watched suburban border. The *porteño* police, it editorialized, were like gardeners trying to eradicate an ant infestation flourishing in the uncared-for garden next door. In the story, an expert asked the homeowner, "If they don't fumigate next door, where the anthills are, what will come of our efforts [over here]?" The story concluded: "The same thing is coming to pass with the police and the population of Buenos Aires . . . [The ants] will continue to devastate his garden . . . as long as the house next door is not fumigated."[52]

Our gardens, their gardens: the insidious infestation destroying this methodical homeowner's garden comes from beyond his own property, from a place where there are no gardeners/policemen, but rather a sordid force that has succumbed to political infighting and that is in league with an underground economy of gambling and prostitution. The parable of the negligent neighbor was echoed in other news reports that described the intervention of *porteño* police in incidents occurring far outside the supposed limits of their jurisdiction.

The reach of that jurisdiction became politically complex in the 1930s. By virtue of its surface area, which (since federalization in 1880) had greatly exceeded what could be effectively inhabited, Buenos Aires had been a city of ill-defined borders. The outline of the territory within the great metropolitan perimeter had been marked out not so much by formal state markers but haphazardly, by the advance of houses "with no sidewalk in front." This diffuse demarcation (if it can even be called that) contrasts with the sixteen police outposts erected between 1932 and 1933 at the intersections of Avenida General Paz and the principal access points to the city. Functioning as ordering landmarks as well as controlling transit from adjoining areas, each one was manned by two officers (three at night) armed with automatic pistols and rifles. Judging from the locations and coordinated appearance of these outposts on the official, administrative border of the city, they can be seen as expressing the importance assigned to monitoring the constant tide of motorized vehicles that crossed, willy-nilly, the porous frontier.

In the southern zones, where the border was not marked by a highway but by a river, one could cross into the capital using two bridges (Alsina

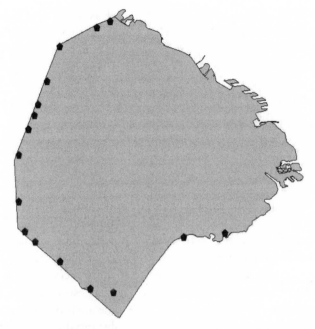

MAP 5. Border outposts, 1933–34. Source: *Memoria del Ministerio del Interior, 1932; Memoria de la Policía de la Capital Federal, 1932–33.*

and Pueyrredón) over the Riachuelo. Here, the Capital Police brought in a fleet of motorcycles with sidecars. Armed with machine guns, these patrols would cross back and forth, monitoring all traffic. Each outpost carried the name of an officer who had been killed in the line of duty.[53]

When the urbanization of Buenos Aires was still incomplete, and the paving of General Paz Avenue (finished in 1936) had not yet consolidated the territorial limits of the city, it was the police that marked out this administrative border, which was also the border of its own jurisdiction.[54] These outposts sprang up at the same time patrol cars and radios were being incorporated into the force (discussed in chapter 4), and were another element in the expansion of police powers of perception.

How should we interpret the effective reach of these outposts? First, their existence acknowledged a *negative* circulation requiring monitoring from within Buenos Aires. In this context, the chain of outposts on the perimeter forms a part of a series of other tools, such as controls at ports and railway stations. The police expanded their function as overseers, supervising the circulation of people and goods.

Second, these posts might be interpreted as a selective barrier for controlling population flows. To what extent did they function as such? We have seen that police maps and blueprints tend to offer a deceptively optimistic visual grammar. They can portray persuasive designs for efficient police intervention, as well as giving the appearance of ubiquity. In certain images, it looked as if the police exerted homogeneous control over the entire city, something that was simply impossible given the limited capacity of their infrastructure and personnel. Indeed, the symbolic (visual) effects of the border outposts were clearer than their concrete implications. Certainly, Buenos Aires continued to be a porous, open city. But now there *were* boundary markers, and the symbolic effect of the police stations should not be underestimated in this regard. A process that defined an "inside" and an "outside" had begun.

Questioning the real effectiveness of border enforcement does not mean one should overlook the initiative's very concrete consequences. Although there is not enough evidence to fully reconstruct how this infrastructure was used, impressionistic data suggests that in the boundary between the city and the most troublesome areas of Greater Buenos Aires, effective monitoring did increase substantially. A squadron of cars regularly crossed the border to drive into nearby provincial jurisdictions (authorities had added twelve Fords and two armored *voiturettes* to the fleet). Each vehicle was manned with three officers trained in using all of the new equipment: the vehicle, the Colt .45, a machine gun, and the radio connecting the patrol car to headquarters. Authorities also provided each station two motorcycle patrols that, beyond "cooperating with security and traffic agents in their diverse duties, [would] also make continual runs through the principal arteries of the city, *especially those that connect to the province.*"[55]

A series of daily orders and press reports issued in the months following the construction of the outposts reveal a concentrated effort on the southern border. For example, we read that at the Alsina Bridge, the police questioned five "suspicious" occupants of a rented car coming from the direction of Avellaneda. Then, "in the vicinity of the bridge over the Riachuelo in the Province of Buenos Aires" shooting broke out between the border police and some passengers, just as they were being patted down.[56] More and more frequently, the Capital Police spilled over the city's border, *outside* the theoretical boundaries of their jurisdiction. Over the course of the 1930s, the power of the *porteño* police and the image of their efficacy expanded across a broader grid that made up a de facto jurisdiction.

The fact that so many newspapers published stories about the *porteño* police operations in the province of Buenos Aires, without making note of the obvious transgression of their jurisdiction, is an indication of the triumph of the institution's own understanding of the territorial reach of its powers. In the miscellaneous daily presses, the police let filter out ways of thinking about city security, its most dangerous areas, the origin of that danger—the places of order and disorder. In the back and forth of rumors and scoops, press reports conveyed a sense that major crime was nourished in conditions that were to be found outside the city, and that the threat to order in Buenos Aires resided in "Greater Buenos Aires." In this light, the major impediment to combating crime no longer appeared to be police corruption or technical inefficiency, but jurisdictional limits. Indeed, the recent modernization had created a sparkling contrast to the corrupt and outdated police of the neighboring province. Thus it was assumed that it was the right—not to mention duty—of the Capital Police to intervene beyond the boundaries of their legal authority.

As a matter of fact, the Buenos Aires city police had *always* intervened in the affairs of other provinces. Now, their newly acquired mobility would only accelerate the process of legalizing their federal jurisdiction (formally established in 1943).

The expansion of political police during the 1930s functioned as a sort of proto-nationalization, with personnel from Buenos Aires intervening as far away as Zárate, Córdoba, and Chaco.[57] In the face of motorized crime, the Division of Investigation routinely cooperated with police in neighboring towns. Abundant evidence suggests that the overall point of these contacts was to defend the capital city, although each episode was different. There were reports of interventions having to do with criminal networks pure and simple (*pistolero* robberies), with politically motivated crime (*pistolero* anarchists), and with activist unions (associated with communism). Raids and forced entries with the new armored trucks, machine guns, and tear gas were some of the most visible instances of this police action. Their targets were shops, local unions, and private homes suspected of hosting the various permutations of common and political criminality. Some raids were spectacular. Some became spectacles.

In one such case, police made a raid on an anarchist group suspected of robbing the Flores branch of the Banco de Londres y América del Sur in January 1933. The robbery had already been reenacted and presented by the press in a series of photographs and illustrated comic strips.

Following confidential leads obtained from wiretaps, Capital Police chief investigator Viancarlos put the operation in motion by sending a unit to the town of Aldo Bonzi. Their truck, stocked with "tear gas and ten agents armed with machine guns and Mauser rifles, ready to back up the detectives at the decisive moment," ended in a blaze of machine-gun fire on both sides. The police finally took control of the situation by using tear gas, forcing the criminals out of their hideaway. "The village was in shock," *El Mundo* reported.[58]

These episodes called attention to the contrast between the technology and professionalism that emanated from the city (the trucks, the weapons and uniforms of the officers, and the elegant suits of the detectives) and the heterogeneous precariousness of the hideouts the police descended upon. The illustrated coverage of another such expedition (this time pursuing a band of counterfeiters in Florencio Varela, fifteen miles from the capital) was accompanied by captions: "Personnel from the province and [Capital Police] Division of Investigation find the machine used to print bills in a shack in Florencio Varela"; and, "The police's trip to Florencio Varela was certainly not an easy drive. Rain had destroyed the roads and they got stuck. Here, the detectives dig the car out of the mud."[59]

In order to investigate the illegal networks thought to be behind crimes occurring downtown, the *porteño* police needed to collaborate with their colleagues on the other side of the border. Members of the city police's Division of Investigation would show up in the province looking for information on the whereabouts of this or that neighbor who might be under suspicion. "By coincidence they [would discover] some important information coming from the [same] provincial authorities who summoned them to inspect those neighborhoods." These operations functioned within a generic framework of mutual cooperation, one that was complemented by specific arrangements with each local police force.[60] Not all of these collaborations went well. Some *caudillos* objected to these incursions, protesting the "clear" violation of jurisdictional limits and the "unsolicited" show of force outside the capital. The chief of the Division of Investigation put into words what everyone already knew: that thuggery and seedy dives were proliferating thanks to the complicity of political structures from *outside*. This was no mere suspicion, he insisted, but a "supposition that smells of certainty." When extra-jurisdictional police interventions culminated in arrests and the suspects were taken to police precincts of the capital, "certain politicians [would arrive], some of them provincial legislators interested in securing the release of these delinquents."[61] More than a few raids on Avellaneda's gambling centers were complicated by such interference. Sometimes accompanying these "criminals, sex traffickers (*tratantes de blancas*), thieves, and other characters of the *bajo fondo*" would be an official who, invoking the power of his office, would call off the operation or take control of the police report so as to protect his *pistolero* allies.[62]

Things functioned much better when officers on both sides of the border worked together. Joint efforts became an underlying premise of a new strategy of sharing intelligence on criminals, though it also worked particularly well when it came to pursuing communists. Some provincial precincts readily cooperated with their *porteño* counterparts, responding to their requests more readily than they did to the heads of their own police force in La Plata. This was quite clear in the case of Habiague, the chief of police in Avellaneda, whose own story sheds light on the ways in which the Buenos Aires Province police became entangled in local *caudillo* politics. Habiague began his career as a journalist writing for *El Diario, La Razón,* and *La Tarde,* then moved into administration at the San Martín racetrack. Soon after, he met Avellaneda's famed *caudillo* Barceló, by whose hand he became a provincial representative (1925–28). From there, always linked to his political boss, he rose to the rank of police commissioner in San Martín (1931), eventually becoming chief commissioner of Avellaneda. He headed the police force there from 1932 until 1939.[63]

Habiague, who often cooperated with the Capital Police, was lauded (in a slew of articles in institutional publications) for "cleaning up" the district.[64] With his permission, informants working for Orden Social and the Sección Especial routinely crossed the bridge to surveil workers' assemblies in Avellaneda's many meatpacking factories. There, they collected data and infiltrated local factions, detained their leaders, and took them back to Buenos Aires.[65] To accomplish this, the Capital Police used their recently expanded powers to make arrests—obtained first in 1932 via the infraction edicts and then extended to include provincial jurisdiction. As we have seen, these tools for maintaining "order" could be successfully appropriated for political agendas. The edict that regulated the carrying of firearms had noticeable repercussions in the city's outskirts.

In a confidential letter, the commissioner of Avellaneda explained to his *porteño* colleagues that the infraction edicts permitted the police to do what otherwise could not be done in his district: arrest and detain (for a month) communist workers in the meatpacking plants of the industrial belt by forcefully transporting them from one jurisdiction to another. Said Habiague:

> Carrying firearms in the Province is regulated by the municipality. [A suspect can be held] for up to four days and fined eight pesos [while waiting] for the Mayor to decide his punishment. Remitting these detainees to the city, it was not requested that they be returned to [this office], because here, in reality, [we] had no case. Moreover, this office keeps in mind that, even though the Capital Police also has no legal justification for detaining them, they do have [one] tool that the provincial police [do not have]. I am referring to the infraction edict against carrying firearms. . . . As the threat from communism would [now] be greater if the first communist-led strike had succeeded, the two police forces have been coordinating their actions on the basis of de facto detentions, as they lack laws permitting them to go after [communist] activities, so dangerous to society.[66]

Thus, *porteño* edicts with jurisdiction in the *porteño* territory were used as a tool of political persecution in Greater Buenos Aires. A 1933 report highlighted the level of discretion granted the police: "The individuals imprisoned in the jurisdiction of the Province of Buenos Aires for activities in that territory should only be granted liberty if so decided by local authorities, administrative or judicial." The report jumpstarted an internal investigation into uncovering the informal collaborations and links between the *porteño* and the Avellaneda police. When questioned about the incident, Chief Habiague and his colleagues in the Division of Investigation responded that province police habitually turned over detained communists to the Capital Police ("without paperwork") at the request of the Sección Especial.[67] "In general, it has been understood that [the Avellaneda police] cannot detain them for very long, and so they send them here extra-legally in order to prolong their detention, where [they remain] until the moment at which habeas corpus obliges us to set them free." The document also alluded to agents from the Division of Investigation directly detaining agitators, "with the consent of local authorities." "The Avellaneda police have not been opposed to this—to the contrary, they have cooperated without ever calling jurisdiction into question when a shared interest of safeguarding public and social order demand it." Everything was managed by telephone: "In general, in these cases, no paperwork is exchanged, although sometimes [the detainees] arrive with a simple delivery note." This routine cooperation was already well established when, in February 1936, Víctor Fernández Bazán, the manager of the *Robos y hurtos* section of the

Capital Police, was named chief investigator of the province police. So began a period infamous for its ruthlessness. By then, the intelligence acquired on either side of the border was indistinguishable.

TWO QUESTIONS REGARDING THE *PORTEÑO* POLICE

The evidence presented in the preceding pages raises questions that go beyond the scope of this inquiry. Two of them have important implications and may be set out for future investigation.

During the 1930s, the police adopted and modified diverse strategies of suburban surveillance. Over the course of the following decade, these practices became well-established conventions. This raises questions about Peronism's master narrative of its own foundational saga, which describes a mass mobilization of residents from the industrial belt entering the city to rescue the workers' new leader. On October 17, 1945, the story goes, vast crowds moved from the "outside" of the city to the "inside," marching unimpeded to the Plaza de Mayo. We know, however, that by this time the police had the capacity to detect—and impede—a movement of this magnitude. Indeed, these masses traveled through the very streets and across the very bridges where police surveillance was most concentrated. These paths, as we have seen, were also equipped with lookout stations that were routinely used to prevent just this kind of situation. Nevertheless, there appears to have been no effort to block, filter, or divert this major incursion of the city's downtown by "outsiders." This *lack of intervention* begs for an explanation, since it contradicts a previous understanding of how order was maintained. The question about the role of the police in the emergence of Peronism is, thus, an open one.

A second line of questioning centers on the metamorphosis of the Capital Police into the Federal Police in 1943. We know that this change was built on a longer history of smaller de facto federalizations and interventions. Although we lack specific studies on this process, evidence suggests that the formal federalization, when it finally arrived, provided a legal foundation for many existing practices. For a long time, the Capital Police had cultivated a national reach, both in terms of its agenda and its geographic scope.

When those informal paths toward federalization are considered, however, they must be contrasted with other deeply rooted territorial rationales that were also at play. Particularly important was the primacy attached to an agenda of *porteño* order as a symbolic focal point for the Capital Police. Thus, when the Capital Police became the Federal Police (Policía Federal Argentina), the new national map crystallized around an existing structure with a clear center. Official federalization occurred as something that was overlaid onto an extended praxis, one that brought its own momentum and inertia stemming from long-standing relationships with provincial police, corporate identities, and deeply rooted interests within the institution. Thus the question arises: when (if ever) did "La Federal" stop being the Capital Police? The distribution of resources, the designing of a "national" agenda centered in Buenos Aires, and certain elements of its police culture all point to strong links and continuities with its *porteño* roots. So it would be for many years to come.

CHAPTER 6

While the City Sleeps

Police and the Social Imagination

The public servant has the obligation to provide information to
those who come to him for aid. Members of the police should
take this culture to a higher level. Even the most modest
individuals within its hierarchy are imbued with exceptional
authority, having the power to temporarily deprive their
citizens of liberty through a simple act of judgment.

—Capital Police, *Orden del Día*, December 20, 1933

THE PEOPLE AND THE POLICE

The police officer is the only agent of the state with direct coercive
power over citizens. Although the use of force accounts for a minimal
portion of his daily activities, this potential—its ever-present threat, the
permanent option to use violence—provides perceptive coherence to a
figure whose activities are, in fact, extraordinarily diverse. What unifies
the social image of the policeman is not what he actually *does* (since
even the most cursory examination sends that definition in many directions), but rather what he represents for the citizen with whom he inter-
acts. What is distinctive about this interaction is the *possibility* of the
use of force—and, more precisely, the use of force against an *us* that
may perceive him as a threat.[1]

Even in contexts of relatively low conflict, the exercise of police
power raises the critical question of its legitimacy. Police power is out-
wardly simple and direct, but its origin is far from obvious. The basis
for its legitimacy has eluded ethnographers of contemporary police
forces and has been the object of considerable critical reflection. "Unlike
law," wrote Walter Benjamin in a celebrated passage, "a consideration

of the police institution encounters nothing essential at all. Its power is formless, like its nowhere tangible, all-pervasive, ghostly presence in the life of civilized states."[2] Police power reveals its essence precisely at the point where the law ends. It is the ultimate admission of the coercive nature of the established order. This is why police power requires a good deal of symbolic artifice; it is an exercise in permanent construction of meaning. Relationships with the civilian population are a key concern for all modern police forces, whose power is euphemized in an abundance of instructions and codes regarding manners and behavior.

Moreover, the use of this coercive force is discretionary. The power to arrest—the most expressive manifestation of a power with many incarnations—results from a decision-making chain that is fragmented and heterogeneous, built on countless micro-decisions that are secret or more or less implicit. Since no police officer enforces the law mechanically (an impossible prospect, given the gap between theoretical tasks and real capacities), this modest guardian of order must decide everyday which incidents or social groups merit his intervention, and how far this intervention will go within the formal or informal frame with which he is provided.[3]

This chapter explores the public opinion strategies adopted by Buenos Aires police in the context of a deep crisis of consensus in the 1920s and 1930s regarding their right to use force. In so doing, it tackles a question transcending this case: how can police forces act as the guardians of a social order they themselves might perceive as unjust, and still earn the respect of those who suffer from its injustice? The answer, I argue here, lies within the process of the symbolic construction of an idealized police officer, one able to remain connected with those he claims to protect. In this case, the connection between the police and *the people* was woven using fiction, mass media, and other key elements of popular culture.

In Buenos Aires, social resistance to the legitimacy of the coercive power of the police is long-standing. Although it is difficult to assess in comparative terms, mass resentment, mockery, and contempt for the police go back to the very foundation of the institution, and have survived every attempt at remedy. In his 1885 report, Police Chief Marcos Paz reflected on this popular animosity, mentioning a problem that many would evoke after him: a notably stubborn "way of being in relation to authority" on the part of the city population. He complained: "The security agent who looks after the life, property and honor of persons, encounters hostility rather than help or acknowledgment in the broad public. Therefore, what could be taken care of by a sole policeman requires the presence of many . . . Contempt always underlies the slightest disorder."[4]

Nowhere was this contempt more eloquently described than in popular journalism, where topics such as police corruption were intertwined with discussions of mistreatment of workers, political dissidents, and common citizens. In the 1920s, this repertoire migrated from the leftist press (anarchist, socialist) to more mainstream mass-market newspapers such as *Crítica*, where the denunciation of police misconduct became an important pillar of the editorial pact between this daily publication and its tens of thousands (soon to become hundreds of thousands) of readers. The defiance of police authority, mockery of police clumsiness, and exposure of police brutality all underlined the commercial success of *Crítica*, "the voice of the people." Its illustrations, rhetorical style, and interviews all constructed a universe in which the abyss between this collective entity called *the people* and the police was a given.[5]

Upon this substratum lay a *hatred* of the police force, which was widely seen as an institution that used intimidation to put down strikes, mistreated and killed workers, and planted false evidence. The police were the absolute *other* in the constitution of the identity of the working classes. For union organizations at the turn of the century (irrespective of their ideological affiliations), the police were *"cosacos,"* or *"mazorqueros"*—in other words, latter-day versions of the bloody enforcers of the Russian tsars or the criminal hordes of the nineteenth-century Argentine dictator Juan Manuel de Rosas. Ubiquitous popular anger against the police produced unease among officials, who were concerned about their image and sought to legitimize their interventions into the "social question." In 1923, for example, Commissioner Romariz recalled arriving at the Federación Obrera Marítima to meet with the union's leader. When he reached the top floor he encountered a wooden artifact that looked like a gallows, from which a police officer had been hung in effigy. During the same period, Romariz remembered, when President Yrigoyen issued orders prohibiting workers' right to assembly, the police charged with monitoring public acts were so mercilessly insulted and threatened that "it was necessary to have the forces of order carry out their mission as far away as possible from the workers' gathering places."[6] Twenty years later, hostility toward the police remained a serious issue: Alberto Bouchez, the official charged with explaining the application of edicts and norms to the public, believed that the police needed to call on a professional publicity service to gain "little by little, a more positive influence on police-public relations."[7]

The impact of Leopoldo Lugones Jr.'s Sección Especial on the institution as a whole and his escalation of communist repression proved costly for the public image of the police, reopening the old question about the legitimacy of its use of force. Almost immediately upon his arrival, Lugones emerged as a controversial, provocative, and conspicuous figure. His speeches against communists, Jews, and his arch-enemy Natalio Botana (*Crítica's* founder) were disseminated in the most intransigent fascist nationalist media. His reputation as an extremist and the stories of his sinister activities seemed to confirm the press's worst suspicions about the police. Expressing the grievance of those officers who opposed the establishment of the Sección Especial in 1930, the magazine *Policía y Justicia* editorialized: "It is an old belief, which has taken root in the public, that the police use an inquisitional system with torture devices similar to those in the Middle Ages. It is unfortunate that the new hierarchy of this institution, instead of correcting this mistaken belief, decided to expand it, even creating a new torture device with all of the technological advancements of the age."[8]

At the same time, a much more problematic breach of public confidence—one that opposed the police and *the people*—was making headlines in the popular press. In this context, generating a sense of unity between the police and society became one of the main missions of police reform during this period. This project brought together officials of different persuasions, including the very same leadership responsible for espionage and political repression.

At the advent of Peronism, the old police utopia of unity with the people was presented as an achievement of the new order. From the balcony of the Casa Rosada, Perón celebrated the historical consolidation of this bond. The police of this new era would be of the people—the "shirtless-ones," *los descamisados,* insisted Evita.[9] The scarcity of research available on this topic suggests that the newly created Federal Police aligned with Perón early on, supporting him during several crucial moments of his rise to power. Indeed, rather than waiting before choosing their political alignment, the Federal Police chose sides quite early, in October 1945. Evidence suggests they even collaborated during the founding mobilization of the October 17 labor demonstration by exhibiting a conspicuous leniency when monitoring worker demonstrations. Some police in uniform were even seen shouting "¡Viva Perón!" The police force, and individual officers, joined the ranks of new Peronist supporters at a time when most areas of government seemed to be going in the opposite direction.[10]

Of course, this by no means implied that the newly "federal" police had renounced their hard-line tactics. During the 1943 de facto regime and the Peronist era that followed, the police force maintained its vast network of political espionage and continued to punish the enemies of the day: communists, political dissidents, and even members of the military who opposed Perón. Between 1948 and 1955, the new Orden Gremial division targeted that branch of the worker movement that still opposed the mandate of the dominant Peronist unions.[11] The idea of a new harmony between the police and the people thus coexisted with the traditional clandestine functions of the police, though the objects of surveillance varied over time. This does not mean that the celebration of change was purely cynical, however. The diagnosis of the political and social situation that Perón offered in 1945, as well as the place reserved in that narrative for the "police of the people," were seen as credible by a significant portion of the rank-and-file because they both resonated with previous core narratives about police and society. The construction of such a system of meaning is the subject of this chapter.

THE TRIUMPH OF THE POLICEMAN ON THE CORNER

Dark deserted streets echo
the slow heel-clicking of passersby;
they give a symphony of alarms
those sentinels on their customary rounds.

*Devuelven las oscuras calles desiertas
el taconeo tardo de las paseantes;
y dan la sinfonía de las alertas
en su ronda obligada los vigilantes.*

—Evaristo Carriego, "El alma del suburbio"

Recent public concern about crime has placed the topic of violence and insecurity at the center of scholarly debates about Latin America's past and present. Finding themselves suddenly involved in discussions on the causes of crime or public policy recommendations, sociologists and anthropologists are pondering the nature of urban imaginaries of fear. Provided with questionnaires and recording devices, they explore the neighborhoods of Buenos Aires and other cities, collecting testimonies ranging from physical and mental sensations to causal interpretations of crime and its consequences.[12] Analyses of the various testimonies have yielded certain remarkably stable topics. One of these seeks to juxtapose the "bad cop" of the present against the noble neighborhood watchman of an idyllic past, an important figure in the nostalgia for order on a human scale. In his study of notions of crime and moral order, for instance, Alejandro Isla singles out the "corner cop" (*vigilante de la esquina*) as implicit in descriptions of what today's police should be. Negative perceptions of the present, he argues, are conceived as a departure from a normative center that remains resistant. At the heart of the denunciation of the corrupt, violent policeman, the longing for that mythical *vigilante* is very much alive.[13] We know little, however, about the genealogy of this emblematic fixture of the *porteño* neighborhood. Let us turn to the genesis of that most long-lived of Buenos Aires policemen, one born in the context of a public opinion crisis at the beginning of the twentieth century.

The figure of the *vigilante porteño* crystalized in the 1920s and 1930s. We might think of him as a local version of the more generic community policeman, well known in many cities of the world, an officer who walked through the neighborhood and interacted with residents face to face. Yet the rise of the *vigilante porteño* is also inseparable from his local context, one that involves the settlement of suburban areas that would become the backdrop for new forms of sociability. Meanwhile, the crisis of public opinion transformed the beat cop into a figure of consensus, untouched by the tensions dividing the institution. By 1933, when public resentment of the role of the police in political repression was a critical problem, the *Revista de Policía* observed: "Of the entire police squad, the street cops are those who inspire the most sympathy and affection from those observant souls who stop to reflect even for a moment on police matters."[14] This pretechnological and depoliticized policeman was the custodian of a vital connection with society, the lifesaving link with the common citizen.

Early concerns about public image were expressed in the many close regulations regarding the *vigilante*'s behavior. Orders and instructions insisted that police power should go hand in hand with a friendly demeanor. Officers were urged to be aware that every instance of discourtesy only served to deepen the citizen's lack of confidence in their authority, already so fiercely attacked in the press. Even the recent street parades, in which the city police displayed their new equipment, began to raise questions, as some perceived them as too intimidating and militaristic to attract the sympathy of the public.[15] In this context, police management of the 1934 Congreso Eucarístico Internacional (which gathered together an unprecedented number of Catholics) was viewed as an opportunity for reconciliation. A flurry of internal directives gave specific guidelines for how those visitors were to be treated.

The main drive to improve the public image of the police did not come from the upper echelons of the institution, however, but from groups of younger policemen who were peripheral to the decision-making centers. These groups were concerned with two fundamental challenges: creating a strong bond of institutional identity within the ranks and projecting an outward image of an efficient, amiable force. Institutional identity, social legitimacy—these were matters that transcended the kind of professional expertise learned at the academy. The campaign to achieve them did not depend upon the most commonly accepted indicators of police modernization, such as the consolidation of training schools, the development of efficient criminalistics, or the expansion of fingerprinting. Nor did it require better weapons or patrol cars. Rather, it was framed in the language of mass culture, and strove for the construction of a moral imagination for policemen.

CULTURE FOR THE "POLICE FAMILY"

The notion of police culture—that is, the aggregate of elements that distinguish a police point of view from that of society at large—has played a major role in explanations of police brutality and police resistance to institutional reform. The assumption is that a shared subculture provides meaning and intelligibility to a job that is not easily integrated into a larger symbolic universe. The stress of having to constantly project an image of effectiveness, along with exposure to danger, tends to generate thick webs of meaning and "canteen" police cultures that provide a sense of belonging. Much has been said, for instance, about the importance of police *machismo,* cultural isolation, political conservatism, sense of mission, and glorification of danger as constituent elements of police identity.[16]

The concept of police culture has proven useful to the task of identifying the "distinctness" of a police point of view. But the same process has contributed to lending it an air of the exotic. When we think about historical periods such as the 1920s and 1930s, when the mechanisms of separation from society were still quite undeveloped, or about police forces whose internal culture is less hermetic, less isolated from the culture at large (as seems to be the case in Buenos Aires), relying on the concept of police culture seems less useful.[17] Indeed, conceiving of the *porteño* policeman's worldview in less exotic terms opens the window for a critical history of the construction of police identity as arising not only from its divorce from the wider culture but also from its familiarity with that culture—that is, from a process of selection and re-signification of topics that are present in popular literature, tango, and mass media.

The construction of bonds of identity within the Capital Police took shape in the 1920s and 1930s around the notion of the "police family," a concept that remains at the center of the institution's ethos to this day.

In the broad community of the police family, concerns about wages and promotion in the hierarchy are intertwined with news about births, weddings, parties, and romantic gossip. Above all, it is a social network.

The main source for the notion of the police as family was *Magazine Policial*, a rank-and-file entertainment review created in 1922. Over the course of its twenty-five-year run, it imitated the miscellaneous style of *Caras y Caretas*, a successful mass-market magazine founded in the nineteenth century by José S. Álvarez. Also known as "Fray Mocho," he was himself a police officer, one who was well attuned to popular culture and graphic media.[18] *Magazine Policial* could be purchased on the street at kiosks and by subscription throughout the country. It sold far more copies than similar institutional publications, and its initial distribution of eighteen thousand during the 1920s went up in the 1930s when police-themed radio theater shows became popular. The new radio-listening audiences pushed the magazine's readership beyond its initial institutional circuit, transforming it into a hybrid product that straddled both its police origins and the wider world of radio entertainment. With a more populist tone—more *tanguera*, more sensational— *La Gaceta Policial* (1926–31) spoke to the ordinary cop on the beat.

At the heart of the *Magazine* project was Ramón Cortés Conde, the author of several police handbooks, the official 1935 *Historia de la Policía de la Ciudad de Buenos Aires,* and a number of imaginative proposals for *porteño* traffic control. Despite his subsequent high standing in the history of institutional figures (a hall in the Museo Policial still carries his name), Cortés Conde was, above all, an advocate for the point of view of the city police, and particularly, its several thousand rank-and file-officers. A "police vanguard" made up of friends and colleagues worked alongside him.[19] Defined in exalted language and expressed through the *Magazine*'s poetic extravagances, the publication's goals reflected classic problems of institutional identity construction—to begin with, the goal of cementing bonds between fellow officers.

The *Magazine* and the *Gaceta* offered a popular and populist way to promote and stay abreast of the concerns and interests of this institution-family, especially in its lower ranks. Salary issues, personal security, and the promotion system were all featured prominently, and always with an eye toward benefiting the most modest agent in the force. Any perceived unfairness toward even the most subordinate street officer on the part of ignorant institutional bureaucrats was met with harsh editorials.

None of these strategies precluded the use of more traditional methods for generating group identity. The *Magazine* also promoted a pantheon of characters that perfectly coincided with the messages sent from official channels. Colonel Ramón Falcón, who (along with his secretary, Lartigau) had been killed in an anarchist bombing attack in 1909, emerged as a main protagonist in these types of stories, figuring as the victim of a cowardly attack. Falcón's elevation to mythic status was the result of initiatives taken long after his death. His statue, unveiled a decade and a half later, was part of this campaign to create a sense of belonging among police. As an illustrious martyr, Falcón presided over a succession of institutional figures, including O'Gorman, Ballvé, Beazley, Capdevila, García, and Denovi. These same names filled the pages of the history books written for police consumption. However, no book could ever aspire to reach the vast audiences or hope to match the graphic resources of *Magazine Policial*. In the 1930s, the fictionalized "Falcón-Lartigau" saga took to the stage as radio theater.[20]

When embracing the cause of group identity, *Magazine Policial* and *Gaceta Policial* served as a complement to official strategies of recruitment and professionalization. Their success stemmed from a combination of strong commitment to the problems of institution building and their deliberate informality, which granted them unofficial credibility. The "family" topics these magazines promoted were formulated in the popular vocabulary of mass culture.

Gaceta Policial offered reading material in a casual, popular tone. Some of its permanent sections, including "Acuarelitas del arrabal" (Watercolors of the *arrabal*) and "La musa popular" (The Muse of the People) celebrated "rough" tango culture. Juan Francisco Palermo (Quico)'s *Diccionario Lunfardo*, published in instalments, began with a dedication: "To Natalio Botana, who plants trees, had children and created *Crítica*: the cradle of this volume. (J.F.P.)." The *Gaceta* even promoted *Crítica*, the "newspaper of the people" (and the main critic of the police) and publicized its collection of sensationalistic literature with full-page ads. Even the *Gazeta*'s crime section was permeated with a truculent style reminiscent of Botana's paper. Pedro de Rojas, the celebrated graphic artist who worked at *Crítica*, illustrated the main articles in this police magazine.

Magazine Policial, for its part, had a more pedagogical slant. Like the miscellaneous publications that it imitated, *Magazine* published fiction in instalments, as well as translations. Writers interested in social issues—Manuel Gálvez, Héctor Pedro Blomberg, and (above all) Juan José de Soiza Reilly—predominated.[21] Like other publications with mass circulation, *Magazine* offered an even more abundant selection of world literature, with a preference for realistic fiction and romantic and naturalist authors: Pérez Galdós, Pío Baroja, Dickens, Anatole France, Paul Bourget, Victor Hugo, Balzac, Maupassant, Daireaux, and Pirandello. *Magazine* also shared the popular press's fondness for Russian social literature (a central pillar of catalogues of other low-priced book collections and popular libraries during this era), offering police readers selections from Andreyev, Chekhov, Averchenko, Tolstoy, and Gorki.

The overlap between the "universal culture" offering of *Magazine Policial* and other popular book collections and catalogues found at neighborhood libraries went far beyond their mutual predilection for Russian writers.[22] These forums also offered readers a selection of authors strongly associated with the cultural milieu of the Left: for example, stories by the anarchist Alberto Ghiraldo[23] and the writer, journalist, and socialist leader Mario Bravo;[24] essays by the anarchist-republican, Spanish journalist-writer Rafael Barrett;[25] a series of headlining essays by Henri Barbusse (a widely distributed standard in communist interwar literary collections); and illustrations by the influential anarchist-pacifist engraver Frans Masereel.[26]

These texts were absorbed into the wide-ranging context of the *Magazine* without any real friction. Pacifism, *filo-comunismo*, "moderate" anarchism, and radical sympathies converged in an eclectic postwar social sensibility. Given the striking degree of similarity with other cultural enterprises of the period, the inclusion of this kind of content brings up the question of the specificity of the social imagination of the police in relation to the society it watched over. In the following section, I argue that the distinctiveness of the police imagination came from a process of selection and re-signification of some of these themes and languages.[27]

WHILE THE CITY SLEEPS: CHRONICLES OF A PLEBEIAN HERO

Police cultures, says Roberto Reiner, do not emerge from didactic manuals read at police academies, but rather from the aggregate mediation of histories transmitted from generation to generation, from everyday jokes and practical commonalities.[28] The popular and populist tone of *Magazine Policial* stemmed from a dense sediment of anecdotes highlighting the qualities of the street cop. He was a small-time urban hero, the embodiment of the highest professional virtues. At the same time, he was the subject of many inside stories. The chronicle of his routine was littered with implicit understandings regarding street lore and certain temptations

FIGURE 24. "Speeding!" *Gaceta Policial*, December 25, 1926.

of the street. The plausibility of the "familial" bond relied upon a combination of the hero-policeman and the morally vulnerable policeman.

A surprisingly large number of these stories took place at restaurants, where the officers participated in the "banquet culture" of the interwar years. Photos of feasts portrayed a sense of family, celebration, and virile camaraderie centered around pasta, wine, and jokes. The highly publicized connection between certain officers and the bohemian groups

FIGURE 25. *Magazine Policial*, August 1929.

of painters, poets, and tango musicians who called themselves the "Republic of La Boca" furthered this image.

"*Mentiras policiales*" (Police Lies) was the title of one humor column in which everything was imbued with a double meaning. Those who knew, took part in, and tolerated the regular run of police tricks could decode the puns instantly. The "*buzón*" (mailbox) section of *Magazine Policial* featured a compendium of private mini-narratives. The police "family" was in on all the jokes.

Among the many implicit understandings was the idea that police work offered ample opportunities for contact with women. In caricatures, jokes, and anecdotes, the juxtaposition of uniformed men and seductive downtown ladies called attention to the pleasures of a job that was usually described in terms of sacrifice. It also constructed, by way of contrast, an

FIGURE 26. *Magazine Policial,* August 1927.

attractive example of masculinity: flirting with prostitutes who passed through the police station, boldly catcalling the modern damsels who strutted down elegant streets, and using the patrol car for sexual conquests. This material also presented a new character on the urban stage, one uniquely suited to exalting the image of the modern policeman's virility: the novice female driver. Her presence introduced a whole range of interactions in which pleasantries gave way to flirting.

In his study on masculine stereotypes in western culture, George Mosse observes that symbols of a virile male body did not emerge in isolation, but rather in relation to the image of the weak and frightened woman.[29] The distressed "modern girl," although more brash than scared, served this function. An archetypical figure of the 1920s, she was independent, open to sexual encounters, often seen smoking a cigarette, and associated with the speed and questionable morality of the automobile. She was also the female figure most frequently seen in the pages of *Magazine Policial*. As we

FIGURE 27. *Magazine Policial,* May 1934.

will see, this game of contrasts was complemented by two other "weak" female characters: the policeman's mother (*la viejita*) and his anxious wife.

In the 1930s, these kinds of lighthearted accounts began to give way to the more serious topic of police mission. Technical modernization and formal recruitment policies brought with them a transformation of the street agent. His image crystallized in the heroic mold. He was now a hermetic figure, honorable, strong, and invulnerable. With the introduction of the radio and automatic weapons, the signifiers of his strength were now to be found in the prominent display of those devices. The humorous appreciation for the beat cop's human fallibility disappeared from public definitions of police mission. Idealized street inter-

FIGURE 28. *Magazine Policial,* October 1933.

actions now involved children or elderly ladies, figures that cast the policeman's virility into sharp relief, leaving no room for jokes and human temptation. In this harder pattern of masculinity (closer to the military model), the policeman was now a step removed from society. He didn't speak to passersby. Rather, he protected them from traffic. He watched over them. He guaranteed that the violence of the city would not disrupt the order of the neighborhood. He had now become expert in the pursuit and apprehension of criminals.

In order to be persuasive, the image of the heroic policeman needed a human dimension, one that was sublime rather than humorous. The construction of the heroic policeman was rounded off by the idea of sacrifice, which developed at various levels, often using the language of popular fiction. He was all at once a victim of his calling for public service, forgotten by a state that paid him little, and at the mercy of the hardships of the street, where he passed more hours than anyone, enduring its relentless pace and cacophony. Rigid with technical efficiency, the uniformed body had its counterpart in the suffering body, the *exposed* body of the policeman-hero.

"The tradition of the Policía de la Capital was to fulfill its mission stoically, through the hard nights of torrential rain and the blazing heat of summer afternoons," observed the director of *Magazine Policial,* Cortés Conde.[30] In addition to inclement weather and bewildering traffic, the policeman was exposed to the ghosts of the night. Here is the ancient connection between police praxis and knowledge about the mysteries of the night, a topic with colonial roots in the figure of the night watchman, who controls the light sources and the identities of passersby. The night was the supreme territory of police authority. It was also the locus of camaraderie: "We were talking one night, some police station workers," recounted commissioner-writer Laurentino Mejías. "There was no news in the area and the *mate*—that perfect companion during the long nights on the watch—passed from hand to hand."[31] Narrated as paternal sacrifice on behalf of an infant society, this vigil imbued the agent with moral superiority. It was the vigil of the "pastoral" police, whose tutelary power was ever watchful over the flock, who knew and protected both the group and its individuals.[32] Like children who could sleep in peace "in warm silk sheets" thanks to the wakefulness of their elders, the citizens of Buenos Aires relied upon the policeman, who endured winter, storms, and threats in order to watch over this carefree, ungrateful society. "And the sleeping city / trusting and at ease / to the cooing of the warning / of the *Ronda Policial* / rests and dreams / dreams without thought."[33]

"While the City Sleeps" was the name of a section of *Magazine Policial* devoted to the everyday experiences of the beat cop, who renounced comfort and personal concerns so that others could enjoy the guarantee of domestic order: a mother could dress her children at home while the rain pattered outside, a pedestrian could return from work safely and rest by the warmth of his stove. A similar stock of anecdotes soon extended to other publications of the "institution-family." Written by both high officials and rank-and-file members, they amassed an anthology of the tragic and picturesque vicissitudes of the job. They fed the sediment of a shared archive of experiential knowledge of the night shift.[34]

The ultimate mission of the agent was to protect citizens from the dangers of urban modernity—from crime, of course, but also from the physical and material violence that loomed at each corner, from noise and speed, from the risks underlying anonymity. This *vigilante,* who owed his name as much to wakefulness (*vigilia*) as to surveillance (*vigilancia*), was more closely related to his colonial ancestor than to his contemporary, the armed and motorized policeman, whom he complemented by opposition. Even if the *vigilante* was also armed, his weapon was never mentioned as an attribute.

The "ignored soldier" attained the peak of heroism when he gave up his own life for the very same society that so disregarded him. As has been shown in classic ethnographic studies of "police culture," station house talk about danger plays a major role in police bonding and camaraderie.[35] But in this case, the dominant meaning resided in the tragic dimension of that risk, since policemen "fallen in the line of duty" injected an intense and morally righteous gravity to that identity. The hero Falcón was reincarnated through the sacrifices of contemporary policemen. For this reason, the homage to fallen officers took place on the anniversary of the Great Fallen One's death. Falcón's name was always invoked next to the coffin and the flowers of the most recently fallen policeman.[36]

The cult of the deceased Buenos Aires policeman developed and expanded during the 1920s and 1930s. The institution erected a monument and named surveillance posts after fallen colleagues (who were remembered again in manuals of institutional history), while the *panteón social* of the cemetery saw a proliferation of rituals. The sacrificial bodies were buried with great pomp in the police mausoleum, built in December 1921. At station houses, small sanctuaries sprang up around the photographs of deceased colleagues. In the mid-1930s, a special section of the cemetery, the "niche of honor," was devoted to those who had died in the line of duty.

"*Nuestros muertos*" (our dead): the gallery of martyrs built a moral counterweight, a balm that made up for the public mockery of the police. *Nuestros muertos:* the possessive defined a sense of belonging, in contrast to *their* dead. *Nuestros muertos* were embraced by an institution-family that constructed itself in the very act of closing ranks around the pain that society refused to acknowledge. Coexistence with an ungrateful public opinion was an essential element of police identity.

Constantly mentioned, the theme of social indifference toward police sacrifice accelerated the seeking of refuge in the peer community. To this day it is present in institutional publications in the form of poems written by rank-and-file policemen. The tragedy of sacrifice constitutes a vital element in the symbolization of police work.[37]

In addition to constructing a corporate "us," the "fallen" gave credence to a (militaristic) notion that police were vulnerable because they incurred risks while fighting crime, ostensibly the primary mission of a modern force. But what caused the deaths of these men, lost in the line of duty? As part of the formalization of tributes, their names, photographs, and an account of the circumstances of their demise were included in a special section of the annual police memorandum. These reports indicate that the risk in police work did not come from crime but rather from generic efforts at maintaining order in the streets. An account of shootings appeared next to a fall from a horse onto the pavement, car or truck accidents, an attack from subjects who resented being scolded for "playing music in front of a house," a bite from a rabid dog, an accident in an unmarked construction site during nightly rounds, knife wounds during a drunken skirmish, or a motorcycle accident suffered while pursuing a speeding car.[38] Behind the image of an institution devoted to catching criminals lay a catalogue of fatalities connected to more traditional tasks.

"Such intimate tragedy is hidden behind each name on the list! How many of these generous officials left behind inconsolable wives, children, parents, all plunged into the despair without reprieve that death brings!" So reads the lament for the "fallen" agents that concludes the *Historia de la policía*—required reading for any aspiring cadet. The construction of the policeman as public servant had the sentimental intensity of melodrama. Similar elements were used to create fables of reconciliation with the people.

POLICE MELODRAMAS: THE SENTIMENTAL BOND BETWEEN STATE AND CITIZEN

During the night watch at a *porteño* police station, two policemen drink *mate*.

Corporal: Police life is a school of pain!

Auxiliary: The police station is where all human calamities converge.

Corporal: It's true, Sir . . .

Auxiliary: Tears and intimate dramas, engraved in the books, between traces of black ink. . . . So much pain and misery in such few phrases.[39]

Between 1934 and 1945 *Ronda Policial* was broadcast every day by Radio Porteña. At its peak, the Radiópolis group—led by Commissioner Cortés Conde—had programs at eleven radio stations on subjects ranging from life in the old city, to famous crime cases, to secret histories of Buenos Aires, to the adventures of the gaucho detective sergeant Venancio.

By then, the "police melodrama" had a long history inside the institution. It flourished in the 1920s and 1930s as a particular version of commercial melodrama that was enormously popular in literature, radio theater, and the movies. Due to its brevity, simple moral structure, and direct relationship with experience, it was the most frequently used genre among police-authors. In the mid-1930s, police melodrama expanded beyond the institution in the form of scripts for radio programs, written by a few officers and civilian collaborators. In doing so, they disseminated the image of the benign night *porteño* watchman.

The police melodrama capitalized on the everyday stories of the officer—the one who knew how to see through the exterior façade of the city, who understood its characters, and who met firsthand the drama of the ordinary. He also heard, in the homelike space of the neighborhood police station, the many stories of its invisible social fabric. The fragmented body of poems, vignettes, and brief anecdotes tended to confirm the fragility and immobility of its characters, where the poor were poor, the rich were rich, and context did not matter. Military coups, the Spanish Civil War, and World War I all occurred far from the misfortunes of the meek, whom the policeman discovered over and over, suspended in time, essentialized in the neighborhood that constituted his stage.

The mild-mannered policeman was a human archive of stories and micro-stories. "I am the counsel with which experience teaches its science to humanity" went the recited message that opened *Ronda Policial.* Described as a knowledge acquired in street-level encounters with these characters, this wisdom was a summary of human nature rather than an analysis of the conflicts and tensions underlying social life. Police culture is not given to abstraction. Its archive of the street is inductive, empirical, and cumulative. It's made of stories and characters, of a very singular incarnation of political or sociological categories. It was precisely his status as inconspicuous observer of the active "school of life" that vested the watchman with moral authority. This strategy fueled the emotive intensity of radio theater, with each episode opening with the reminder: "I know of the mother . . .; I know of the sick . . .; I know of the good man, of the alcoholic." The very name of the program, *Ronda Policial* (Police Rounds), evoked a world and established a point of view: that of the agent who *walked* the city, who related to its street corners in all of their emotional dimension, marked by concrete references (the dance hall, the café, the street names). His concrete knowledge thus complemented more abstract descriptions of police space, represented in blueprints, maps, and construction design.

The police melodrama took its cues from the tragic sadness with which hunger and poverty were vividly represented both in popular newspapers and in police magazines. During the night shift at the station, agents read poems about a mother's suffering, about the imprisonment of her son, punished for stealing a piece of bread to feed her; about sickness, death, or solitude. This police-school-of-pain relied on the languages and images of "proletarian fiction," which in this reframing underwent an ideological reversal: here, the social critique persisted, but the policeman was no longer a subject of otherness. Instead, he was the ally of those who suffered.[40] Indeed, he shared their sense of social injustice.

"Would you let me stay the night?" an unfortunate soul asked the officer on duty in the story "Pernoctar!" (To Spend the Night!), written by police officer Natalio Castro.[41] Here, in a Buenos Aires darkened by the global economic crisis, the police station is depicted as a refuge. The same background had set the stage for writer and journalist Enrique González Tuñón's book *Camas desde un peso* (Beds Starting at One Peso), where a stream of marginal characters (bohemians, the unemployed, the homeless) circulated through *boliches* and shady boarding houses. In his collection of night-shift anecdotes, Officer Castro imitated this model (one of the stories was titled "Beds at a Half-Peso"). But unlike González Tuñón and other authors writing about the secrets of the city, Castro had firsthand experience. His story's protagonist, instead of being a mere agent of order, was able to empathize with and actively embrace the down-and-out individuals who haunted the inns and public spaces; they were not there because of their ideological beliefs, as González Tuñón would have it, but because they were victims of the economic crisis. In this way, the officer helped (rather than punished) those who violated the legal order of the day, and of the night.[42]

These magazines included traces of sympathy and familiarity with the cultural universe of the Left, the exhibition of which could even help to cement a certain kind of street credibility inside the institution. But since police knowledge resisted abstraction, it remained exterior to the point of view of dissident culture and leftist formulations of social conflict. The society that paraded before the *vigilante* was made up of characters whom he knew firsthand. His knowledge was not sociological. Rather, he was directly acquainted with the experience of suffering and the injustices of the world. He harbored a certain tragic view of human nature, one that relied upon a moral conception that saw the world as irrevocably divided between the weak and the strong. In a society consisting of bad wolves and little red riding hoods, the job of the police was to intervene wherever groups of predators lay in wait, ready to attack the helpless and the vulnerable.

These stories occurred in the Buenos Aires of the 1920s and 1930s, where upward mobility was, despite some oscillations, a dominant trend. The *barrio* was the most emblematic product of this process, and the patrolman who watched over it represented the guarantee of an order that was identified with the values of upwardly mobile social groups. Nevertheless, the narratives of the humane policeman described a society that was static and dichotomous, an essentially unfair order of asymmetrical and irreconcilable poles. This society resembled that of popular fiction rather than the real social context: it belonged to a "melodramatic nation" where the aesthetics and languages of those "from below" were exalted at the expense of values associated with the well-to-do.[43]

The hero of the "police melodrama" had distinctive class origins. His moral force stemmed from his otherness in relation to the rich and powerful, and from his display, anecdote by anecdote, of empathy for the weak. The world of the rich was remote territory, mined with moral hazards, a place that promised little more than humiliation for the policeman who was required to travel through it:

> "You have to quiet the vices and miseries of the empty aristocracy," says a Divine Voice to the street officer. "Still, you must defer to them, hiding the repugnant blight they carry into the street [whenever they] cross the thresholds of their palaces. You see them passing in their luxurious automobiles, their squalid faces stupefied by alcohol and alkaloids as they return from their orgies, and you must tolerate their imbecilic whims, help them if you must, to walk up to their doorways and place the key in the lock. You are everything, dear officer, and you are nothing."[44]

With manly disdain, the policeman portrayed the artificial and fundamentally corrupted world in which the privileged lived. "Surrounded by aristocratic palaces," he stood at the corner enduring the cold and the rain, proudly keeping his chin up.[45] *Gaceta Policial* never tired of telling the story of the moral bankruptcy of the powerful—their cocaine addictions, their dark financial maneuvers. An editorial in its anniversary edition of 1930 opened thus: "*Gaceta Policial* is a solid supporter of the social order, as long as it is understood that the powerful are not the only ones in need of protection."[46] Police sensibility was anti-revolutionary and anti-bourgeois. But most of all, it was anti-elitist.

The radio theater show *El hijo del vigilante* (The Watchman's Son) described the discrimination suffered by Calixto, a poor policeman's son who went to school with wealthy children. Insolent and lacking in manners, Calixto's schoolmates ridicule him:

> *Juancito:* (Yelling from far away) Che, *vigilante*, pass me the ball!
>
> *Pedrito:* (Laughing) Ha-ha! . . . *vigilante!* . . .
>
> *Juancito:* My father's a doctor. I think they're going to make him a congressman."

During recess, Calixto listens quietly to conversations about family *estancias* and vacations in Mar del Plata. The boy belongs to a class that does not enjoy such luxuries. He is, moreover, the son of a policeman—the most questioned of lower-class occupations. The great moral revelation occurs in the final act: Calixto's father died defending the victim of a robbery. In the end, the officer's sacrifice wins the child the admiration of his wealthy companions. The resolution is cloaked in the language of heroism:

> It seemed like right at that moment the social and economical differences had ended forever. Now, in the midst of that scene, there was only one difference between them, both true and profound, the real difference that distinguished one man from another: heroism. And the son of Agent Sánchez was, for all of his classmates, the son of a hero. THE END.[47]

In this imaginary world, then, empathy did not entail closeness with the upper classes. But neither did it bring policemen closer to organized labor. The territory of intervention of the *porteño* cop was not the factory, the union, the barricade, or the assembly. His stage was the *barrio* street, where the *characters* of injustice—those who needed his protection—walked by. When an anarchist entered that scene, his political condition was immediately absorbed into that same world of moral melodrama in which an encounter was possible because, ultimately, he was just another victim—more idealistic, perhaps more cultivated, but a victim nonetheless. Police melodrama was infused with the emotions of the social diminutive. It was an effort to reconcile the law of the state and human law (understood in densely sentimental terms).

It was not easy to integrate the police "snitch" into the pantheon of virtuous characters that made up the "police family." He was an invisible figure, alluded to only in passing and largely thought to contaminate the institution's image. Only once did *Magazine Policial* take on this figure, publishing the modest "Elogio del botón reo" (In Praise of the Rough Snitch) in 1933. Written in Lunfardo and signed by "Armando Escolaso" (Armando Gambling), the ode dedicated a few words of encouragement to this figure. "We need to somehow thank you for all you do in the saintly ministry of your caging [*encanadora*] profession."[48] In this view, the informant was seen as another proletarian: he lived in "a dive in the distant suburb, on a street you'd need to look up in the *Peuser* atlas." He got up "when the hands on the *reló de lata* [tin clock] hadn't even dreamed of striking shabby old 5 in the morning." He drank his *mate* quickly and kissed his wife, who responded: "Come home early, *papito*." He walked twelve blocks to "catch the bus that dropped [him] off right at the [police] station." Then the snitch began his eight-hour shift walking the streets, keeping an eye out for any information that might be of use. Meanwhile, when children walked by on their way to school, he was reminded of his own son. A drunk appeared, but the snitch pretended not to notice. He didn't want to have to carry him back to the station. He smoked a *pucho* (cigarette), taking his time. Throughout the day there would be many occasions to look the other way. However, the snitch followed his contract with the police to the letter when "the filthy rich owner of an ostentatious car" tried to bribe him, hoping to avoid being reported for an infraction. "You closed your eyes so as not to fall into the temptation of taking that money, and grumpily, you knew how to be more honorable than the rich slob [*bacán*] that tried to pay you off."

The motif of maternal sacrifice, so typical of tango lyrics and mass-market literature, is a fixture of police narrative to this day. Its leading character is the *mater dolorosa*, the policeman's suffering mother, who made the ultimate sacrifice for the good of society. The widowed elderly lady, who before he started his rounds would warn her son about the dangers of the street, was a cornerstone of the great institutional theme of the fallen cop. She presided over the commemoration of "our dead" and was an essential element of every anecdote aimed at solidifying a sense of belonging based on "common pain."

In other respects, the *mater dolorosa* was linked to the criminal. In this world—the school of pain (*escuela del dolor*)—the affective bond was more important than anything else, including the law. Insofar as life found them sharing the same emotions, the suffering of mothers (and fathers) was conceived in terms that joined those on both sides of the law. Likewise, it was this sentimental empathy that connected the model officer with the subjects under his power (a relationship also described as that of an adult watching over sleeping children).

Thus, the police melodrama recounted time and again the discovery of a virtue that had been invisible or dismissed, hidden under misleading appearances. In his study of the genre, Peter Brooks sees melodrama as placing virtue at the center of the scene. It is a spectacular tribute to virtue, a demonstration of its power and its effects. It is also the story of the concealment of virtue, and therefore the drama of its discovery.[49] What was it that was impeding the social perception and recognition of police virtue? Perhaps it was the uniform, or the intimidating weapons. It might also have been the very humbleness of this public servant, who was *erroneously* feared. Also, the humbleness of his class and his vocation contrasted with the frivolous characters of the prideful metropolis. In this universe of blazing moral clarity, each was in his place, and the reader knew who was who.

Underlying the tale of the discovery of police virtue, however, was an ambivalent relationship with the law, one in which the emphasis on the human sensitivity of the good policeman constructed a form of authority that resided above, or in the interstices, of the law. He was capable of making imperceptible legal accommodations, always based on his human experience and tutelary mission. Here is where the theme of the pact between policeman and transgressor arose, made in the name of an unwritten moral code that connected these two street-level actors beyond their standing in the eyes of the law. (This virtuous pact was the counter-figure to the spurious pact represented as "police shenanigans," or corruption, a regular feature in *Crítica*'s headlines).

The plausibility of the pact between the thief and the benign policeman lay in its power to distinguish between those who committed crime with evil intent and those who did so out of necessity. Such was the case of the official who crossed paths with the criminal Bloisi in the radio program "La captura." In the opening scene, listeners are made aware of the fact that the much-feared Bloisi has his own "poor, suffering mother." At the very moment when the hero of the story has trapped the criminal, a character enters the scene to announce that the criminal's mother has died:

(TIN, TAN, TÓN)

Policeman (Soft voice, tender): Bloisi . . .

Bloisi (Overwhelmed): Take me away, sir. . . . It doesn't matter anymore.

Policeman (Moved): No, Bloisi. You are still a man. I have a mission to follow. But . . . promise me that you will not escape and . . .

Bloisi (Hopeful): And what, Sir? What? . . .

Policeman: And . . . I will allow you to see your poor mother.[50]

This decision to postpone Bloisi's punishment is rewarded when the thief, honoring his part of the deal, turns himself in the next day, allowing the rule of law to take its course. The policeman tells him: "I have lied for you. Perhaps I've done something wrong . . . I haven't done my duty . . . but it doesn't matter. I too am a son and, like you, have an old mother." The emotional identification between the criminal and policeman is finally sealed when Bloisi confesses, telling the tale of his descent into crime. The policeman encourages this frankness by refusing to arrest him and by letting slip that he himself is a writer. The thief's story includes all the tropes of social melodrama: the impoverished upbringing, his sister's tuberculosis, his mother's suffering, and the inhuman working conditions at his factory job. The guilty party is not the alleged thief, but the cigar-smoking factory boss, indifferent to human suffering.

The idea of an opposition between the thief and the policeman no longer depended on the equivalence between the moral and the legal. In the world of melodrama, the best cop was not the one who used modern techniques or diligently applied the law, but rather the one who had the same notions of justice and injustice as the rest of society: on the side of the "good and weak" and against the "bad and strong." Upon these concepts rested the sustainability of the alliance between the listeners of the *Ronda Policial* and the state agents of order. On either side of the radio receiver, listeners knew that carrying out police duties meant, at times, deciding not to punish the offender. Like Radio Porteña's audiences, the police officer was sensitive to human suffering. Between them, understanding was possible because his commitment to easing pain was stronger than his allegiance to the law.

Here is where the crucial question of police discretion reappeared. Those who would idealize the *vigilante* did not counter press accusations with fables of attachment to legal order. Far from covering up the beat cop's discretionary leeway, those fables exalted it as providing the very margin of decision required to display an understanding of what was socially fair. These police melodramas pointed not to the law, but rather to the *benign* use of discretion as that which allowed the policeman to decide when to use force and when to forgive. Police abuse coexisted with the wise discretion of the corner policeman, with the virtuous *restriction* of a power that was not amorphous, but informed by the landmarks of a just sentimental order.

POLICE AND SOCIAL CONFLICT

If melodrama situated the policeman in a logic of clear moral superiority, his role in social conflict introduced much more resistant ideological and narrative tensions. The coexistence of the watchman as friend-of-the-dispossessed and the policeman as guardian-of-the-status quo (whose task consisted of spying on those who dissented with this unfair order) brought up the obvious question of the moral foundations of the institution's mission. As we have seen, consensus around the repression of protest cannot be explained through class identification. The question about the place of the political enemy in the moral universe of the ideal policeman needs to take into account a fact that is often overlooked: the police's role as guarantor of the established order did not in itself create an identity in tune (or in economic alliance, or aesthetic fascination) with the upper classes. On the contrary, the evidence points to a marked otherness in relation to the tastes and sensibilities of the wealthy, whose interests were protected as a duty rather than as a calling.

How could the surveillance and control of the working classes be seen as legitimate when the class and vital concerns of the working poor were presented as being identical to those of the policeman? One clue lies in the religious elements of this imaginary. The influence of Catholic social thought of the 1920s and 1930s in police discourse became apparent as time went on, as the eclectic tolerance of the 1920s gave way to the emergence of a Christian renaissance. Monsignor Dionisio Napal (the army's vicar) was, in the mid-1930s, the cultural and ideological star of *Magazine Policial,* the same publication that had not long before looked favorably upon certain anticlerical voices. Napal's *El imperio soviético,* an anti-communist manual republished at various points over the course of the 1930s, gradually displaced—both in column-inches and editorial emphasis—every other reading recommendation proffered to the "police family." By then, the above-mentioned Russian authors included dissidents denouncing the abuses of the communist regime.

The stigmatization of the political activist might be attributed to this greater ideological context and linked to other examples of polarization in the 1930s, a period when nuances were erased and positions hardened. By then, however, the symbolic construction of the left-wing activist had an endogenous tradition that preceded Catholic anti-communism. The singular levels of repression during this period were part of a long history of police intervention in the political arena. The expulsion of the dissident had roots in a police culture that was *complemented* by the context of the anti-liberal and anti-communist reaction of the 1930s, but was quite compatible with other ideological frames of reference.

Here a line was drawn, setting artists and writers apart from the broader cultural field of the Left (whose knowledge might be useful or even enjoyed by the metropolitan policeman), apart from leftist agitators who were incompatible with his most fundamental ideals of order. This explains the presence of communist or anarchist authors in police magazines. Another line distinguished the idiosyncratic details of *this* agitator (whose misadventures might be narrated with sympathy in police anecdotes) from those of the abstract activist, with whom no association was possible. A third separation occurred between the weak members of society (who deserved a better world and relied on an alliance with the policeman to protect them from harm) and those who *pretended* to save the weak by going on strike and throwing bombs. If the law was not a dominant theme in the imaginary of the police, order was. One last opposition completed the system: that existing between *criollo* familiarity with the point of view of the worker-ally of the police—justly indignant, conservative in his resigned view of the world—and the exotic jargon of the worker who had been colonized by foreign interests. The Ukrainian Argentine worker and anarchist Simón Radowitzky served as a foil for police identity insofar as he was juxtaposed with the greatest police martyr, Falcón, and was constantly resignified as an emblem of "foreignness." Far from putting at risk the alliance between the police and the people's point of view, the war against Radowitzky (and his emulators) consolidated it.

This perspective found its most articulate representation in police historiography. Eager to control its institutional memory, the Capital

Police had always tended toward laborious reconstructions of its past. In the Peronist years, when the idea of a utopia of unity between the people and the police conquered the mainstream official discourse (in which the good policeman of the present was contrasted with the wicked policeman of the past), the question of the prior handling of social conflict became critical.

In those years, three police officers published testimonial books about the Semana Trágica (Tragic Week), a traumatic massacre of workers following a strike in January 1919:[51] *La Semana Trágica: Enero de 1919,* by Commissioner Cortés Conde; *La Semana Trágica,* by Commissioner José R. Romariz; and *Los orígenes y la Semana Trágica de enero de 1919,* by police officer Octavio Piñero.[52] These authors were of different political persuasions. Cortés Conde had opposed the rise of Peronists within the institution and was, in fact, a somewhat solitary ally of those members of the military who resisted Perón's rise in 1945. Romariz's version of events, which relied upon an opposition between a dark past and a shining present, showed his full commitment to the Peronist order installed in 1946. Piñero, for his part, was a Radical Yrigoyenist. Despite these differences, all three narratives bore the mark of the advent of Peronism, and thus greater recognition for the working classes. Uncomfortable questions arose regarding the former police alliance with the established political and economic powers. Thus, the narrative of the Semana Trágica was invested with a paradigmatic quality that allowed it to organize themes of police identity and propose an ideal version of the relationship between the police and the people.

That narrative can be summarized as follows. In January 1919, pushed by miserable working conditions, meager wages, and greedy bosses, the workers of the Vasena factory went on strike. The reasonable demands of *real* workers were co-opted and exploited by foreign agitators and an irresponsible leftist press. The real culprits were the bosses, the agitators, and the yellow journalists. The well-meaning majority was dragged along by a small group: "Working people of this country, who are naturally peaceful and traditionally honest, were poorly equipped to distinguish between their own needs and the ambitions of the leaders."[53] Romariz sketched out workers' desolate conditions with imagery that was reminiscent of Russian social literature, even citing Gorki when describing the "non-men" of the dispossessed groups. Here, the "authentic" workers were gentle people opposed to extremist ideas.[54]

All three authors strove to establish their personal sympathy for even the most politically involved workers. Piñero praised the pioneer initiatives of early twentieth-century socialism. Cortés Conde explained the distinction between professional agitators and "the idealist who dreams of a better humankind." Romariz talked about his enthusiastic participation in the socialist demonstrations of his youth, "enjoying my role as bourgeois-hater."[55] There were many just and sincere participants in the Semana Trágica. The cause of the outbreak of violence was the opposition between the false workers and the bad bosses. Misled in their loyalties, the police were instructed by their superiors to align themselves with the latter, while everything in their nature and social composition pulled them in the opposite direction (the same direction that had prevailed in the form of Peronism, according to Romariz).

Exposed to the explosive results of the war between capital and labor were rank-and-file policemen (as distinct from *the* police) who were human, scared, confused, and lost in a chaotic landscape of shootings. In certain passages, the patrolmen were portrayed as victims in terms similar to those used to describe fallen civilians, everyone trapped in a confusing theater of forces that overwhelmed them. "We, the modest officials and humble agents of the institution, didn't count at all in the game of opposing interests," said Romariz.[56] The erasure of the line between repressors and repressed was clear in his description of the disposition of corpses: at the morgue, dead policemen were identified in a rush to be thrown inside a truck full of dead bodies. "There they piled up in grotesque positions and their identification papers fell in a mess at the bottom. What did it matter? The poor souls who lost their lives in the Semana Trágica, even the police officers who were sacrificed for the sake of the mission, had no flowers, tears, prayers recited over their tombs." Those who had opposed each other at the barricades—working-class activists and rank-and-file policemen—were now materially mixed in the crematorium.[57]

Police narratives of the Semana Trágica confirmed that despite appearances, there was a deep connection between the police and the people. Ultimately, the heart of this tale of social conflict lay in the minute experiences of its actors, highlighting their helplessness in the grand scheme of alignments. The common policeman emerged morally intact. The only measure of his heroism was the extent of his sacrifice. His enemies—the unscrupulous upper classes, the foreign agitators—were no different from the enemies of the working majorities. Any repressive initiative led by the institutional hierarchy would have to take into account this distinction between good and bad workers, weak and strong, the interests of the people and those of the oligarchy. When

Peronism redefined the targets of surveillance as communist militants, dissident students, and politicians allied with the rich, it was only making official this preexisting symbolic configuration of the relationship between people and police.

Persuading society about the rightness of using force in order to maintain the established order has always been a major challenge for modern police agencies. To be effective, police interventions require that civilians be convinced about the fundamental justice of this power—a difficult task, considering the precarious legal foundations of police power and its obvious use of force. Just as important, police agencies require that rank-and-file policemen—recruited mostly from the working classes—be certain about the legitimacy of their right to repress social protest.

The history of the police construction of the figure of the virtuous Buenos Aires neighborhood cop reveals the complexities involved in this task of persuasion. Contrary to the widespread notion of a police culture cut off from mainstream culture, the successful mythology of the *vigilante*—born in the 1920s and 1930s and alive still to this day—functioned in connection with (rather than separation from) the symbolic universe of popular culture and mass entertainment.

Of course, the ideological success of the *vigilante* did not translate into widespread acceptance of the Buenos Aires police, whose power has always been (and still remains) routinely contested. But current opinion polls show that even the most critical discourses tend to distinguish the "good" neighborhood cop from the abusive, corrupt cop. Moreover, there is ample evidence for the key role played by this figure in the informal mechanisms of identity building within the institution. The notion of a deep bond between rank-and-file policemen and the most vulnerable members of society, routinely reinforced in accounts of instances of social sensitivity, was critical in reconciling even the most traumatic episodes, including massacres of workers, with notions of social justice. In times of social harmony, the picture of the policeman as micro-manager of neighborhood conflicts consolidated the notion that good police discretion is often better than impersonal law enforcement.

Notes

INTRODUCTION

1. Richard Walter, *Politics and Urban Growth in Buenos Aires, 1910–1942* (Cambridge: Cambridge University Press, 1993); Francis Korn, *Buenos Aires: Los huéspedes del 20* (Buenos Aires: Sudamericana, 1974); Francis Korn and Luis A. Romero, eds., *Buenos Aires/entreguerras: La callada transformación* (Buenos Aires: Alianza, 2006); Francis Korn, *Buenos Aires: Mundos particulares* (Buenos Aires: Sudamericana, 2004).

2. In the 1890s, 14 percent of the U.S. population, compared to more than 25 percent in Argentina, were immigrants. In 1910, the percentage was still 14.5 in North America, whereas the 1914 Argentine census showed that 30 percent of the population had been born elsewhere. This average proportion was much higher in the city of Buenos Aires. Fernando Devoto, *Historia de la inmigración en la Argentina* (Buenos Aires: Sudamericana, 2003), 49.

3. Cited by Walter, *Politics and Urban Growth*, 84.

4. Horacio Torres, "Evolución de los procesos de estructuración espacial urbana: El caso de Buenos Aires," *Desarrollo Económico* 15, no. 58 (July–September 1975): 281–306; James Scobie, *Buenos Aires: Plaza to Suburb (1870–1910)* (Oxford: Oxford University Press, 1974), chaps. 3 and 5.

5. Leandro Gutiérrez and Luis A. Romero, *Sectores populares, cultura y política: Buenos Aires en la entreguerra* (Buenos Aires: Sudamericana, 1995); Adrián Gorelik, *La grilla y el parque: Espacio público y cultura urbana en Buenos Aires, 1887–1936* (Bernal: UNQ, 1998); Diego Armus, ed., *Mundo urbano y cultura popular: Estudios de historia social Argentina* (Buenos Aires: Sudamericana, 1990); Luciano De Privitellio, *Vecinos y ciudadanos: Política y sociedad en la Buenos Aires de entreguerras* (Buenos Aires: Siglo XXI, 2003); Ezequiel Adamovsky, *Historia de la clase media argentina: Apogeo y decadencia de una ilusión, 1919–2003* (Buenos Aires: Planeta, 2009).

6. The Capital Police was established in 1880, when Buenos Aires became the nation's capital. Until then, the old Policía de Buenos Aires had jurisdiction over the city and the province of Buenos Aires—a major district covering 10 percent of the country's territory. Throughout the period covered in this book, the Capital Police's legal jurisdiction covered the city of Buenos Aires only, while the province of Buenos Aires had its own, separate, Buenos Aires Province Police. In 1943, the Capital Police became the Argentine Federal Police (Policía Federal Argentina), retaining its jurisdiction over the city. This situation would last until 2010, when the Policía Metropolitana was created, with specific municipal jurisdiction.

7. Beatriz Sarlo, *Una modernidad periférica: Buenos Aires 1920 y 1930* (Buenos Aires: Nueva Visión, 1988); Beatriz Sarlo, *La imaginación técnica: Sueños modernos de la cultura argentina* (Buenos Aires: Nueva Visión, 1992).

8. Pierre Bourdieu, *Outline of a Theory of Practice,* translated by Richard Nice (Cambridge: Cambridge University Press, 1977), 3.

9. Even if things don't have meaning beyond the one attributed by human interaction, says Arjun Appadurai, this does not preclude the fundamental question about the historical circulation of objects. For that purpose, one needs to follow the trail of things themselves, desciphering the meanings embedded in their shape, uses, and trajectories. Arjun Appadurai, ed., *The Social Life of Things: Commodities in Cultural Perspective* (Cambridge: Cambridge University Press, 1988), 4.

10. Susana Torrado, "Estrategias de desarrollo, estructura social y movilidad," in *Una historia social del siglo XX,* vol. 1 (Buenos Aires: Edhasa, 2007), 37.

11. Peter Fritzsche, "On Nostalgia, Exile, and Modernity," *American Historical Review* 16, no. 5 (December 2001): 1587–1618.

12. María Teresa Gramuglio, "Estudio preliminar," in *El diario de Gabriel Quiroga,* edited by Manuel Gálvez (Buenos Aires: Taurus, 2001), 9–52; Jean Delaney, "Imagining *El ser Argentino:* Cultural Nationalism and Romantic Concepts of Nationhood in Early Twentieth-Century Argentina," *Journal of Latin American Studies* 34, no. 3 (August 2002): 625–58.

13. On 1920s Argentine mass Catholicism, see Miranda Lida: "Católicos Roaring Twenties," in *Historia del catolicismo en la Argentina, entre el siglo XIX y el XX* (Buenos Aires: Siglo XXI, 2015), 91–117.

14. On the distributive effect of the 1920s bonanza, see Pablo Gerchunoff and Horacio Aguirre, "La economía argentina entre la gran guerra y la depresión," *Estudios y perspectivas* no. 32 (CEPAL, Buenos Aires, May 2006), 42; on the recovery from the 1930s crisis, see Claudio Bellini, "El proceso económico," in *Argentina: Mirando hacia dentro,* edited by Alejandro Cattaruzza (Madrid: Mapfre/Taurus, 2012), 144–46.

15. Tulio Halperín Donghi, *La Argentina y la tormenta del mundo: Ideas e ideologías entre 1930 y 1945* (Buenos Aires: Siglo XXI, 2003).

16. The description of the 1930s as an era of fraudulent politics is quite justified. On September 6, 1930, democratically elected Radical president Hipólito Yrigoyen (1916–22 and 1928–30) was ousted by a military coup led by General José Félix Uriburu. His short administration would end in 1932, with the rise of General Justo (1932–38), leader of a coalition that won elec-

tions as a result of the abstention of the Radical Party. After 1935, when Radical candidates began to participate, elections were grossly manipulated. In this context of explicit fraud, Justo's presidency was followed by those of two other Conservatives, Roberto Ortiz (1938–40) and Ramón Castillo (1940–43). The politics of fraud would end with a new military coup, in 1943, and the rise to power of Colonel Juan Perón. Luciano De Privitellio, "La vida política," in *Mirando hacia dentro*, 39–66.

17. On the theoretical premises of cultural criminology, see J. Ferrell, K. Hayward, and J. Young, *Cultural Criminology: An Invitation* (London: Sage, 2008), 1–29.

18. Lila Caimari, *Apenas un delincuente: Crimen, castigo y cultura en la Argentina, 1880–1955* (Buenos Aires: Siglo XXI, 2004), 124–35.

19. Ricardo Rodríguez Molas, *Historia de la tortura y el orden represivo en la Argentina* (Buenos Aires: CEAL, 1985). Laura Kalmanowiecki's pioneering work also asks hard questions about the political police of the late twentieth century: "Military Power and Policing in Argentina, 1900–1955" (PhD diss., New School for Social Research, 1995). See also Martin Edwin Andersen, *La policía: Pasado, presente y propuestas para el futuro* (Buenos Aires: Sudamericana, 2002).

20. In his critical assessment of this state of affairs, Marcelo Sain points to the unproductive overlap between the common sense of social science and the generic critique of the police among the politically progressive. A system of mutual reinforcement, he argues, has conspired to confuse the most basic questions about the institution; see "La policía en las ciencias sociales: Ensayo sobre los obstáculos epistemológicos para el estudio de la institución policial en el campo de las ciencias sociales," in *Estudiar la policía: La mirada de las ciencias sociales sobre la institución policial*, edited by Mariana Sirimarco (Buenos Aires: Teseo, 2010), 27.

21. Michel Foucault, *Seguridad, territorio, población: Curso en el Collège de France (1977–1978)* (Buenos Aires: Fondo de Cultura Económica, 2006), 374 (my translation). For the English version see *Security, Territory, Population: Lectures at the Collège de France, 1977–78,* edited by Michel Senellart, translated by Graham Burchell (Basingstoke: Picador, 2009).

22. On the challenges faced by researchers who work with Argentine police archives, see Lila Caimari and Mariana Nazar, "Detrás de una puerta gris: Notas sobre los archivos policiales públicos argentinos," in *From the Ashes of History: Loss and Recovery of Archives and Libraries in Modern Latin America*, edited by Carlos Aguirre and Javier Villa-Flores (Raleigh, NC: Ed. A Contracorriente, 2015), 117–44.

23. Eric Monkkonen, "From Cop History to Social History: The Significance of Police in American History," *Journal of Social History* 15, no. 4 (Summer 1982): 577.

24. Mark Neocleous, *The Fabrication of Social Order: A Critical Theory of Police Power* (London: Pluto Press, 2000), 5.

25. I borrow the notion of "domestic police" from Hélène L'Heuillet, *Baja política, alta policía: Un enfoque histórico y filosófico de la policía* (Buenos Aires: Prometeo, 2010), 152. Like L'Heuillet and other authors, I draw from

Norbert Elias's seminal *The Civilizing Process: Sociogenetic and Psychogenetic Investigations* (Oxford: Blackwell, 2000 [1936]) for my analysis of police surveillance of customs and habits.

26. Michel Foucault, "'*Omnes et singulatim*': Vers une critique de la raison politique," *Dits et écrits II, 1976–1988* (Paris: Quarto-Gallimard, 2001), 955.

27. J-M. Berlière et al., eds., *Métiers de police: Être policier en Europe, XVI-IIe–XXe siècle* (Rennes: Presses Universitaires de Rennes, 2008); C. Emsley and B. Weimberg, *Policing Western Europe: Politics, Professionalism and Public Order (1850–1940)* (Westport, CT: Greenwood Press, 1991); Clive Emsley, *The English Police: A Political and Social History* (London: Longman, 1996); Monkkonen, "From Cop History to Social History." I also consulted the studies available on the Criminocorpus website about the history of the French police: http://www.criminocorpus.cnrs.fr

28. Caimari, *Apenas un delincuente,* chap. 5.

CHAPTER 1. *PISTOLEROS*

1. "Asaltaron a un pagador de las obras sanitarias: Atacaron a balazos al auto en que viajaba, robando 286.000 pesos," *Crítica,* October 3, 1930, 1.

2. *RP,* January 16, 1927, 70.

3. Ibid.

4. Edwin Sutherland's classic study *Principles of Criminology* (Chicago: Lippincott, 1934) was published in the postcrisis period and avoided depicting the Depression as an exclusive factor in its explanations of urban crime.

5. M. Fishman, "Crime Waves as Ideology," *Social Problems* 25 (1978): 531; J. Sheley and C. Ashkins, "Crime, Crime News, and Crime Views," *Public Opinion Quarterly* 45 (1981): 492.

6. The epigraph is from Jorge Luis Borges, *Evaristo Carriego: A Book about Old-Time Buenos Aires,* translated and introduced by Norman Thomas Di Giovanni (New York: E.P. Dutton, 1984 [1930]), 116.

7. Raúl García Heras, *Automotores norteamericanos, caminos y modernización urbana en la Argentina, 1918–1939* (Buenos Aires: Libros de Hispanoamérica, 1985).

8. Fernando Rocchi, "La americanización del consumo: Las batallas por el mercado argentino, 1926–1945," in *Americanización: Estados Unidos y América Latina en el siglo XX: Transferencias económicas, tecnológicas y culturales,* edited by M. Inés Barbero and Andrés Regalsky (Buenos Aires: EdunTref, 2003), 149; Anahí Ballent, "Kilómetro cero: La construcción del universo simbólico del camino en la Argentina de los años treinta," *Boletín del Instituto de Historia Argentina y Americana "Dr Emilio Ravignani,"* 3rd ser., 27 (2005): 108–37.

9. "Candidatos a millonarios," *EM,* December 21, 1929.

10. "La invasión de los automóviles," *CC,* April 9, 1927.

11. Manuel Gálvez, "La tragedia de un hombre honrado," in *Una mujer muy moderna* (Buenos Aires: Tor, 1927), 153.

12. OD, July 20, 1934, 873.

13. Borges, *Evaristo Carriego,* 113–14. Adrián Gorelik has noted the antitechnological underpinnings of this story in *La grilla y el parque: Espacio*

público y cultura urbana en Buenos Aires, 1887–1936 (Bernal: Universidad Nacional de Quilmes, 1998), 409. On Borges's encounter with the city in the 1920s, see Beatriz Sarlo, "Orillero y ultraísta," in *Escritos sobre literatura argentina* (Buenos Aires: Siglo XXI, 2007), 149.

14. On the association between the automobile and sexual freedom, see Guillermo Giucci, *La vida cultural del automóvil: Rutas de la modernidad cinética* (Bernal: Universidad Nacional de Quilmes/Prometeo, 2007), 187.

15. "La División Investigaciones realiza una importante pesquisa con motivo de los numerosos robos de automóviles," *RP,* June 1, 1929, 658. On the "spiantadores" see M. Barrés, *El hampa y sus secretos* (Buenos Aires: Imprenta López, 1934), 126.

16. Roberto Arlt, "El arte de robar automóviles," *EM,* May 22, 1929.

17. "Delincuentes audaces," *RP,* September 16, 1927, 769.

18. "Será posible detener ahora la marcha de los automóviles," *EM,* January 14, 1932, 12.

19. Ramón Cortés Conde, *Cómo nos roban: Los secretos del mundo delincuente; Los más famosos cuentos del tío; Ardides, engaños, sistemas y métodos que utilizan los malhechores para estafarnos* (Buenos Aires: Editorial Olivé, 1943), 70.

20. "Una sola hipótesis: El raid fue el resultado del miedo," *EM,* January 27, 1937, 26; "Característica de la banda: El raid," *EM,* January 28, 1937, 10.

21. On the "road bandits" of the 1930s in the United States, see Claire Bond Potter, *War on Crime: Bandits, G-Men, and the Politics of Mass Culture* (Rutgers, NJ: Rutgers University Press, 1998), 57–73.

22. "De un momento a otro caerá en poder de la policía la banda de El Pibe Cabeza," *EM,* January 28, 1937, 10.

23. Ibid.

24. "Nuevas formas de la delincuencia," *RP,* January 1, 1906, 120.

25. Ramón Cortés Conde, *Historia de la policía de la ciudad de Buenos Aires: Su desenvolvimiento, organización actual y distribución de sus servicios* (Buenos Aires: Imprenta López, 1933), 318; "Sobre Policía Federal habló el Inspector General Viancarlos," *Radiópolis–MP,* August 1938; Martin Andersen, *La Policía: Pasado, presente y propuestas para el futuro* (Buenos Aires: Sudamericana, 2002), 127. The initiatives to create the Gendarmería and the Federal Police were modeled on the FBI, which was redesigned by Hoover at the beginning of the 1930s in reaction to U.S. "automobile bands." See Bond Potter, *War on Crime,* chap. 4.

26. On the expansion of the road network during the 1930s see A. Ballent and A. Gorelik, "País urbano o país rural: La modernización territorial y su crisis," in *Crisis económica, del estado e incertidumbre política, 1930–1943,* edited by Alejandro Cattaruzza (Buenos Aires: Sudamericana, 2001), 156.

27. The epigraph is from Élmer Mendoza, *Silver Bullets,* translated by Mark Fried (London: MacLehose Press, 2016), 11.

28. Sandra Gayol, *Honor y duelo en la Argentina moderna* (Buenos Aires: Siglo XXI, 2008); Hilda Sabato, *Buenos Aires en armas: La revolución de 1880* (Buenos Aires: Siglo XXI, 2008).

29. Robert Harkavy, *The Arms Trade and International Systems* (Cambridge, MA: Ballinger, 1975), 35. Complaints urging more regulation of the

arms trade can be found in H. C. Engelbrecht and F. C. Hanighen, *Merchants of Death: A Study of the International Armament Industry* (New York: Dodd, Mead, 1934).

30. "Las armas de precisión," *SH*, November 19, 1912.

31. Laurentino Mejías, *Policíacas (mis cuentos)* (Buenos Aires: Tor, 1927), 133.

32. *CC*, May 4, 1929.

33. In English in the original text.

34. Pablo Piccato, *City of Suspects: Crime in Mexico City, 1900–1931* (Durham, NC: Duke University Press, 2001), 99. In this case, the turn to firearms should be understood in the context of revolution and civil war, which accelerated the circulation of arms among vast portions of the population. On the case of São Paulo see Boris Fausto, *Crime e cotidiano: A criminalidade em São Paulo (1880–1924)* (São Paulo: Editora Brasilense, 1984), 95.

35. Rafael Barrett, "El revólver," *MP*, March 1928, 33.

36. This summary comes from a range of newspapers from Buenos Aires and the southern outskirts of the city. On gun use during political rallies, see Marianne González Alemán, "¿Ciudadanos en la calle? Violencia, virilidad y civilidad política en la campaña presidencial porteña de 1928," http://historiapolitica .com/datos/biblioteca/6jornadas/melon_jvi.pdf. The allusion to picnics came from *La Protesta* and *La Antorcha*, quoted in Osvaldo Bayer, *Los anarquistas expropiadores y otros ensayos* (Buenos Aires: Planeta, 2003), 33–34.

37. Dominique Monjardet, *Lo que hace la policía: Sociología de la fuerza pública* (Buenos Aires: Prometeo, 2010), 27.

38. *OD*, July 2, 1932, 1032.

39. Law 11.284 in *OD*, March 20, 1933, 302; *OD*, May 18, 1937, 492. Decrees in 1936 and 1938 are no. 89.159 (August 28, 1936) and no. 102.082 (March 29, 1937), partially reproduced in "Portación de armas," *Revista de Policía de la Provincia de Buenos Aires* 1, no. 9 (January 1942): 69. In 1910, the city police raised the penalty for using and carrying arms to the maximum, although evidence suggests the regulation was not enforced. Ministerio del Interior, *Memoria del Ministerio del Interior, 1920–21*, 178–79. The first national arms registry, the Registro Nacional de Armas (RENAR), was created in 1973.

40. John Ellis, *The Social History of the Machine Gun* (Baltimore: Johns Hopkins University Press, 1975), 152.

41. Narciso Robledal, "La policía lucha contra el enemigo público," *Atlántida*, December 26, 1935, 2; "La represión de la delincuencia," *LL*, January 27, 1933, 2. The ruling on machine guns can be found in "Decreto del Poder Ejecutivo del 23 de septiembre de 1932," in *OD*, September 29, 1318.

42. *Ahora*, March 1, 1940.

43. Jorge Luis Borges, "Death and the Compass," in *Labyrinths: Selected Stories and Other Writings*, translated by Donald A. Yates (New York: New Directions, 1962 [1944]), 79.

44. José María Slavarría, "La muerte del cuchillo," *LN*, June 8, 1911, 6. I owe this reference to Sandra Gayol.

45. Domingo F. Sarmiento, *Facundo: Civilización y barbarie* (Madrid: Letras Hispánicas, 1997 [1845]), 98.

46. *LN*, June 8, 1911.

47. Jack Katz, *Seductions of Crime: Moral and Sensual Attractions in Doing Evil* (New York: Basic Books, 1988); Pat O'Malley and Stephen Mugford, "Crime, Excitement and Modernity," in *Varieties of Criminology: Readings from a Dynamic Discipline,* edited by Gregg Barak (Westport, CT: Praeger, 1994), chap. 10.

48. "Como en el far west: Cuatro hombres armados, uno de los cuales tenía un Winchester, asaltaron al habilitado de la Aduana," *LR,* 4th ed., May 2, 1921, 1.

49. "En Bahía Blanca fue asaltado un pagador del F.C.S.," *LN,* December 10, 1932; "Asaltaron un tren," *Crítica,* December 9, 1932, 1; "El transporte de caudales en camiones blindados," *RP,* January 16, 1933. On Mate Cosido see Osvaldo Aguirre, *Enemigos públicos: Los más buscados en la historia criminal argentina* (Buenos Aires: Aguilar, 2003), chap. 6.

50. Another important instance of ethnic mafias, which does not fit in the framework of *pistolerismo* but does converge with the magnitude of organized crime, was Zwi Migdal, the Jewish-Polish "mutual benefit association" that beginning in 1906 administered an extensive international sex trafficking network. In 1930, after several formal complaints and extensive coverage in the media, the Zwi Migdal was disbarred, and those responsible were convicted.

51. "En pleno día fue perpetrado ayer un audaz asalto en la explanada de acceso al Hospital Rawson," *LN,* October 4, 1927, 7; "Esta tarde, poco antes de las 13, se produjo un audaz asalto frente al Rawson," *LR,* October 3, 1927, 1.

52. Bayer, *Los anarquistas expropiadores;* Luciana Anapios, "Terrorismo o propaganda por el hecho: Los debates sobre la utilización de la violencia en el anarquismo argentino a fines de la década del '20" (paper presented at the Segundas Jornadas de Historia Social, La Falda, Córdoba, May 2009).

53. Luciana Anapios, "El anarquismo argentino en los años veinte: Tres momentos en el conflicto entre *La Protesta* y *La Antorcha*" (IDAES working paper no. 3), http://www.idaes.edu.ar/papelesdetrabajo/paginas/n_anteriores /articulos03.html.

54. A critical profile of "Facha Bruta" can be found in Aguirre, *Enemigos públicos,* chap. 4.

55. *LO,* January 10, 1933. *La Opinión* was a Conservative newspaper published in the suburban town of Quilmes, with circulation in the province of Buenos Aires.

CHAPTER 2. LANGUAGES OF CRIME

1. *CC,* October 15, 1927.

2. Adolfo Prieto, *El discurso criollista en la formación de la Argentina moderna* (Buenos Aires: Sudamericana, 1988); Alejandra Laera, *El tiempo vacío de la ficción: Las novelas argentinas de Eduardo Gutiérrez y Eugenio Cambaceres* (Buenos Aires: Fondo de Cultura Económica, 2003); Josefina Ludmer, *El cuerpo del delito: Un manual* (Buenos Aires: Perfil, 1999).

3. On *Revista Criminal* see Máximo Sozzo, "Retratando al 'Homo criminalis' esencialismo y diferencia en las representaciones 'profanas' del delincuente

en la *Revista Criminal* (Buenos Aires, 1873)," in *La ley de los profanos: Delito, justicia y cultura en Buenos Aires (1880–1940),* edited by Lila Caimari (Buenos Aires: Fondo de Cultura Económica–UdeSA, 2007), 23. On *Tribuna,* see Álvaro Abós, *El crimen de Clorinda Sarracán* (Buenos Aires: Sudamericana, 2003).

4. Various authors have discussed Georg Simmel's hypothesis regarding the neurological dimension of modernity—described in his seminal 1903 article "The Metropole and Mental Life"—as a basis for the analysis of the sensationalistic press of the early twentieth century. On the North American case, see Ben Singer, "Modernity, Hyperstimulus, and the Rise of Popular Sensationalism," in *Cinema and the Invention of Modern Life,* edited by Leo Charney and Vanessa R. Schwartz (Berkeley: University of California Press, 1995), 72; on Berlin, see Peter Fritzsche, *Reading Berlin, 1900* (Cambridge, MA: Harvard University Press, 1996), chap. 4.

5. William Hannigan, "News Noir," in *New York Noir,* 19.

6. Luc Sante, introduction to *New York Noir: Crime Photos from the Daily News Archive* (New York: Rizzoli, 1999), 7. The tabloid format was relatively rare in Argentina; in Buenos Aires, *El Mundo* and *El Pueblo* adopted it in the 1930s.

7. Helen MacGill Hughes, *News and the Human Interest Story* (New Brunswick, NJ: Transaction Books, 1981), 221.

8. [Arthur Fellig] Weegee, *Naked City* (New York: Da Capo Press, 1973 [1945]), 78. On Weegee, see V. Penelope Pelizzon and Nancy M. West, "'Good stories' from the Mean Streets: Weegee and Hard-Boiled Autobiography," *Yale Journal of Criticism* 17, no. 1 (2004): 20–50.

9. Ramón Cortés Conde, *Cómo nos roban* (Buenos Aires: Editorial Olivé, 1943), 71.

10. *Ahora,* March 5, 1940.

11. On *Crítica,* see Sylvia Saítta, *Regueros de tinta: El diario "Crítica" en la década de 1920* (Buenos Aires: Sudamericana, 1998), chap. 6; Lila Caimari, *Apenas un delincuente: Crimen, castigo y cultura en la Argentina moderna* (Buenos Aires: Siglo XXI, 2004), chap. 6.

12. Marcela Gené, "Periodistas del dibujo: Representaciones de crímenes y delincuentes en el diario *Crítica;* Buenos Aires, 1925," *Intercambios* 6 (June 2003), http://www.jursoc.unlp.edu.ar. For a profile of Taborda, see Helvio Botana, *Memorias: Tras los dientes del perro* (Buenos Aires: Peña Lillo, 1985), 44.

13. *Crítica,* October 3, 1932, 7.

14. Jacques Wolff, "Structure, fonctionnement et évolution du marché international des nouvelles: Les agences de presse de 1835 à 1934," *Revue économique* 42, no. 3 (1991): 575–601.

15. Neil Clark, *Stranger Than Fiction: The Life of Edgar Wallace, the Man who Created King Kong* (Stroud, UK: History Press, 2014), 95. In Buenos Aires, the mystery novel and the *noir* novel became popular via the 1940s "Yellow Series" (Editorial Tor), which produced inexpensive translations of works by J.S. Fletcher, Sax Rohmer, Edgar Wallace, Arthur Conan Doyle, Edgar Allan Poe, Gaston Leroux, and Georges Simenon. The masters of the hard-boiled genre, Raymond Chandler and Dashiell Hammett, were also published in Spanish in a number of collections and in the magazine *Leoplán.* When Borges and

Bioy Casares launched their famous series "The Seventh Circle" in 1945, they were bestowing intellectual "dignity" on a genre that was already very popular. Jorge Lafforgue and Jorge B. Rivera, eds., *Asesinos de papel: Ensayos sobre narrativa policial* (Buenos Aires: Colihue, 1996), 14–15.

16. *Crítica*, September 23, 1932, 5.

17. David Ruth, *Inventing the Public Enemy: The Gangster in American Culture, 1918–1934* (Chicago: University of Chicago Press, 1996); Thomas Doherty, *Pre-Code Hollywood: Sex, Immorality, and Insurrection in American Cinema, 1930–1934* (New York: Columbia University Press, 1999), chap. 6.

18. The 1922 data comes from the magazine *La Película*, cited in Andrés Levinson, "Serie argentina de Cinematografía Valle: Comentarios sobre el cine mudo en la Patagonia" (paper presented in the roundtable discussion "Historia, medios y sociedad: Argentina desde fines del siglo XIX hasta la actualidad," XIII Jornadas Interescuelas Departamento de Historia, Catamarca, August 10–13, 2011). On the importation of film material in the Argentine market, see Fernando Rocchi, "La americanización del consumo: Las batallas por el mercado argentino, 1926–1945," in *Americanización: Estados Unidos América Latina en el siglo XX; Transferencias económicas, tecnológicas y culturales,* edited by M.I. Barbero and A. Regalsky (Buenos Aires: EdunTref, 2003) 151. The information on movie theaters in Latin America is from Gaizka Usabel, *The High Noon of American Films in Latin America* (Ann Arbor: UMI Research Press Studies in Cinema, 1982), 126.

19. *El Heraldo del Cinematografista*, April 13, 1932, 163.

20. "En el barrio de Flores, seis pistoleros asaltaron la sucursal de un banco," *LN*, January 3, 1933.

21. Jack Bilbo, *Memorias de un pistolero,* translated by Luis Klappenbach (Buenos Aires: El Ombú, 1933).

22. Roberto Arlt, "Un argentino entre gangsters: Cuento policial," *El Hogar,* February 26, 1937, 6–7; "Está loco o se hace el loco Al Capone?" *EM*, February 12, 1938. Sylvia Saítta discusses Arlt in *El escritor en el bosque de ladrillos: Una biografía de Roberto Arlt* (Buenos Aires: Sudamericana, 2000), 189.

23. "Un émulo de Al Capone," *LN*, January 30, 1931, 1; "Como en Chicago, contra Al Capone," *Crítica*, October 9, 1932, 2. Argentina's first crime movies also imitated Capone. In *Fuera de la ley* (1937, Manuel Romero), the protagonist joins a gang of thieves and kidnappers after reading Capone's biography.

24. Osvaldo Aguirre, *Enemigos públicos: Los más buscados en la historia criminal argentina* (Buenos Aires: Aguilar, 2003), chap. 5.

25. The Ayerza case inspired three movies: *Bajo las garras de la mafia* (1933, Ugo Anselmi), *Asesinos* (1933, José García Silva), and *La maffia* (1972, Leopoldo Torre Nilsson). R. Blanco Pazos and R. Clemente, *De La Fuga a La Fuga: El policial en el cine argentino* (Buenos Aires: Corregidor, 2004), 12.

26. Osvaldo Aguirre carefully reconstructs some of these crimes, which are presented as both the apex and crisis of the Rosario Sicilian mafia. The central questions of my analysis are unrelated to the internal history of the mafia underworld, but I make use of Aguirre's research into the Favelukes and Ayerza cases. Osvaldo Aguirre, *Historias de la mafia en la Argentina* (Buenos Aires: Aguilar, 2000).

27. "Horas de angustia," *Crítica*, October 5, 1932, 2.

28. *EM*, October 8, 1932, 8; *LN*, October 7, 1932, 1; *Crítica*, October 7, 1932, 1.

29. The version of events offered by Favelukes did not correspond to the expectations of the public, and for a few days, his innocence was questioned. "Favelukes lo habría simulado," *Crítica*, October 11, 1932, 1.

30. "El alegre secuestrado," *EM*, October 13, 1932, 6.

31. Some suggest there was an attempt to extort the mafia capo Juan Galiffi by asking for money in exchange for a set of compromising documents. Pretending to accept, the mafioso arranged an interview and riddled the journalist with bullets when he was about to deliver the evidence, according to the story. According to another theory, Alzogaray had reported on the corrupt practices of the Santa Fe police and knew too much about mafia families' connections. Gustavo Germán González, a legendary journalist from *Crítica*'s crime section, affirmed that Alzogaray was killed while extorting Galiffi. *El hampa porteña: 55 años entre policías y delincuentes* (Buenos Aires: Prensa Austral, 1971), vol. 1, 66. Aguirre questions this hypothesis in *Historias de la mafia*, 296. For a retrospective report on the case, see *Ahora*, March 17, 1938.

32. "La bella secuestrada," *Crítica*, October 19, 1932, 18; "¿Qué hay del secuestro de Abel Ayerza?" *Crítica*, December 14, 1932, 9; "¿Abel Ayerza se oculta?" *Crítica*, December 29, 1932, 7.

33. *LN*, February 24, 1933, 7.

34. Ibid., 5.

35. For a pioneering systematic study of this phenomenon, see James Davis, "Crime News in Colorado Newspapers," *American Journal of Sociology* 57, no. 4 (January 1952): 325–30. Examining St. Louis newspapers, E. T. Jones shows that crimes against people received thirty-five times more attention than crimes against property, and that homicide received ninety times more coverage than any other major crime. E. T. Jones, "The Press as Metropolitan Monitor," *Public Opinion Quarterly* 40 (Summer 1976): 239–44.

36. In the 1920s, an ongoing fascination with the miraculous was spurred by the technological "miracles" of communication. Beatriz Sarlo proposes that instead of reducing the attraction of occult knowledge, the radio confirmed the validity of the "modern marvel." Beatriz Sarlo, *La imaginación técnica: Sueños modernos de la cultura argentina* (Buenos Aires: Nueva Visión, 1997), 135.

37. *Crítica*, October 6, 1932, 1.

38. *Crítica*, October 9, 1932, 1 and 3. The police investigation was prolonged two more years. In 1934, the Division of Investigation published a list of those responsible for the kidnapping. The gang members (Simón Samburgo, José Canicatti, Salvador Chiarenza, Felipe Tomaselli, and Miguel Angel Amorelli) were arrested in November. Policía de la Capital, *Memoria de Investigaciones*, 1934, Sección Defraudaciones y Estafas, 81.

39. *LN*, February 25, 1933, 5.

40. Leonardo Castellani, *Martita Ofelia y otros cuentos de fantasmas* (Buenos Aires: Penca, 1944), 33; Franceschi presents this idea in his prologue to *Martita Ofelia*, 13–25.

41. *BA*, October 26, 1932, 1.

42. Castellani, *Martita Ofelia,* 45.

43. The project, discussed in the Senate three months after the burial of Ayerza, took elements from the positivist toolkit, such as the concept of social defense and the legalization of the right to pre-criminal institutionalization of individuals categorized as "dangerous." At the same time, it combined these proposals with a restoration of the death penalty with an air of social retribution that was completely foreign to the theoretic framework of penal positivism.

44. *BA,* October 27, 1932; "Ante el crimen," February 23, 1933; "El apremio y la reforma penal," March 3, 1933.

45. "La urgencia de las reformas," *LN,* December 7, 1932, 6; "El proyecto de reforma del Código Penal," *LP,* December 7, 1932, 11; "La terrible lección," *LR,* February 23, 1933, 1; "Influye en el desborde de la delincuencia la lenidad de nuestra ley penal," *EM,* October 26, 1932, 4.

46. Rodolfo Rivarola, *La justicia en lo criminal: Organización y procedimiento* (Buenos Aires: Félix Lajouane, 1899), 48.

47. Rodolfo Moreno Jr., *El problema penal* (Buenos Aires: Talleres Gráficos Argentinos de L. J. Rosso, 1933), 10.

48. Congreso Nacional, Cámara de Senadores, *Diario de Sesiones,* June 22, 1933, 338. Senator Villafañe's speech contained the most extreme use of ideological terms in the debate. Alfredo Palacios was the main opponent of the project.

49. Eugenio R. Zaffaroni, *Tratado de derecho penal: Parte general I* (Buenos Aires: EDIAR, 1995), 436; Sebastián Soler, *Derecho penal argentino* (Buenos Aires: Tipográfica Editora, 1951), 116. A detailed analysis of the debate can be found in José Peco, *La reforma penal en el Senado en 1933* (La Plata: Instituto de Criminología de la UNLP, 1934).

CHAPTER 3. ORDER AND THE CITY

1. Darío Macor, "Imágenes de los años treinta: La invención de la década del treinta en el debate político intelectual de la Argentina sesentista" (PEIHS working paper no. 3, Centro de Estudios Históricos, Facultad de Formación Docente en Ciencias, Universidad Nacional del Litoral, Santa Fe, 1995).

2. Leandro Gutiérrez and Luis Alberto Romero, *Sectores populares, cultura y política: Buenos Aires en la entreguerra* (Buenos Aires: Sudamericana, 1995); Francis Korn and Luis Alberto Romero, eds., *Buenos Aires/Entreguerras: La callada transformación* (Buenos Aires: Alianza, 2006); Luciano De Privitellio, *Vecinos y ciudadanos: Política y sociedad en la Buenos Aires de entreguerras* (Buenos Aires: Siglo XXI, 2003).

3. Diego Armus, ed., *Mundo urbano y cultura popular: Estudios de historia social argentina* (Buenos Aires: Sudamericana, 1990); Carolina González Velasco, *Gente de teatro: Ocio y espectáculo en la Buenos Aires de los años veinte* (Buenos Aires: Siglo XXI, 2012).

4. Pablo Gerchunoff and Horacio Aguirre, "La economía argentina entre la gran guerra y la depresión" (*Estudios y perspectivas* no. 32, CEPAL, Buenos Aires, May 2006), 42.

5. The state of siege began by decree on September 5, 1930, and continued in the capital for thirty days. On September 6, a proclamation reinstated the

death penalty for an undefined period of time (the measure was used to justify the execution of the anarchist "expropriator" Severino Di Giovanni). On October 4, a new decree prolonged the state of siege "until there is a new resolution." (It was suspended for one day in November 1931, for the elections to take place.) When Justo took power, the state of siege was lifted but it was put back in place that December and then extended though July 6, 1936. Thanks to Mariana Nazar for her help reconstructing this timeline.

6. Yrigoyen was the charismatic leader of the Unión Cívica Radical (UCR), the first democratically elected party after the 1912 passage of the Sáenz Peña electoral law, which regulated universal male suffrage. With a wide base of popular support, Yrigoyen's UCR was elected twice (in 1916 and 1928), with a six-year interlude led by another Radical president, Marcelo T. de Alvear. The UCR was ousted from power by the military coup led by José Félix Uriburu (the first coup of many in modern Argentine history) in September 1930.

7. Policía de la Capital, *Orden del Día Reservada*, February 23, 1932, 3.

8. The División Investigaciones (Division of Investigation) was a descendent of the Comisaría de Pesquisas; it was created and directed by José S. Álvarez (the future writer and journalist Fray Mocho) in 1885 and remained a critical part of the Capital Police. It was headquartered in the Central Department, and its jurisdiction covered the entire city. Beyond the specific areas targeted for political repression, the division included offices on intelligence, such as "Frauds and Scams" and "Robberies and Thefts." An important section specializing in identification was also part of this branch. Other offices included Information, Special Laws, Personal Security, Wharfs, Banks and Theaters, Presidential Custody, Judicial Photography, and so on. The division's archives remained inaccessible when this book was written; its history is yet to be written. A "brief" official history of the División Investigaciones was published in the institutional magazine *Mundo Policial* (nos. 54–76).

9. Hernán Camarero, *A la conquista de la clase obrera: Los comunistas y el mundo del trabajo en la Argentina, 1920–1935* (Buenos Aires: Siglo XXI–Ed. Iberoamericana, 2007).

10. Adolfo Rodríguez, *Historia de la Policía Federal Argentina* (Buenos Aires: Editorial Policial, 1978), vol. 7, 207.

11. Lila Caimari, *Apenas un delincuente: Crimen, castigo y cultura en la Argentina, 1880–1955* (Buenos Aires: Siglo XXI, 2004), 124–35. For a collection of accounts about the Sección Especial, see *Los torturados: La obra criminal de Leopoldo Lugones (hijo); Relato de las víctimas* [Buenos Aires: Editorial Estampa, 1932]. On the human rights organizations of the late 1930s, see Virginia Vecchioli, "La invención de una causa: Un encuentro entre notables y recién llegados del derecho y la política," in *PolHis: Boletín Bibliográfico del Programa Buenos Aires de Historia Política del Siglo XX,* http://historiapolitica.com/datos/biblioteca/JCM_Vecchioli.pdf.

12. The language problem would persist over time: the Sección was often in need of employees who could read Hungarian, Albanian, Lithuanian, Latvian, Armenian, and Turkish.

13. Policía de la Capital, *Memoria de investigaciones,* "Sección Especial," 1932, 78; *Memoria,* 1933, 180.

14. AGN, Ministerio del Interior, Fondo Agustín P. Justo, boxes 45, 46, 47, and 48. Laura Kalmanowiecki reconstructs the opposing sectors' system of control in *Military Power and Policing in Argentina, 1900–1955* (PhD diss., New School for Social Research, 1995), 100; "Origins and Applications of Political Policing in Argentina," *Latin American Perspectives* 27, no. 2 (March 2000): 36–56; and "Police, Politics and Repression in Modern Argentina," in *Reconstructing Criminality in Latin America,* edited by Carlos Aguirre and Robert Buffington (Wilmington, DE: Scholarly Resources, 2000), chap. 9.

15. García assumed leadership of the Capital Police when Justo took power in February 1932. He remained in this position until his death three years later, occupying a relatively long and effective term of leadership. The typical tenure for police chiefs was brief during this period, revealing the position's instability: E. González (1/1919–9/1921), Denovi (9/1921–10/1921), Laguarda (10/1921–11/1921), E. González (11/1921–3/1922), Laguarda (3/1922–3/1922), Bortagaray (3/1922–10/1922), Fernández (10/1922–5/1927), Wright (5/1927–10/1928), Etcheverry (10/1928–10/1928), Graneros (10/1928–9/1930), Hermelo (9/1930–12/1930), Pilotto (12/1930–2/1932), García (2/1932–2/1935), Danieri (2/1935–3/1936), Vacarezza (3/1936–2/1938), Sabalain (2/1938–12/1940), Rosas (12/1940–12/1941), Martínez (12/1941–6/1943).

16. On the problematic legal underpinnings of modern policing, see Paolo Napoli, *Naissance de la police moderne: Pouvoir, normes, société* (Paris: La Découverte, 2003), introduction. On the edict as a source of police power in Buenos Aires, see Sofía Tiscornia, *Activismo de los derechos humanos y burocracias estatales: El caso Bulacio* (Buenos Aires: CELS, 2008), 24.

17. Ana Cecchi, "Esfera pública y juegos de azar: Del meeting contra el juego al allanamiento de domicilio privado; Prensa y parlamento en Buenos Aires, 1901–1902," *Cuadernos de Antropología Social* 32 (2010): 169–94.

18. Edicto de policía, Reuniones públicas, Cámara de Diputados de la Nación, *Diario de Sesiones,* May 11, 1932, 262. The edict on public gatherings would be extended and altered several times over the following years. Ministerio del Interior, Policía de la Capital, *Disposiciones de policía,* book 2 (Buenos Aires: Biblioteca Policial), 1943, 434. For an analysis of this measure's significance in the political context of the new decade, see Marianne González Alemán, "¿Qué hacer con la calle? La definición del espacio público porteño y el edicto policial de 1932," *Boletín del Instituto de Historia Argentina y Americana Dr. Emilio Ravignani* 34 (January 2012): 107–39.

19. AGN, Fondo Ministerio del Interior, 1933, leg. 28, doc. 27.742.

20. Ibid.

21. *Versiones taquigráficas de las sesiones del Honorable Concejo Deliberante de la Ciudad de Buenos Aires,* November–December 1933, 3496. On the origins of Puerto Nuevo's founding, linked to the arrival in 1930 of a boat of unemployed Polish people, see Lidia de la Torre, "La ciudad residual," in *Buenos Aires: Historia de Cuatro Siglos,* by J. L. Romero and L. A. Romero (Buenos Aires: Altamira, 2000), vol. 2, 273.

22. Roberto Arlt, "Desocupados en Puerto Nuevo," *Actualidad: Económica, Política, Social* 3 (June 1932). On the ties between Arlt and Elías Castelnuovo and other communist intellectuals, see Sylvia Saítta, *El escritor en el bosque de*

ladrillos: Una biografía de Roberto Arlt (Buenos Aires: Sudamericana, 2000), chap. 7.

23. *EM*, October 21, 1933, 3; November 4, 1933, 8; November 9, 1933, 12; November 15, 1933, 10; November 23, 1933, 10.

24. Letter from the chief of police, Luis J. García, to the minister of the interior; AGN, Fondo Ministerio del Interior, 1933, leg. 28, doc. 27.742. For an account of regular arrests and requisitions at the Campamento de Desocupados (Camp for the Unemployed), see Natalio Castro, "Recorriendo el campamento de desocupados," in *Relatos de la Oficina de Guardia* (Buenos Aires: Biblioteca Policial, 1937), 47. For a description of the activities of the Sección Especial in Puerto Nuevo, see Kalmanowiecki, *Military Power and Policing*, 190.

25. The lack of documentation makes an evaluation of this strategy difficult, but the press mentions effective "preventative" arrests: "Three individuals were about to commit a criminal act when they fell into the hands of the police"; *EM*, January 15, 1933, 8. The first human rights organizations in the country were established to counter this power—Socorro Rojo and the Liga Argentina por los Derechos del Hombre, both tied to the Communist Party. Evidence suggests that the use of habeas corpus allowed lawyers to mitigate the edicts' effects.

26. The quotes from the 1932 edicts appear in Policía de la Capital, *Nuevos edictos policiales y su reglamentación,* 2nd ed., rev. (Buenos Aires, 1932). In the years following their publication, some were amended or expanded as specific Órdenes del Día.

27. Police records indicate 32 deported in 1932, 448 in 1933, 423 in 1934, and 197 in 1935. Policía de la Capital, *Memoria de Investigaciones,* 1932, 1933, 1934, and 1935, Sección Embarcaderos. The Justo archives record 140 deported between December 19, 1932, and April 28, 1933, plus another 51 in the ten months prior; AGN, Fondo Agustín P. Justo, box 48, docs. 31 and 33. In 1937, the police published a list with another 28 individuals deported through the Ley de Residencia. OD, November 6, 1937, 1070. An example of routine newspaper coverage of these deportations can be found in "Tenebrosos y ladrones son deportados," *EM,* February 9, 1933, 12.

28. *Crítica,* November 21, 1932.

29. "Amigos de la institución y defensores de su causa," *RP,* April 16, 1933, 148; *Radiópolis–MP,* August 1939; Luis Cortés Conde, "Reseña histórica de los Hogares Policiales," *Radiópolis–MP,* May 1945. The police housing project is covered in the magazine *Hogar Policial* (1929–1937).

30. Kalmanowiecki, *Military Power and Policing*, 127–28.

31. Adolfo Rodríguez, *Historia de la Policía Federal Argentina* (Buenos Aires, Editorial Policial, 1978), vol. 7, 230; Ramón Cortés Conde, "El día de la Seguridad Pública y el acercamiento del pueblo a su policía," *MP,* July, 1931, 16; "Radio Nacional es una colaboradora de nuestra policía," *MP,* August 1933.

32. *EM*, July 7, 1931; *RP,* June 16, 1931, 609; *LN*, July 7, 1931, 8.

33. "El pueblo en todas sus esferas ha demostrado su confianza y simpatía a la institución tutelar del orden," *EM,* July 8, 1931, 6.

34. "Memorial dirigido al Honorable Congreso por los señores representantes de las sub-comisiones vecinales de las 46 secciones policiales de la Capital

Federal," June 1933; AHCDN, Particulares, Comisión de Hacienda y Presupuesto, Expediente no. 1336 (01336-P-1934); "La colecta pro-armamento de la policía: Se espera la contribución de los bancos y las fuertes casas de comercio," *RP*, March 16, 1933, 222; "Colecta pro-adquisición de armas para la policía," *RP*, July 1, 1933, 509; OD, July 24, 1931, 706.

35. "Memorial dirigido."

36. "Carta de empresas comerciales de Retiro y Puerto Nuevo solicitando aumento de efectivos policiales"; "Carta apoyo de Federico Devoto, Leopoldo Costa, Matías Ramos Mejía, Ricardo Lavalle, Horacio Rodríguez Gaete, Ing. Antonio Devoto, Dr. Juan Carlos Llames Massini y Manuel Muchio, domiciliados en Callao N 930, componentes de las comisiones que han actuado en jurisdicción de la sección 17ª de Policía denominadas pro-adquisición de pistolas Colt y pro-adquisición de material para el cuerpo de bomberos de la capital," AHCDN, Expediente no. 1336 (P-1934).

37. Luis A. Romero, "1920–1976: El estado y las corporaciones," in *De las cofradías a las organizaciones de la sociedad civil: Historia de la iniciativa asociativa en la Argentina, 1776–1990,* by R. Di Stefano, H. Sabato, L. A. Romero, and J. L. Moreno (Buenos Aires: Edilab, 2002).

38. Archivo de la Honorable Cámara de Diputados de la Nación, Expediente no. 1335, November 8, 1934, "Congreso de Sociedades de Fomento."

39. Public support of an increase in policemen is described in Archivo de la Honorable Cámara de Diputados de la Nación, Legajos 00823-P-1924, 0027-P-1934, 00547-P-1934, 00547-P-1934, 00638-P-1934, 00640-P-1934, 00733-P-1934, 00682-P-1934, 00831-P-1934, 00979-P-1934, 00982-P-1934, 01301-P-1934, 01310-P-1934, 01316-P-1934, 01316-P-1934, 1321A-P-1934, 01322-P-1934, 01324-P-1934, 01326-P-1934, 01335-P-1934, 01336-P-1934, 01369-P-1934, 01396-P-1934, 00492-P-1935.

40. "Vecinos de la seccional 27ª," in "Memorial dirigido al Honorable Congreso."

41. Ibid.

42. On the rise of Argentine Catholicism in the 1920s and 1930s, see Miranda Lida and Diego Mauro, eds., *Catolicismo y sociedad de masas en la Argentina, 1900–1950* (Rosario: Prohistoria, 2009); Miranda Lida, *Historia del catolicismo en la Argentina, entre el siglo XIX y el XX* (Buenos Aires: Siglo XXI, 2015), 91–117.

43. I borrow Elias's concept of civilization to understand "low" police power. See Hélène L'Heuillet, *Baja política, alta policía: Un enfoque histórico y filosófico de la policía* (Buenos Aires: Prometeo, 2010), chap. 4; Norbert Elias, *El proceso de la civilización: Investigaciones sociogenéticas y psicogenéticas* (Mexico City: Fondo de Cultura Económica, 2009 [1939]); Michel Foucault, "'Omnes et singulatim': Vers une critique de la raison politique," in *Dits et écrits II, 1976–1988* (Paris: Quarto-Gallimard, 2001), 955.

44. Emphasis added.

45. On noise in the ancient city, see Yi-Fu Tuan, *Landscapes of Fear* (New York: Pantheon, 1979), 147.

46. "Epílogo la disputa: Los protagonistas sostuvieron una disputa por las molestias de un aparato radiotelefónico," *EM*, January 13, 1933, 12; "Ruidos

molestos e innecesarios" (editorial), *EM*, February 18, 1933, 4; "Hubo anoche en el radio céntrico dos desfiles ruidosos," *LN*, October 14, 1929, 3.

47. OD, June 6, 1938, 555. One symptom, among many, of the impotent regulation of noise is found in a municipal regulation that required the use of pneumatic tires for all vehicles that did not "run slowly"; OD, July 10, 1934, 813. Trajano Brea, "Los ruidos nocturnos," *MP*, August 1929, 7.

48. Prostitution was initially regulated by municipal law in 1875, and it would remain regulated until 1936. Nevertheless, there are many traces of growing public opinion against prostitution in the 1920s and 1930s. In 1925, brothels were banned from the streets in a series of repressive measures against sex workers on the street, pimps, and sex traffickers. Evidence on the enforcement of the Ley de Residencia in the 1930s indicates that numerous foreigners were deported for *proxenetismo* (pandering).

49. OD, February 2, 1937, 120; "Servicios especiales con motivo de carnaval," OD, February 19, 1939, 181.

50. Dominique Monjardet, *Lo que hace la policía: Sociología de la fuerza pública* (Buenos Aires: Prometeo, 2010), chap. 2.

51. The moderate curve in the rise of the application of the contravention edicts preceding the rise in the 1930s likely reflects the efforts of Jacinto Fernández, chief of police from December 1922 to May 1927, who focused police efforts on drunkenness and panhandling. In 1923 and 1926, Fernández increased the police's ability to punish these offenses (thirty days of incarceration). Rodríguez, *Historia de la Policía Federal Argentina*, 118.

52. The figures are taken from Policía de Buenos Aires, Capital Federal, *Memoria correspondiente al año 1933*, 391; Policía de Buenos Aires, Capital Federal, *Memoria correspondiente al año 1934*, 459.

53. Julia K. Blackwelder, "Urbanization, Crime, and Policing: Buenos Aires, 1870–1914," in *The Problem of Order in Changing Societies: Essays on Crime and Policing in Argentina and Uruguay, 1750–1940*, edited by Lyman Johnson (Albuquerque: University of New Mexico Press, 1990), 80.

CHAPTER 4. DETECTING DISORDER

1. The epigraph is from Ezequiel Martínez Estrada, *La cabeza de Goliat* (Buenos Aires: Centro Editor de América Latina, 1968 [1940]), 145.

2. On the constructed symbolism of police ubiquity in Buenos Aires, see Diego Galeano, *Escritores, detectives y archivistas: La cultura policial en Buenos Aires, 1821–1910* (Buenos Aires: Teseo/BN, 2009), 42. The image of the eye was also used by other police forces and private detective agencies (hence the name "private eye"), including the legendary Pinkerton agency.

3. Cited in Viviana Barry, *Orden en Buenos Aires: Policías y modernización policial, 1890–1910* (MA thesis, UNSAM/IDAES, 2009), 139.

4. For more on *Crítica*'s campaign, see Sylvia Saítta, *Regueros de tinta: El diario "Crítica" en la década de 1920* (Buenos Aires: Sudamericana, 1998), 199.

5. "El bailongo," in *Puñado de emociones* (Buenos Aires: Plus Ultra, 1977 [1941]), 76.

6. Marcos L. Bretas, *Orden na cidade: O ejercicio cotidiano da autoridade policial no Rio de Janeiro: 1907–1930* (Rio de Janeiro: Rocco, 1997). For a revision of British and U.S. historiography on this point, see Eric Monkkonen, "History of Urban Police," *Crime and Justice* 15 (1992): 547–80.

7. On the practice of disguise among police at the turn of the century, see Sandra Gayol, "Entre lo deseable y lo posible: Perfil de la Policía de Buenos Aires en la segunda mitad del siglo XIX," *Estudios Sociales* 6, no. 10 (1996): 131.

8. Federico Gutiérrez [Fag Libert], *Noticias de policía* (Buenos Aires, 1922 [1907]); Ricardo Rodríguez Molas, "Policía, poeta y anarquista en 1900," *Desmemoria: Revista de Historia* 5, no. 19/20 (September–December 1998): 236. For an intellectual profile of Gutiérrez, see Horacio Tarcus, ed., *Diccionario biográfico de la izquierda argentina: De los anarquistas a la "nueva izquierda" (1870–1976)* (Buenos Aires: Emecé, 2007), 302.

9. Budget data from Ministerio del Interior, *Memoria del Ministerio del Interior,* 1936–37, 918. Data on salaries from *Revista de la Caja de Socorros de la Policía y Bomberos de la Capital,* September 1935, 25.

10. Barceló was elected mayor of the town of Avellaneda in 1909, 1917, 1924, 1927, and 1932. During the period analyzed here, he was the Conservative "boss" of the area, controlling important (legal and illegal) economic and political resources.

11. "Last Reason," in "Radio *La Nación*," *MP*, January, 1936; Oral History Project, Instituto T. Di Tella, interview with Esteban Habiague, 74.

12. ODR, August 10, 1931, 33.

13. "Lack of zeal" in enforcing gambling regulations was the reason given in the majority of reprimands issued to officers. This and other cases can be found in ODR, 1934.

14. *MP*, August 1925; *MP*, March 1926. In the early 1930s, the Órdenes del Día "Reservadas" increased as a result of the punishments allotted to *quinieleros*.

15. On the "invitational edges of corruption" and patterns of police abuse of authority, see P. A. Waddington, *Policing Citizens: Authority and Rights* (London: University College London Press, 1999), chap. 5.

16. *LN*, July 14, 1931.

17. ODR, January 14, 1933, 12; "Vigilancia ordinaria y permanente en la ciudad," *PA*, January 16, 1934, 53.

18. "Copia del informe producido por el Señor Asesor Letrado Dr. Ignacio C. Olmedo, en el sumario instruido al Comisario Juan C. Correa de la Sección 31ª," AGN, Archivo Agustín P. Justo, box 45, doc. 75.

19. Julio Angel Méndez, *Organización de la escuelas de policía* (Buenos Aires, 1936), 9. For Cadet School admission requirements, see OD, November 27, 1930 (followed by successive modifications).

20. In her study of the composition of the Capital Police at the beginning of the twentieth century, Viviana Barry shows that young cadets trained to represent the metropolitan police commingled with a population of recruits in the lowest ranks of the army, making up a roaming population formed by these hurried expeditions to the northern provinces. *Orden en Buenos Aires,* chap. 1.

21. Gutiérrez, *Noticias de policía,* 10.

22. "Nuestra policía," *LV,* August 24, 1901, 2. "We will say it again," said this socialist newspaper a decade later. "The police employees, even those that are not armed with machetes, are for the most part far from being models of culture. . . . One of them, of dark complexion like his conscience, and whom we only know by the name of León, demonstrated by his torpid behavior to be the perfect brute"; "Gesta policial," *LV,* January 16, 1910; "¡Esa primera del mundo!" *LV,* September 12, 1903, 2. On the characterization of the police in the anarchist periodical *La Protesta,* see Pablo Ansolabehere, *Literatura y anarquismo en la Argentina (1879–1919)* (Rosario: Beatriz Viterbo, 2011), 110.

23. Méndez, *Organización de la escuelas de policía.* According to Ricardo Salvatore, the height difference between the inhabitants of the pampas and those of the northeast (which reflects differences in nutrition) was 2.75 inches. "Heights, Nutrition and Well-Being in Argentina, ca. 1850–1950, Preliminary Results," *Journal of Iberian and Latin American Economic History* 25, no. 1 (2007): 53.

24. "La ineficacia de la acción policial," *EM,* October 9, 1932, 1; "Hay que vigilar más y mejor el territorio de la capital," *RP,* June 1, 1933, 345.

25. On the transformation of urban police during this period see Robert Fogelson, *Big City Police* (Cambridge, MA: Harvard University Press, 1977); Nathan Douthit, "Police Professionalism and the War against Crime in the United States, 1920s-30s," in *Police Forces in History,* edited by George L. Mosse (Beverly Hills, CA: Sage, 1975), 317–33.

26. On street service in Buenos Aires during the nineteenth century, see Mercedes García Ferrari, *Ladrones conocidos/Sospechosos reservados* (Buenos Aires: Prometeo, 2010), chap. 1.

27. Waddington, *Policing Citizens,* chap. 1.

28. AGN, Fondo Ministerio del Interior, 1933, leg. 22, doc. 22.413; "La Jefatura ha reglamentado el servicio de las reservas de la Policía de la Capital," *EM,* December 1, 1933, 16.

29. "Cómo se resta vigilancia a la ciudad," *EM,* December 31, 1933.

30. Municipal regulation on bicycle traffic, OD, January 31, 1931, 111; municipal regulation on pedestrian traffic, OD, February 6, 1939, 128.

31. By the mid-1930s, the traffic section was issuing twelve thousand sanctions annually for "disobedience." Policía de la Capital, *Memoria correspondiente al año 1934,* "Contravenciones municipales," 52.

32. Nicolás Labanca, *Recuerdos de la Comisaría 3era: Ambiente y acción policial hace 50 años* (Buenos Aires: Ediciones Viomar, 1969), 44. On urban policing and the automobile age, see Clive Emsley, "Mother, What *Did* Policemen Do When There Weren't Any Motors? The Law, the Police, and the Regulation of Traffic in England, 1900–1939," *Historical Journal* 36, no. 2 (1993): 357–81.

33. Horacio Torres, "Evolución de los procesos de estructuración espacial urbana: El caso de Buenos Aires," *Desarrollo Económico* 15, no. 58 (July–Septempber 1975): 281–306.

34. *RP,* August 1, 1925, 394.

35. Policía de la Capital, *Memoria, antecedentes y datos estadísticos correspondientes al año 1923*, 11. (These are institutional reports compiled by Jacinto Fernández, Capital police chief between 1922 and 1927.)

36. *MP*, May 1930. Policía de la Capital, *Memoria de Investigaciones*, 1933, 242. The greatest rise in the number of police districts (from twenty-eight to forty) occurred under Falcón's administration (1906–9). Barry, *Orden en Buenos Aires*, 33. For statistics on police distribution in neighborhood districts, see Ministerio del Interior, *Memoria del Ministerio del Interior*, 1926.

37. Gutiérrez, *Noticias de policía*, 44.

38. In his comparative study of the police presence in twenty North American cities between 1880 and 1970, Eric Monkkonen detects a sustained growth in the proportion of police per inhabitant. The average ratio in the 1930s was slightly higher than in Buenos Aires during the same years. "From Cop History to Social History: The Significance of the Police in American History," *Journal of Social History* 15, no. 4 (Summer 1982): 575–91.

39. In his analysis of the jurisdictional map of 1870, Diego Galeano has shown that plans to place police units at a "central point" went unfulfilled, clearly shown by the disparate locations of Buenos Aires stations; "La policía en la ciudad de Buenos Aires, 1867–1880" (Master's thesis, San Andrés University, 2010), 124.

40. OD, August 3, 1932, 1102.

41. AGN, Fondo Ministerio del Interior, July 1933; "Límites de comisarías y ubicación de paradas," OD, April 20, 1937, 374. The new law did not alter the distribution of street posts.

42. OD, June 4, 1938, 548.

43. The video could be found on the Federal Police website until 2011, when it was replaced. It is still available (February 2016) at http://www.youtube.com/watch?v = bal1a0a7Avc&feature = related.

44. AGN, Fondo Ministerio del Interior, 1932, doc. 32280.

45. "Certamen Internacional de Tiro de Pistola," *Radiópolis–MP*, August 1938.

46. Jorge Eduardo Coll, "La defensa del orden público y la acción de la policía," *RP*, October 1937, 977.

47. "Gases como arma policial," *MP*, August 1933, 37. For how to administer tear gas, see OD, August 29, 1933, 927.

48. Barry, *Orden en Buenos Aires*, 131.

49. Policía de la Capital, *Memoria: Antecedentes, datos estadísticos; Crónica de actos públicos; Correspondiente al año 1925*, 10.

50. Ibid., 336; *Revista de la Caja de Socorros de la Policía y Bomberos de la Capital*, December 1936, 17.

51. For studies of the "patrol car effect," see Robert Reiner, *The Politics of the Police*, 3rd ed. (Oxford: Oxford University Press, 2000), 116.

52. In the United States, the history of interwar police reforms is directly linked to a search for explanations about the alienation of the contemporary police; Albert Reiss Jr., "Police Organization in the Twentieth Century," *Crime and Justice* 15 (1992): 51–97.

53. "Ahí viene la cana," *EM*, July 20, 1929. "Lunfardo" was the term originally used to designate the marginal lexicon related to the crime and prison underworld. By the 1920s, however, so many Lunfardo terms had spread widely into common speech that the term came to designate generic street slang.

54. Martínez Estrada, *La cabeza de Goliat*, 146.

55. Laurentino Mejías, "Los atracos," *RP*, June 16, 1932, 513–14.

56. *La patrulla policial: Aventuras del Sargento Venancio, Radiópolis–MP*, December 1938. The scripts are signed by "three Argentine detectives"—Cortés Conde, Bellini, and García Ibáñez.

57. Characters like Don Frutos Gómez (Delmiro Ayala Gauna) and Father Metri (Leonardo Castellani) contributed to the creolization of the Argentine literary languages of crime detection. Their authors were intent on showing that the man of the countryside possessed powers of observation that were comparable to those of Sherlock Holmes. D. Ayala Gauna, *Los casos de Don Frutos Gómez* (Buenos Aires: Centro Editor de América Latina: 1969), 34; L. Castellani, *Las muertes del Padre Metri* (Buenos Aires: Dictio, 1978 [1942]).

58. Ley de Telégrafos Nacionales no. 750 1/2, 1875, in Ministerio del Interior, Policía de la Capital Federal, *Disposiciones de Policía*, book 3 (Buenos Aires: Biblioteca Policial, 1943), 139. The information obtained had the character of judicial proof.

59. "La transmisión diaria del 'Boletín,'" *RP*, January 1, 1933, 20.

60. Ibid.

61. "Lo que no debe ser propalado en nuestra 'Broadcasting Policial,'" *RP*, January 16, 1933, 44; "Los servicios de radiocomunicaciones de la policía de la capital," *RP*, April 1, 1933, 235.

62. In 1909, the police had a telegraphic network that extended across 1,288 blocks and served to communicate between forty-four police stations, as well as a public assistance communication network and two direct lines to the national and provincial telegraph system. In 1908 they added a central switchboard to coordinate communication between all units; Barry, *Orden en Buenos Aires*, 131. On the telegraph as a method of inter-police cooperation between Buenos Aires and Rio de Janeiro, see Diego Galeano, "¿Quiénes eran los indeseables? Controles policiales de extranjeros entre Brasil y Argentina a comienzos del siglo XX" (paper presented at Fuera de la Ley: Jornadas de Discusión sobre Delito, Justicia y Policía en Perspectiva Histórica [siglos XIX y XX], San Andrés University, Buenos Aires, June 19, 2010).

63. Rafael Montenegro, *Historial de la Policía de la Capital Federal* (Buenos Aires: Policía de la Capital, 1934), 49.

64. "La Radio al servicio de la policía," *RP*, November 16, 1929, 1349.

65. Directives for the use of radiotelephone services in OD, March 17, 1933, 293–94.

66. "Servicios especiales con motivo del 1º de mayo," OD, April 28, 1937.

67. "Permitió la captura del asaltante el anuncio por radio del delito," *EM*, December 17, 1933; "Un invento extraordinario que nuestra policía debe aprovechar," *RPo*, September 1935, 7.

68. Narciso Robledal, "La policía lucha contra el enemigo público," *Atlántida,* December 26, 1935, 21. Also see "La radio cumple una elevada función social contra la delincuencia," *Antena,* February 2, 1935, 12.

CHAPTER 5. THE PLACES OF DISORDER

1. The epigraph is from Hélène l'Heuillet, *Baja política, alta policía: Un enfoque histórico y filosófico de la policía* (Buenos Aires: Prometeo, 2010), 93.

2. *Apenas un delincuente: Crimen, castigo y cultura en la Argentina, 1880–1945* (Buenos Aires: Siglo XXI, 2004), chaps. 5 and 6.

3. For a study of the crime section in *La Nación,* see M. Aron, J.J. Canavessi, and C. Müller, "Delito y seguridad en el diario *La Nación* en el año del Centenario," *Cuadernos de Seguridad* 12–13 (August 2010): 49.

4. On the transnational circulation of "underworld" imagery, see Dominique Kalifa, *Les bas-fonds: Histoire d'un imaginaire* (Paris: Seuil, 2013).

5. For more on the spacial distribution of *porteño* cafés at the end of the nineteenth century, see Sandra Gayol, *Sociabilidad en Buenos Aires* (Buenos Aires: Ediciones del Signo, 2000), 36 and 42. For the location of brothels, see Donna Guy, *Sex and Danger in Buenos Aires: Prostitution, Family, and Nation in Argentina* (Lincoln: University of Nebraska Press, 1991), chap. 3; Horacio Caride, "Una aproximación a la historia prostibularia de Buenos Aires en tiempos de la 'legalidad'" (paper presented at Fuera de la Ley: Jornadas de Discusión sobre Delito, Policía y Justicia en Perspectiva Histórica [Siglos XIX y XX], San Andrés University, Buenos Aires, June 17 and 18, 2010). On the distribution of police surveillance at the end of the nineteenth century, see Diego Galeano, "La policía en la ciudad de Buenos Aires: 1867–1880" (Master's thesis, San Andrés University, 2010), 132–37.

6. Fernando Aliata, *La ciudad regular: Arquitectura, programas e instituciones en el Buenos Aires posrevolucionario, 1821–1835* (Bernal: UNQ/Prometeo, 2006), 102.

7. Jorge Fondebrider, ed., *La París de los argentinos* (Buenos Aires: Bajo la Luna, 2010), 426.

8. Raúl Vergara, *Historia del alumbrado público de la Ciudad de Buenos Aires* (Buenos Aires, 1946).

9. According to data from Vergara, *Historia del alumbrado público,* in Caballito Norte, Flores Sud, Chacarita, and Parque Patricios, fifteen hundred oil lamps were destroyed, three hundred electric arc lamps were destroyed, and among electric lamps then being installed, more than a thousand were destroyed; Octavio A. Piñero, *Los orígenes y la Trágica Semana de enero de 1919* (Buenos Aires, 1956), 79; José R. Romariz, *La Semana Trágica* (Buenos Aires: Editorial Hemisferio, 1952), 88.

10. On the cultural constructions around the "reo" and "cordial" neighborhood of the interwar period, see Adrián Gorelik, La grilla y el parque: Espacio público y cultura urbana en Buenos Aires (1887–1936) (Bernal: Universidad Nacional de Quilmes, 1998), pt. 3, chap. 2.

11. César Vapñarsky, *La Aglomeración Gran Buenos Aires: Expansión espacial y crecimiento demográfico entre 1869 y 1991* (Buenos Aires: EUDEBA, 2000), chap. 8.

12. Horacio Caride, *La idea del conurbano bonaerense, 1925–1947* (working paper no. 14, Instituto del Conurbano, UNGS, San Miguel, 1999).

13. Carlos O. Bunge, *Los envenenados (escenas de la vida argentina de fines del siglo XIX* (Madrid: Espasa-Calpe, 1926), 72. On turn-of-the-century suburban ranches, see Graciela Silvestri, *El lugar común: Una historia de las figuras del paisaje en el Río de la Plata* (Buenos Aires: Edhasa, 2011), 186.

14. Roberto Arlt, "Pueblos de los alrededores," EM, March 31, 1929.

15. Yi-Fu Tuan, *Topophilia: A Study of Environmental Perception, Attitudes, and Values* (New York: Columbia University Press, 1990 [1974]), chap. 14.

16. On the police as a selective regulator of circulation, see Michel Foucault, class held January 18, 1978, in *Seguridad, territorio, población: Curso en el Collège de France* (1977–1978) (Buenos Aires: Fondo de Cultura Económica, 2006), 45.

17. Ramón Cortés Conde, *Historia de la policía de la ciudad de Buenos Aires* (Buenos Aires: Biblioteca Policial, 1937), 396.

18. Policía de la Capital, *Memoria de Investigaciones*, 1935, 230.

19. CC, March 16, 1929. On the concept of the weekend, see Anahí Ballent, "La 'casa para todos': Grandeza y miseria de la vivienda masiva," in *Historia de la vida privada en la Argentina,* edited by F. Devoto and M. Madero (Buenos Aires: Taurus, 1999), vol. 3, 26.

20. Ezequiel Martínez Estrada, *La cabeza de Goliat* (Buenos Aires: Capítulo/CEAL, 1968 [1940]), 253; "Desbordes de incultura," EM, December 3, 1933, 4.

21. The *porteño* brothels closed in 1934, with the end of legal prostitution. Two years later, the Proflaxis Social Law made them illegal in the rest of the country. In her research on prostitution in Buenos Aires, Donna Guy found an increase in the number of licensed bordellos in the 1920s, followed by a sharp decline after 1927, as Prohibition approached; Guy, *Sex and Danger,* 109.

22. "Candidatos a millonarios," EM, December 21, 1929.

23. On horse racing as popular entertainment in Buenos Aires in the early twentieth century, see Roy Hora, *Historia del turf argentino* (Buenos Aires: Siglo XXI, 2014).

24. Roberto Arlt, "Risorgimiento de la timba localizada," EM, December 2, 1930; *Last Reason, A rienda suelta* (Buenos Aires: Biblioteca Nacional/Colihue, 2006 [1925]); Ana Cecchi, "Last Reason y Roberto Arlt: Crónicas y aguafuertes en los años veinte y treinta," in *La timba como relato de pasaje: La narrativa del juego en la construcción de la modernidad porteña* (Buenos Aires, 1900–1935) (Buenos Aires: Teseo/BN, 2012).

25. Roberto Arlt, "La mujer que juega a la quiniela," EM, December 9, 1928.

26. Marcelo Pedetta, "Cara y cruz: Estado, juego oficial y juego clandestino antes de 1936" (paper presented at Fuera de la Ley: Jornadas de Discusión sobre Delito, Policía y Justicia en Perspectiva Histórica [Siglos XIX y XX], San Andrés University, Buenos Aires, June 2010).

27. "La represión del juego," *LP*, February 15, 1931; reprinted in LL, February 16, 1931, 3.

28. Anahí Ballent, "Country Life: Los nuevos paraísos, su historia y sus profetas," *Block*, no. 2, 1998, 88–101.

29. Interview with a former employee of the Mar del Plata casino, Ricardo N. Lombardi, conducted in May 2008 by Marcelo Pedetta, Archivo de Historia Oral, Departamento de Historia, Facultad de Humanidades, UNMdP. Thanks to Marcelo Pedetta for access to the source.

30. "El desarrollo del juego" (editorial), *LL*, July 8, 1933, 3.

31. *LP*, March 2, 1933.

32. Policía de la Provincia de Buenos Aires, OD no. 12.594, January 4, 1932.

33. Jorge Schvarzer, "La implantación industrial," in *Buenos Aires: Historia de cuatro siglos*, edited by J.L. Romero and L.A. Romero (Buenos Aires: Altamira, 2000), vol. 2, 209.

34. Nicolás Iñigo Carrera, *La estrategia de la clase obrera*, 1936 (Buenos Aires: La Rosa Blindada, 2000), 68. Though not as close to the capital, Quilmes exhibited similar characteristics.

35. "Servicios policiales en Avellaneda," *LN*, October 14, 1929.

36. *LP*, March 2, 1933. "Con la complicidad de la policía sujetos apañados por el oficialismo violan descaradamente determinada ley: Sólo falta un hipódromo," *LL*, September 13, 1932, 1; *LP*, April 3, 1933, reprinted in *LL*, April 4, 1933, 3; "Funcionan clandestinos en el corazón de Avellaneda: En locales no muy distantes de la comisaría 1era numerosas mujeres ejercen la prostitución," *LL*, August 9, 1933, 5.

37. *"Escolaso"* is a Lunfardo term for gambling.

38. Adrián Pignatelli, *Ruggierito: Política y negocios sucios en la Avellaneda violenta de 1920 y 1930* (Buenos Aires: Nueva Mayoría, 2005), 47.

39. On Fresco's reform efforts, see Osvaldo Barreneche, "La reorganización de las policías en las provincias de Buenos Aires y Córdoba, 1936–1940," in *Procesos amplios, experiencia y construcción de las identidades sociales: Córdoba y Buenos Aires, siglos XVIII–XX*, edited by B. Moreyra and Silvia Mallo (Córdoba: Centro de Estudios "Prof. C. Segreti"/UNC, 2007).

40. Jorge Luis Borges, "Death and the Compass," in *Collected Fictions of Jorge Luis Borges*, translated by Andrew Hurley (New York: Penguin, 1999), 152.

41. Suprema Corte de Justicia de la Provincia de Buenos Aires, *Justicia criminal y delincuencia del siglo XX*, 135. The data reflects the number of registered episodes in the provincial justice system in relation to proportional demographic growth. Given that the judicial proceedings register a minor proportion of the crimes committed, we must assume that they reflect a very attenuated picture.

42. *EM*, February 6, 1933, 12.

43. *EM*, October 22, 1933, 12.

44. "Informaciones de Avellaneda: Un contratista de obras fue ayer asesinado a balazos por individuos que desaparecieron inmediatamente," *LN*, October 25, 1929; "Hubo ayer un violento tiroteo en Valentín Alsina: Entre dos bandos se cambiaron más de 20 tiros; Resultó herido gravemente el sujeto

conocido como 'Gallego López,'" *LL,* February 11, 1933, 5; "Explotó otra bomba en una panadería," *LL,* August 24, 1931, 1.

45. "Fue asesinado el mayor Rosasco," *LL,* June 12, 1931, 1; "Acribillado a balazos fue asesinado el mayor José W. Rosasco," *LO,* June 12, 1931, 1.

46. This is Osvaldo Bayer's hypothesis; Osvaldo Bayer, *Los anarquistas expropiadores y otros ensayos* (Buenos Aires: Planeta, 2003), 75–80. On anti-communist repression in Avellaneda, see Hernán Camarero, *A la conquista de la clase obrera: Los comunistas y el mundo del trabajo en la Argentina, 1920–1935* (Buenos Aires: Siglo XXI–Ed. Iberoamericana, 2007), 165.

47. "Como los gangsters de Chicago, los pistoleros criollos de Morón utilizaron ametralladoras: Hay muchos puntos de contacto en los procedimientos usados en esas bandas," *Crítica,* February 20, 1935, 12; "En Avellaneda, los muertos matan," *Ahora,* August 1, 1935, 28.

48. I have consulted the morning edition of *La Libertad,* edited in Avellaneda with coverage in the southern suburban towns of Lanús, Villa Dominico, Sarandí, Valentín Alsina, and Wilde. The visibility granted to violent incidents depended on political context. A Radical paper, *La Libertad* described the problems linked to Conservative Barceló's management, reestablished in 1930. The second local newspaper consulted, the conservative *La Opinión,* followed similar political lines in its interpretation of local violence.

49. *LL,* October 17, 1929. The link between the hardening of the porteño police and the rise of organized crime in Avellaneda is underlined in La Opinión in a summary of Rosasco's trajectory; *LO,* June 13, 1931, 1.

50. The thriving Avellaneda community, *LL* editorialized, had no luck: "People are on their own, and the fate of their life and property is random"; "Seguridad pública" (editorial), *LL,* June 16, 1931; "Campañas contra el juego de azar en Avellaneda" (editorial), *LL,* July 8, 1931; "Avellaneda vive a merced de su magestad [sic] el delincuente" (editorial), *LL,* September 26, 1932; "Avellaneda se halla a merced de la delincuencia," *LL,* November 8, 1932, 5; "La complicidad del silencio policial: Valentín Alsina a merced de la delincuencia," *LL,* September 10, 1932, 5; "Es alarmante la sucesión de asaltos y robos en Lanús Oeste," LL, February 15, 1933, 5.

51. "En Morón, para defenderse de los delincuentes, organizarán los vecinos un cuerpo de policía," *EM,* May 23, 1933; "Debe mejorarse la vigilancia en San Fernando: El servicio policial resulta deficiente por la escasez de personal," *LN,* March 2, 1927, 7; "La subcomisaría de Ciudadela necesita aumento de agentes," *LN,* March 6, 1927, 6; "La eterna cuestión: Falta de policía," *LL,* August 4, 1033, 5; "La Sociedad de Fomento de V. Alsina se queja por la falta de policía," LL, January 16, 1933, 4.

52. "Meterle máquina: Y para qué?" *EM,* January 31, 1933, 3.

53. Ministerio del Interior, Memoria del Ministerio del Interior, 1932–33, 492.

54. On expert knowledge and plural meanings in the construction of General Paz Avenue, see Valeria Gruschetsky, "Una aproximación a la acción estatal a través de su producción material: El proyecto de la Avenida General Paz (Buenos Aires, 1887–1941)," Boletín Bibliográfico Electrónico del Programa Buenos Aires de Historia Política del Siglo XX, no. 6 (September 2010): 18.

55. "Modernos sistemas adoptados por la Prefectura General de Policía contra la delincuencia," *MP*, June 1931, 26. Emphasis added.

56. OD, December 19, 1934, 1536; OD, May 12, 1933, 514.

57. Laura Kalmanowiecki, "Military Power and Policing in Argentina, 1900–1955" (PhD diss., New School for Social Research, 1995), 187.

58. "Los pistoleros al verse perdidos tiraron a matar a los pesquisas," EM, January 20, 1933, 9.

59. *EM*, December 22, 1933.

60. Policía de la Capital, Disposiciones de policía, book 3 (Buenos Aires: Biblioteca Policial), regulation 1254.

61. Policía de la Capital, Memoria de Investigaciones, 1932, 14.

62. "Auge de la delincuencia en la Prov. de Buenos Aires," *EM*, January 30, 1933, 1.

63. Norberto Folino, *Barceló y Ruggierito patrones de Avellaneda* (Buenos Aires: CEAL, 1971), 100. Folino adds that during the Peronist period, Domingo Mercante called upon the veteran Habiague to work as an experienced assistant in the repression of communist workers.

64. "El Comisario Inspector Esteban Habiague y el personal de Avellaneda han sido calurosamente felicitados por la jefatura de Policía de la Provincia," *Radiópolis–MP*, November, 1938.

65. "Allanamiento de un local obrero: En los allanamientos, tomó parte la policía de la capital federal," LL, August 11, 1932, 5.

66. Letter from Habiague to Jefe de la Policía de la Capital, AGN, Fondo Ministerio del Interior, 1932, "Investigación en la misma con motivo publicación diario La Prensa," leg. 15, doc. 22403.

67. Policía de la Capital, *Informe de Investigaciones*, 1933, 171.

CHAPTER 6. WHILE THE CITY SLEEPS

1. P. A. J. Waddington, *Policing Citizens: Authority and Rights* (New York: Routledge, 1999), 23.

2. Walter Benjamin, "Critique of Violence," in *Reflexions: Essays, Aphorisms, Autobiographical Writings*, edited and introduced by Peter Demetz, translated by Edmund Jephcott (New York: Schocken, 1986), 287.

3. Waddington, *Policing Citizens*, 15–16; Dominique Monjardet, *Ce que fait la police: Sociologie de la force publique* (Paris: La Découverte, 1996), chap. 2.

4. *Memoria del Departamento de Policía de la Capital, 1884–85*, 7, quoted in Mercedes García Ferrari, *Ladrones conocidos/sospechosos reservados: Identificación policial en Buenos Aires, 1880–1905* (Buenos Aires: Prometeo, 2010), 39.

5. Lila Caimari, *Apenas un delincuente: Crimen, castigo y cultura en la Argentina, 1880–1955* (Buenos Aires: Siglo XXI, 2004), chap. 6.

6. José Ramón Romariz, *La Semana Trágica* (Buenos Aires: Editorial Hemisferio, 1952), 73.

7. Alberto R. Bouchez, "La propaganda y la policía," *Radiópolis–MP*, August 1944.

8. *Policía y Justicia*, no. 56, 1933, 2; *Policía y Justicia*, no. 92, 1933, 3–4; *Policía y Justicia*, no. 59, 1933, 1–3; *Policía y Justicia*, no. 60, 1933, 5, cited in

Martin Andersen, *La policía: Pasado, presente y propuestas para el futuro* (Buenos Aires: Sudamericana, 2002), 109.

9. Andersen, *La policía*, 146.

10. Ibid., 143.

11. Ricardo Rodríguez Molas, *Historia de la tortura y el orden represivo en la Argentina* (Buenos Aires: EUDEBA, 1985), 120. On the reactivation of the Sección Especial during Peronism and the creation of Orden Gremial, see Laura Kalmanowiecki, *Military Power and Policing in Argentina, 1900–1955* (PhD diss., New School for Social Research, 1995), 111, 128. On the application of the Ley de Residencia (Residential Law) to the expulsion of communist workers during Peronism, see Mariana Nazar, "Estado de derecho y excepcionalidad: Algunas prácticas de control social sobre trabajadores durante el primer peronismo" (February 2016), http://historiapolitica.com/datos/biblioteca/nazar1.pdf.

12. Lucía Dammert, ed., *Seguridad ciudadana: Experiencias y desafíos* (Valparaíso: Municipalidad de Valparaíso, 2004); Teresa Caldeira, *City of Walls: Crime, Segregation and Citizenship in São Paulo* (Berkeley: University of California Press, 2001); Javier Auyero and María Fernanda Berti, *La violencia en los márgenes: Una maestra y un sociólogo en el conurbano bonaerense* (Buenos Aires: Katz, 2013); Gabriel Kessler, *El sentimiento de inseguridad: Sociología del temor al delito* (Buenos Aires: Siglo XXI, 2009).

13. Alejandro Isla, "La calle, la cárcel y otras rutinas de los ladrones: Tradición y cambio en el mundo del delito," in *Seguridad ciudadana*, 59–101.

14. *RP*, December 16, 1933, 923.

15. *OD*, March 1, 1933, 229; *OD*, March 13, 1934, 293; "El 'Día de la Policía,'" *RP*, November 1937, 1018.

16. Robert Reiner, *The Politics of the Police* (Oxford: Oxford University Press, 2000), chap. 3. For a thorough analysis of the concept of "police culture," see Tom Cockcroft, *Police Culture: Themes and Concepts* (New York: Routledge, 2013).

17. On the singular connection between the police point of view and public opinion in Argentina, see Ruth Stanley, "Conversaciones con policías en Buenos Aires: En busca de la 'cultura policial' como variable explicativa de abusos policiales," in *Estado, violencia y ciudadanía en América Latina* (Madrid: Entinema, 2009), 77–105; Sabina Frederic, "Oficio policial y usos de la fuerza pública: Aproximaciones al estudio de la policía de la Provincia de Buenos Aires," in *Un estado con rostro humano: Funcionarios e instituciones estatales en la Argentina desde 1880*, edited by Ernesto Bohoslavsky and Germán Soprano (Buenos Aires: Prometeo, 2010), 281–307.

18. *Magazine Policial* initiated a great burgeoning of police magazine offerings, including traditional magazines like *Revista de Policía* (1897–1939), *Gaceta Policial* (1926–31), *Policía y Justicia* (1930–33), *Revista Policial* (1932–35), *Revista de Policía y Criminalística de Buenos Aires (1934–48)*, *Policía Argentina* (1934–35), *Actuación Policial* (1939–45), and *Carnet Policial* (1941–44). The police welfare society's publication, the *Revista de la Caja de Socorros de la Policía y Bomberos de la Capital*, developed an editorial agenda that went far beyond its initial functions as a police union bulletin. *Hogar Policial* (1929–37) promoted Police Homes within different jurisdictions.

19. Editors included Ángel Cacuri, Alberto Godel, Baldomero López, Aníbal Assali, Antonio Lofiego, José Cabrera, and Ángel Mentido. Several members of the Cortés Conde family participated in *Magazine Policial*: Oscar, the nominal director, was a professor of literature and the author of professional texts and poems (and likely in charge of the more literary sections of the publication). Luis was the editor of the bibliography section, while Ángela and Julia contributed poems and short texts. The Verbum Press belonged to the Cortés Conde family; it republished in book form most of the material that originally appeared in the magazine.

20. Ramón Cortés Conde, *Falcón-Lartigau* (Buenos Aires: Verbum); *Inauguración del monumento al Coronel Ramón Falcón en la Escuela de Policía* (Buenos Aires: Imprenta y Encuadernación de la Policía, 1925).

21. Manuel Gálvez, "El indio viejo," *MP*, March 1936; Héctor Pedro Blomberg, "El ausente," *MP*, June 1931, 5; "Las gaviotas," *MP*, January 1932, 13; H.P. Blomberg and Julio C. Viale Paz, "Los caminos de la historia" (radiotheater script), *MP*, November 1937; Juan José de Soiza Reilly, "Los libros viejos," *MP*, November 1926, 5; "La maestra de los perritos," *MP*, May 1927, 5; "Ironías del amor," *MP*, April 1930, 3; "El zorro matrero," *MP*, March 1934; "La historia de un libro," *MP*, March 1936.

22. In her study of the "Los Pensadores" collection (an Editorial Claridad project to publish "high" literature), Graciela Montaldo underlines the centrality of Russian writers, as well as Henri Barbusse and Anatole France, both of whom were often published in *Magazine Policial*; Graciela Montaldo, "La literatura como pedagogía, el escritor como modelo," *Cuadernos Hispanoamericanos* 445 (July 1987): 41–64. On communist libraries' catalogues, see Hernán Camarero, *A la conquista de la clase obrera: Los comunistas y el mundo del trabajo en la Argentina, 1920–1935* (Buenos Aires: Siglo XXI-Ed. Iberoamericana, 2007), 226. On the popular libraries, see Leandro H. Gutiérrez and Luis A. Romero, "Sociedades barriales y bibliotecas populares," in *Sectores populares, cultura y política: Buenos Aires en la entreguerra* (Buenos Aires: Sudamericana, 1995), 69.

23. Alberto Ghiraldo, "La evasión," *MP*, January 1926, 5.

24. Mario Bravo, "Canción de las cosas tristas," *MP*, February 1932, 9; "Canción de las cosas del camino," *MP*, May 1932, 16.

25. Rafael Barrett, "Vacuna," *MP*, September 1924, 65; "El sueño de Rodín," *MP*, January 1925, 51; "Máscaras," *MP*, February 1925, 60; "Los médicos," *MP*, April 1925, 16; "Dactiloscopía," *MP*, May 1925, 13; "Los lentes del indio," *MP*, September 1925, 9; "Gorki y Tolstoi," *MP*, November 1925; "Inmoralidad de los examines," *MP*, October 1927; "El revólver," *MP*, March 1928, 33; "El amante," *MP*, May 1930. Barrett (1876–1910) was a longtime contributor to *Caras y Caretas* and *Ideas*. His anarchist and republican convictions put him in conflict with the director of *El Correo Español*, prompting him to move to Asunción. For a profile of Barrett, see *Diccionario biográfico de la izquierda argentina: De los anarquistas a la "nueva izquierda" (1870–1976)*, edited by Horacio Tarcus (Buenos Aires: Emecé, 2007), 50.

26. Henri Barbusse, "Crimen pasional," *MP*, May 1925, 3; "La derrota," *MP*, June 1925, 3; "El Idiota," *MP*, July 1925; "El niño (algunos secretos del

corazón)," *MP*, November 1925, 3; "Ayer y mañana (algunos secretos del corazón)," *MP*, October 1926, 5.

27. The selection of readings suggests an informed understanding of the local literary world. In the 1920s (when *Magazine Policial* was most audacious) there were signs of interest in the avant-garde, with poems by Norah Lange (a "friend and contributor"), Eduardo González Lanuza, and Jorge Luis Borges, together with several articles on Ultraísmo. Eduardo González Lanuza, "Nocturno," *MP*, July 1927, 34; Norah Lange, "Calle," *MP*, September 1926, 1.

28. Reiner, *Politics of the Police*, 87.

29. George L. Mosse, *The Image of Man: The Creation of Modern Masculinity* (New York: Oxford University Press, 1996), 53.

30. Ramón Cortés Conde, "¡Mientras la ciudad duerme! . . .," *MP*, April 1934.

31. Laurentino Mejías, "Chirino," in *La policía . . . por dentro: Mis cuentos (I)* (Barcelona: Imprenta Viuda de Luis Tasso, 1911), 170.

32. Michel Foucault, "'Omnes et singulatim': Vers une critique de la raison politique," *Dits et écrits II, 1976–1988* (Paris: Quarto Gallimard, 2001), 953–80.

33. Marciana C. de Algaba, "Ronda policial," *Radiópolis-MP*, November 1939.

34. In the "Sección del Agente," the very official *Revista de Policía y Criminología* provided monthly street anecdotes. Begun in July 1935, this publication accompanied efforts to raise police standards, as championed by Chief García's reforms. It was directed by Enrique Fentanes and distributed for free to the subscribers of the *Biblioteca Policial*, also led by Fentanes. Its reported circulation totaled five thousand copies.

35. Reiner, *Politics of the Police*, 87.

36. "La Caja del Socorro rindió homenaje a los servidores de la policía sacrificados en aras del orden pública," *RCSP*, January 1936, 20. The annual homage to Falcón and Lartigau, held every December 15, is mentioned in *OD*, October 24, 1934.

37. Agente Jerónimo Melantoni, "Sacrificio," Sección "Literarias," *Radiópolis-MP*, November 1939.

38. *Memoria de la Policía de la Capital*, 1932, 203.

39. "Lo que se transmite por Ronda Policial," *Radiópolis–MP*, September 1938.

40. On "proletarian fiction," see Nicolás Rosa, "La ficción proletaria," *La Biblioteca* 4–5 (Summer 2006): 33–51.

41. Oficial Principal Natalio Castro, "Pernoctar!" in *Relatos de la Oficina de Guardia* (Buenos Aires: Biblioteca Policial, 1937), 67.

42. Castro, "Camas a 0.50," in *Relatos de la Oficina de Guardia*, 99; Enrique González Tuñón, *Camas desde un peso* (Buenos Aires: Ameghino, 1998 [1932]).

43. Matthiew Karush uses the phrase "melodramatic nation" in his study of the social imagery of Argentine cinema in the 1930s: "The Melodramatic Nation: Integration and Polarization in the Argentine Cinema of the 1930s," *Hispanic American Historical Review* 87, no. 2 (2007): 293–326.

44. Oficial Thermidor, "El agente de policía," *MP*, December 1924, 9.

45. Ibid.

46. *GP,* May 31, 1930, 7; "Los agentes financieros: La alta sociedad en sus diversas actividades," *GP,* May 1, 1926, 2; "Quiso matarlo porque no la dejó que comprara cocaína," *GP,* August 20, 1927, 9.

47. "El hijo del vigilante," *Radiópolis–MP,* August 1938; "Escuela de cadetes," *Radiópolis–MP,* August 1937.

48. Armando Escolaso, "Elogio del botón reo," *MP,* August 1933.

49. Peter Brooks, *The Melodramatic Imagination: Balzac, Henry James, Melodrama, and the Mode of Excess* (New Haven: Yale University Press, 1995 [1976]), 27.

50. "La captura," in R. Cortés Conde, C. Novaro, and J. González, *Relatos policiales: Episodios, sketchs, anécdotas, relatos, historietas y glosas teatralizadas especialmente para el micrófono* (Buenos Aires: Verbum, 1935), 67.

51. The Semana Trágica began with a strike at the Vasena Metal Workshops on January 7, 1919, during the Radical presidency of Hipólito Yrigoyen. Fueled by the much-polarized context of the postwar era, the conflict soon became violent and was dominated by the most intransigent groups—anarchists on the one hand and extreme nationalists on the other. It soon became apparent that the initial police repression of the crowds was insufficient, and the army was called to restore order. Over the course of three days, military groups, the police, and armed factions fueled by the anti-Semitic far right moved freely in a chaotic city, killing hundreds of people and leaving many thousands wounded. Edgardo Bilsky, *La Semana Trágica* (Buenos Aires: CEAL, 1985); Julio Godio, *La Semana Trágica de enero 1919* (Buenos Aires: Hyspamérica, 1985).

52. Ramón Cortés Conde died soon after finishing the book. Several chapters appeared as advance copies within *Magazine Policial,* but the full text was never published. I am grateful to Sonia Cortés Conde, who helped me to access the unedited manuscript. José Ramón Romariz, *La Semana Trágica: Antecedentes sociales, económicos y políticos; Episodios y relatos históricos de los sucesos sangrientos de enero del año 1919* (Buenos Aires: Editorial Hemisferio, 1952); Octavio A. Piñero, *Los orígenes y la Trágica Semana de enero de 1919* (Buenos Aires, 1956).

53. Cortés Conde, *La Semana Trágica* (unpublished manuscript), 6.

54. Romariz, *La Semana Trágica,* 37.

55. Ibid., 60.

56. Ibid., 91.

57. Ibid., 154.

Index